Nervous States

ALSO BY WILLIAM DAVIES

The Limits of Neoliberalism
The Happiness Industry

NERVOUS STATES

Democracy and
the Decline of Reason

WILLIAM DAVIES

W. W. NORTON & COMPANY
Independent Publishers Since 1923

Originally published in Great Britain under the title
Nervous States: How Feeling Took Over the World

Manufacturing by LSC Communications, Harrisonburg

Library of Congress Cataloging-in-Publication Data

Names: Davies, William, 1976– author.
Title: Nervous states : democracy and the decline of reason / William Davies.
Description: First American edition. | New York : W. W. Norton & Company, [2018] | Originally
published: London : Jonathan Cape, 2018. | Includes bibliographical references and index.
Identifiers: LCCN 2018049347 | ISBN 9780393635386 (hardcover)
Subjects: LCSH: Emotions—Political aspects. | Communication in politics—Psychological aspects. |
Democracy—Psychological aspects. | Political psychology.
Classification: LCC JA74.5 .D39 2018 | DDC 320.01/9—dc23
LC record available at https://lccn.loc.gov/2018049347

ISBN 978-0-393-35794-3 pbk.

W. W. Norton & Company, Inc.
500 Fifth Avenue, New York, N.Y. 10110
www.wwnorton.com

W. W. Norton & Company Ltd.
15 Carlisle Street, London W1D 3BS

1 2 3 4 5 6 7 8 9 0

To Martha

Contents

Introduction

On a late Friday afternoon in November 2017, police were called to London's Oxford Circus for reasons described as "terror-related." Oxford Circus Underground station was evacuated, producing a crush of people as they made for the exits. Reports circulated of shots being fired, and images and video appeared online of crowds fleeing the area, with heavily armed police officers heading in the opposite direction. Eyewitnesses described screams and chaos, with people huddling inside shops for safety.

Amidst the panic, it was unclear where exactly the threat was emanating from, or whether there might be a number of attacks going on simultaneously, as had occurred in Paris two years earlier. Armed police stormed Selfridges department store, while shoppers were instructed to evacuate the building. Inside the store at the time was the pop star Olly Murs, who tweeted to his 8 million followers "Fuck everyone get out of Selfridge now gun shots!!" As shoppers in the store made for the exits, others were rushing in at the same time, producing a stampede.

Smartphones and social media meant that this whole event was recorded, shared, and discussed in real time. The police attempted to quell the panic using their own Twitter feed, but this was more than offset by the sense of alarm that was engulfing other observers. Former leader of the far-right English Defense League Tommy Robinson tweeted that this "looks like another jihad attack in London." The *Daily Mail* unearthed an innocent tweet from ten days earlier, which had described a "lorry stopped on a pavement in Oxford Street," and inexplicably used this as a basis on which to tweet "Gunshots fired" as armed police officers surrounded Oxford Circus station after "lorry ploughs into pedestrians." The media was not so much reporting facts, as serving to synchronize attention and emotion across a watching public.

Around an hour after the initial evacuation of Oxford Circus, the police put out a statement that "to date police have not located any trace of any suspects, evidence of shots fired or casualties." It subsequently emerged that nine people required treatment in hospital for injuries sustained in the panic, but nothing more serious had yet been discovered. A few minutes later, the London Underground authority tweeted that stations had reopened and trains were running normally. Soon after that, the emergency services were formally stood down. There were no guns and no terrorists.

What had caused this event? The police had received numerous calls from members of the public reporting gunshots on the Underground and on street level, and had arrived within six minutes ready to respond. But the only violence that anyone had witnessed with their eyes was a scuffle on an overcrowded rush-hour platform, as two men bumped into each other, and a punch or two was thrown. While it remained unclear what had caused the impression of shots being fired, the scuffle had been enough to lead the surrounding crowd to retreat suddenly in fear, producing a wave of rapid movement that was then amplified as it spread along the busy platform and through the station. Given that there had been two successful terrorist attacks in London earlier in the year and seven others reportedly foiled by the police, it is not hard to understand how panic might have spread in such confined spaces.

Ghost disturbances like this had happened before. New York's JFK airport had witnessed a similar occurrence the previous year. On that occasion, stampedes broke out in numerous terminals across the airport, with reports on Twitter of an "active shooter" on the loose. One explanation was that the crowd had started to knock over the metal poles which organize lines of passengers, and the cumulative sound of these hitting the floor resembled gunfire. A small accident or misunderstanding was rapidly exaggerated, thanks to a combination of paranoid imagination and social media.

Following the Oxford Circus incident, local shopkeepers demanded a "Tokyo-style" loudspeaker system to be installed in the surrounding streets to allow the police to communicate with entire crowds all at once. The idea gained little traction but did diagnose the problem. Where events are unfolding rapidly and emotions are riding high, there is a sudden absence of any authoritative perspective on reality. In the digital age, that vacuum of hard knowledge becomes rapidly filled by rumors, fantasy, and guesswork, some of which is quickly twisted and exaggerated to suit a preferred narrative. Fear of violence can be just as disruptive a force as *actual* violence, and it can be difficult to quell once it is at large.

In statistical terms, the chance of dying in a terrorist attack or mass shooting in London or New York is extremely small indeed. But this type of cool objective perspective is not available—nor particularly useful—to the person who is in immediate fear for their life. After a panic has ended, it is up to political authorities, newspaper reporters, and experts to try and establish the facts of what has taken place. But nobody would expect people to act in accordance with the facts in the heat of the moment, as a mass of bodies are hurtling and screaming around them. Where rapid response is essential, bodily instinct takes hold.

Events such as these typify something about the times in which we live, when speed of reaction often takes precedence over slower and more cautious assessments. As we become more attuned to "real time" events and media, we inevitably end up placing more trust in sensation and emotion than in evidence. Knowledge becomes more valued for its speed and impact than for its cold objectivity, and emotive falsehood often travels faster than fact. In situations of physical danger, where time is of the essence, rapid reaction makes sense. But the influence of "real time" data now extends well beyond matters of security. News, financial markets, friendships, and work engage us in a constant flow of information, making it harder to stand back and construct a more reliable portrait of any of them. The threat lurking in this is that otherwise peaceful situations can come to feel dangerous, until eventually they really are.

The modern world was founded upon two fundamental distinctions, both inaugurated in the mid-seventeenth century: between mind and body, and between war and peace. These binaries have been gradually weakening for over a hundred years. As we will see, the rise of psychology and psychiatry in the late nineteenth century brought mind and body into closer proximity to each other, demonstrating how our thoughts are influenced by nervous impulses and feelings. The invention of aerial bombing in the early twentieth century meant that war came to include techniques for terrifying and policing civilian populations, well beyond the limits of combat.

These two distinctions—between mind and body, and war and peace—appear to have lost credibility altogether, with the result that we now experience conflict intruding into everyday life. Since the 1990s, rapid advances in neuroscience have elevated the brain over the mind as the main way by which we understand ourselves, demonstrating the importance of emotion and physiology to all decision making. Meanwhile, new forms of violence have emerged, in which states are attacked by non-state groups, interstate conflicts are fought using nonmilitary means (such as cyberwarfare), and the distinction between policing and military intervention becomes blurred. As society has been flooded by digital technology, it has grown harder to specify what belongs to the mind and what to the body, what is peaceful dialogue and what is conflict. In the murky space between mind and body, between war and peace, lie nervous states: individuals and governments living in a state of constant and heightened alertness, relying increasingly on feeling rather than fact. Mapping that condition and identifying its origins is the task of this book.

*

When we speak of *feeling* something, this can mean two different things. First, there is physical sensation, including pleasure and pain, which is crucial for navigating our environment. Our nervous system receives sensations from the outside world, which are used to coordinate our bodies and instinctive movements. The brilliance of our neurological network is that it facilitates immediate response to new information, whether that be from our physical circumstances or our internal organs. The brain manages sensory impressions extremely rapidly, offering among other things a crucial defense against external threats.[1] The brain is itself a complex sensory organ, which learns to organize impressions over time and extract patterns from them. Individual sensations may not count as knowledge, but they are an indispensable form of data, which we rely on almost constantly.

Second, there are feelings in the sense of emotions. These are experiences that we are capable of consciously reflecting on and articulating. We have a wide vocabulary for naming and expressing these feelings. We communicate them physically in our facial expressions and body language. They tell us important things about our relationships, lifestyles, desires and identities. Feelings of this sort present themselves to our minds, such that we actually notice them, even if we can't control them. Emotions can now be captured and algorithmically analyzed ("sentiment analysis") thanks to the behavioral data that digital technologies collect. And yet feelings of this sort are not welcome everywhere. In public life, an accusation of being "emotional" traditionally carries the implication that someone has lost objectivity and given way to irrational forces.

Feelings are how we orient ourselves, while also providing a reminder of shared humanity. Our capacity to feel pain and love is fundamental to how and why we care about each other. But as the stories of Oxford Circus and the JFK stampede demonstrate, survival instincts and nerves are not always reliable. The information feelings convey in the moment can conflict starkly with the facts that are subsequently established. The crucial quality of feelings—their immediacy—is also what makes them potentially misleading, spawning overreactions and fear. Unscrupulous politicians and businesses have long exploited our instincts and emotions, to convince us to believe or buy things that, on more careful reflection, we needn't have done. Real-time media, available via mobile technologies, exacerbates this potential, meaning that we spend more of our time immersed in a stream of images and sensations, with less time for reflection or dispassionate analysis.

During the seventeenth century, a number of European scholars produced ideas and institutions which aimed to regulate feelings, on the basis that they were untrustworthy and possibly dangerous. The French philosopher René Descartes treated physical sensations with great suspicion, in contrast to rational principles belonging to the mind. The English political theorist Thomas Hobbes argued that the central purpose of the state was to eradicate feelings of mutual fear that would otherwise trigger violence. In the same era, pioneering communities of merchants and gentlemen introduced strict new rules for how their impressions should be recorded and spoken of, to avoid exaggeration and distortion, using numbers and public record-keeping. They would later become known as experts, and their ability to keep personal feelings separate from their observations was one of their distinguishing traits.

This period of history produced the intellectual building blocks of the modern age. Contemporary notions of truth, scientific expertise, public administration, experimental evidence and progress are all legacies of the seventeenth century. The elevation of reason above feeling was hugely productive, indeed world-changing in its implications. And yet it wasn't simply knowledge that was being sought; it was also peace. To this day, much of the value of objectivity in public life, as manifest in statistics or economics, is that it provides a basis for consensus among people who otherwise have little in common. The German philosopher Hannah Arendt observed that the West's "curious passion" for "objectivity" can be traced back originally to Homeric narrative, which recounted tales of war from the highly unusual position of a disinterested observer.[2] A society that recognizes the authority of facts must also establish certain professions and institutions that are beyond the fray of politics, sentiment, or opinion.

This book tells the story of how that seventeenth-century project has run aground, with the results we see today. Experts and facts no longer seem capable of settling arguments to the extent that they once did. Objective claims about the economy, society, the human body and nature can no longer be successfully insulated from emotions. In 82% of countries around the world, less than half of the public express trust in the media, and this is contributing directly to rising cynicism toward governments.[3] The governmental institutions of the European Union and Washington, DC, are viewed as centers of elite privilege, which serve themselves rather than the public. Such feelings often hold greatest sway among communities that also benefit economically from those governments' policies.

Some feelings have greater political potency than others. Feelings of nostalgia, resentment, anger, and fear have disrupted the status quo. Populist uprisings, as manifest in the victories of Donald Trump, the Brexit campaign, and a wave of nationalist surges across Europe, are cases of this, and have been widely criticized for their denigration of expertise and harnessing of emotional discontents. But these are symptoms of a problem, and not a cause. Individual leaders and campaigns will come and go, but the conditions that enabled them will endure.

We can respond either by hurling more facts at these disturbances or by diagnosing their underlying drivers. This book pursues the latter path, bringing the history of ideas to bear on our bewildering present, in the hope that we might be able to understand it better. There are facts and figures used along the way, but only as a starting point to explore and interpret historic upheavals, and never as the final word on things. My argument is in two parts. The first part examines how the seventeenth-century ideal of expertise came about, and why it has been losing credibility, especially since the 1990s. In particular, mounting inequality in the West means that, in certain ways, the facts produced by experts and technocrats simply do not capture lived reality for many people. Objective indicators of progress, such as GDP growth, conceal deep fractures within society. Crucially, these divisions are not merely economic, but have acquired a bodily and existential dimension: people's lives are being shaped by divergent health, life expectancy and encounters with physical and psychological pain. Pessimism emanates most strongly from bodies that are aging faster and suffering more.

One could leave the story there, and simply lament the decline of modern reason, as if emotions have overwhelmed the citadel of truth like barbarians. The most vehement defenders of scientific rationality claim that alien forces—liars, demagogues, Kremlin trolls, or the uneducated public—have been granted too much power, and need to be eliminated from politics all over again. That response ignores a subsequent historical development, which is no less important for shaping the modern world, and which the second part of this book explores. The desire to harness emotions and physical instincts for political purposes also has a long history, producing its own centers of elite control, but with one crucial difference: it operates in the service of conflict rather than of peace. At the height of the Enlightenment, as reason appeared to be triumphing once and for all, the French Revolution demonstrated the immense power that could be unleashed by popular sentiment. The ability to mobilize ordinary people en masse was a revelation that would soon be harnessed by Napoleon.

Modern warfare produces miasmas of emotion, information, misinformation, deception, and secrecy. It mobilizes infrastructure, civilian populations, industry, and intelligence services in innovative ways. The rise of aerial warfare meant that problems of civilian morale and real-time decision making acquired greater urgency, producing new techniques for managing popular sentiment and sensing incoming threats. It was this paranoia that led to the invention of the digital computer and later the

Internet. War places strategic importance on feeling in both senses of the term: the right kind of emotions need triggering, while enemy movements and plans need sensing as rapidly as possible. Information becomes valued for its speed as much as its public credibility. This is a whole new way of handling the question of truth which often runs entirely counter to the original scientific ideal of reason and expertise.

Since the late nineteenth century, nationalists have sought to manufacture popular mobilizations by conjuring up memories of past wars and enthusiasm for future ones. But something else has happened more recently, which has quietly fed the spirit of warfare into civilian life, making us increasingly combative. The emphasis on "real time" knowledge that was originally privileged in war has become a feature of the business world, of Silicon Valley in particular. The *speed* of knowledge and decision making becomes crucial, and consensus is sidelined in the process. Rather than trusting experts, on the basis that they are neutral and outside the fray, we have come to rely on services that are fast, but whose public status is unclear. A 2017 survey, for example, found that more people were willing to trust search engines than human editors.[4]

The promise of expertise, first made in the seventeenth century, is to provide us with a version of reality that we can all agree on. The promise of digital computing, by contrast, is to maximize sensitivity to a changing environment. Timing becomes everything. Experts produce facts; Google and Twitter offer *trends*. As the objective view of the world recedes, it is replaced by intuition as to which way things are heading *now*. This nervous state offers more emotional stimulation and sensitivity, but for the same reason it is unsettling and disruptive of peaceful situations. In some circumstances, it can generate conflict and upheaval out of nothing. Meanwhile the question lurks in the background of *who* might be seeking to trigger specific feelings and *why*.

The ultimate danger of this situation is the one identified by Hobbes in the seventeenth century. If people don't *feel* safe, it doesn't matter whether they are objectively safe or not; they will eventually start to take matters into their own hands. Telling people that they are secure is of limited value if they *feel* that they are in situations of danger. For this reason, we have to take people's feelings seriously as political issues, and not simply dismiss them as irrational. Individual and collective worlds have been taken over by feeling. We don't have to speak the language of "culture war" or adopt violent rhetoric in order to recognize that politics is becoming increasingly framed and approached in quasi-militaristic terms. The political task is to feel our way toward less paranoid means of connecting with one another.

Populism is a threat, but it also contains opportunities. What kinds of opportunity? As I'll explore, many of the forces transforming democracies today stem from aspects of the human condition that lie deep in our psyches and bodies, beyond matters of fact: physical pain, fear of the future, a sense of our own mortality, the need to be cared for and protected. These features of humanity might sound a little dark, even macabre, but they are also things that we hold in common. As it becomes harder to establish widespread consensus through facts and expert testimony, we may have to dig deeper into our emotional and physical selves in search of a common world. If those committed to peace are not prepared to do this work of excavation, then those committed to conflict will happily do so instead.

When reason itself is in peril, there is an understandable instinct to try to revive or rescue something from the past. The question is what. What was so great about those innovations and revolutions of seventeenth-century Europe anyway? It has become a cliché to celebrate the rugged individualism, cold rationality, and truth-seeking courage of the scientific pioneers. But in our current age, when intelligence and calculation are performed faster and more accurately by machines than by people, an alternative ideal is needed. Perhaps the great virtue of the scientific method is not that it is smart (which is now an attribute of phones, cities, and fridges) but that it is slow and careful. Maybe it is not more intelligence that we need right now, but less speed and more care, both in our thinking *and* our feeling. After all, emotions (including anger) can be eminently reasonable, if they are granted the time to be articulated and heard. Conversely, advanced intelligence can be entirely unreasonable, when it moves at such speed as to defy any possibility of dialogue.

Democracies are being transformed by the power of feeling in ways that cannot be ignored or reversed. This is our reality now. We can't reverse history, and nor can we circumvent it; this historical era needs to be traversed with unusual judgment and care. Rather than denigrate the influence of feelings in society today, we need to get better at listening to them and learning from them. Instead of bemoaning the influx of emotions into politics, we should value democracy's capacity to give voice to fear, pain, and anxiety that might otherwise be diverted in far more destructive directions. If we're to steer through the new epoch, and rediscover something more stable beyond it, we need, above all, to understand it.

PART ONE

The Decline of Reason

I

DEMOCRACY OF FEELING

The new era of crowds

The presidency of Donald J. Trump began with a quarrel over a number, the one in question being the number of people at his inauguration. On the evening of the inauguration, the *New York Times* published an estimate that the crowd was only a third as big as that which attended Obama's inauguration in 2009, which some had put at 1.8 million. Images of the 2017 crowd from overhead, showing much larger areas of unoccupied space along the National Mall than in 2009, appeared to confirm this. This provoked the first of many extraordinary press conferences hosted by then White House press secretary, Sean Spicer, in which he accused the press of seeking to "minimize the enormous support" that Trump had attracted, and claimed that the crowd was in fact "the largest audience ever to witness an inauguration, period." The same day, Trump informed a gathering at CIA headquarters that the crowd was somewhere between 1 million and 1.5 million.

Ridicule descended on Spicer from various corners of the press and social media, not least because his press conference had been conducted in the manner of a bumbling propagandist reciting a party line, with no questions permitted from the press corps. But the White House line only hardened as a result, with some startling new philosophical justifications employed along the way. Trump adviser Kellyanne Conway strongly denied that Spicer had lied, but had simply offered "alternative facts" to the ones believed by the journalists. At another press conference the next day, Spicer said "sometimes we can disagree with the facts." Within seventy-two hours of Trump's being sworn in, it appeared that the White House had suspended basic criteria of truth.

This conflict with the media seemed to energize Trump, allowing him to return to the moral and emotional gambits that had proved so effective over the course of his election campaign. Within the media's seemingly factual statements about crowd sizes, Trump saw injustice, elitism, and persecution. "They demean me unfairly," he told an ABC News interviewer a few days later, before leading him to a wall-mounted photograph of the inauguration, apparently showing the vast size of the crowd from a more accurate angle. "I call it a sea of love," he said, gesturing to the image. "These people traveled from all parts of the country—maybe the world— hard for them to get here. And they loved what I had to say." For Trump this was no mere disagreement over "facts." It was an opposition between two emotions: the arrogant sneer of his critics and the love of his supporters. On this, at least, he was right.

There is no official data on the size of inauguration crowds. The National Park Service no longer provides its own estimates of crowd sizes, after it became embroiled in a controversy over the size of the "Million-Man March" that drew African American men to Washington in 1995. On that occasion, the Park Service had estimated that 400,000 attended, which (for obvious reasons) cast mild doubt upon the success of the event. The political heat that surrounds such issues meant that the Park Service subsequently withdrew from offering any calculations.

Even without the politics, crowd sizes produce wildly different estimates: numbers given for the crowd that turned out in London for the royal wedding of William and Kate in 2011 vary from 500,000 to over a million. Photographs taken from satellites and balloons have always provided the most authoritative guide, adapting techniques first developed to spy on Soviet weaponry, but these suffer from various defects. Satellite imagery is vulnerable to clouds getting in the way, and the density of people in the crowd can be distorted by the amount of shadow their bodies cast and the color of the ground beneath them.

One of the key features of crowds is that they appear radically different in size and density, depending on where one is standing. It is no doubt the case that Trump *did* see a densely packed crowd, reaching into the far distance, as he spoke in front of the Capitol Building that day as the newly sworn-in president of the United States. That's how it would have looked. He may have felt that, if only journalists could have seen his view, they would have agreed with him. Organizers of marches and protests always have a vested interest in inflating the numbers in attendance, but crowds also appear (or feel) far larger to those who are part of them than to those who aren't. This may be something of an optical illusion, but it is not necessarily dishonest.

The spread of smart devices into the urban environment produces more data for estimating crowd movements from one moment to the next, but this is not quite the same thing as offering a conclusive figure. You can study the number of mobile-phone signals in a given place at a given time, or equip urban infrastructure (such as street lights) with smart sensory devices, but the data that is captured remains fleeting in nature. It's good for sensing surges of activity and movement, which is what such "smart city" interventions are principally designed for, but a crowd remains an intrinsically difficult thing to grasp objectively.

As absurd as the statements of Trump, Spicer, and Conway may have sounded, there is something telling about the fact that this inaugural spat arose around this particular topic: a matter of great emotional significance, but where experts are comparatively powerless to resolve differences. It is not simply that crowds are resistant to scientific techniques of observation and measurement. There are too many voices who don't *want* them to be defined in that way, including the organizers, speakers, and members of large gatherings. A neutral objective perspective is hard to come by and difficult to defend.

Public rallies are as old as politics itself. But they have taken on a fresh sense of purpose since the global financial crisis of 2007–9, especially on the left. The Occupy movement that emerged in 2011 to protest against the banks made public assembly its central political purpose, and took the cold, scientific language of statistics and turned it into a mobilizing identity with the famous slogan "we are the 99%." Left-wing leaders, such as Alexis Tsipras in Greece, Pablo Iglesias in Spain and Jeremy Corbyn in the UK, have placed renewed political emphasis on the ability to bring large numbers of people together in public spaces. Here too, the size of rallies stirs a range of emotions from both supporters and opponents: exuberance, scorn, empathy, misinformation, hope, and resentment. Corbyn's rallies have frequently provoked complaints from his supporters that they are not being adequately covered by the mainstream media, despite their apparently vast scale.

But again, what yardstick would one use to assess a crowd's significance? How big does a rally need to be before it counts as newsworthy? And what qualifies as evidence? Circulation of photographs on Twitter, claiming to show one march but actually showing a different (usually much larger) one altogether, adds to the fog that surrounds the politics of crowds. Mockery follows from those who dismiss rallies as politically irrelevant, with contrasts being drawn between success on the streets and success at the ballot box. On the other hand, analysis following Corbyn's unexpectedly high polling result in Britain's 2017 general election showed that his rallies *did have* a positive effect on voting behavior in the vicinity.[1] But who could say exactly how or why?

A sense that we have entered a new age of crowds is heightened by the growth and rising influence of social media. Since the seventeenth century, newspapers and publishers have provided a "one to many" form of communication, serving public audiences and readerships with information. The recipients were largely passive in this relationship, and somewhat predictable as a result. Since the early 2000s, social media has supplemented (and in some ways co-opted) this system with a "many to many" style of communication, in which information moves like a virus through a network, in far more erratic ways. Certain ideas or images can spread seemingly of their own accord, taking experts by surprise, and triggering some extraordinary electoral upsets in the process. New techniques of marketing and messaging have arisen to try and influence viral and mimetic processes of content-sharing. Crowds have been a feature of politics since ancient times, but they never possessed real-time coordination tools until the twenty-first century.

The controversy surrounding Trump's inauguration crowd size may look on the surface like a laughable conflict between facts and fiction, reality and fantasy. It may look like the kind of issue that could be easily settled by expert authority, if only experts were treated with sufficient deference. But it serves us with an entry point to understanding the uneasy new political terrain that we have entered, in which neutral perspectives falter and feelings carry greater weight. The significance of a crowd is largely in the eye of the beholder. Where does this leave politics? And is there any discernible logic running through this chaotic new environment?

There is a logic here, but to grasp it we need to take feelings seriously. At the same time, we have to put comfortable assumptions about representative democracy on hold. Our familiar idea of mass democracy is the one in which most people are content to stay home and let someone else speak on their behalf—an elected representative, a judge, a professional critic, expert, or commentator. It involves professionally managed parties, agencies, newspapers, and publishers, through whom matters of importance are safely routed, and where everyone plays by the same rules. But in order for this to work, the vast majority of people must be content to stay quiet most of the time, and to trust those who speak in place of them. That, it seems, is something that people are increasingly reluctant to do. As trust in professional politicians and the media declines around the world, support for direct democracy has been rising.[2] There is no reason to assume this trend will dissipate in the near future.

Where politics becomes infused by the logic of crowds, it becomes less about peaceful political representation and more about mobilization. Whether on the street or online, crowds are not a proxy for something else, as, for example, a parliament is meant to be a proxy for its electorate or a judge is the face of the justice system. They don't purport to *represent* society as a whole, in a way that a "representative sample" is treated by an opinion pollster as a means of discovering what the whole nation thinks. If crowds matter at all, it is because of the depth of feeling that brought so many people into one place at one time. As in the wars that dominate the nationalist imagination, crowds allow every individual to become (and feel) part of something much larger than themselves. This needn't be a bad thing, but it carries risks and plays on our nerves.

The critical political question is who or what has the power to mobilize people. As numerous mainstream political campaigns have discovered in recent years after losing to insurgents and newcomers, appealing to objectivity and evidence rarely moves people physically or emotionally. So what *is* it that prompts people to engage in such a direct fashion, and what governs them once they do? This question preoccupies advertisers, brand consultants, and public-relations experts, as well as politicians. Social media platforms compete for the "engagement" of audiences, seeking to hold our attention for as long as possible, with "content" merely the bait. Once words and images are merely tools with which to mobilize and engage people, it ceases to matter so much if they are valid or objective reflections on reality. This is the anxiety that now surrounds "fake news" and propaganda. But we have been here before.

Bodily congregations

In 1892, a French doctor, medical researcher, and occasional anthropologist called Gustave Le Bon was thrown from his horse while riding in Paris and nearly killed. Le Bon became fixated on why this had happened. Was there anything that could be discerned about a horse's temperament by studying it? He began to inspect photographs of horses in search of clues, seeking signs of animal psychology in their physical form. He was strongly influenced by Charles Darwin, whose work on animal expression had also relied on photography to analyze their emotions. The birth of photography had opened up new scientific possibilities, allowing faces and expressions to be scrutinized with an objective eye. For the first time, a fleeting glance could be captured and studied, making way for a more methodical science of emotions where previously there had been only theories and descriptions. Le Bon's horse study led him further toward questions of psychology, and how human behavior might be explicable in terms of physical and biological cues. The area of psychology that he was most concerned with understanding was the one for which he is now best known: crowd behavior.

Le Bon had experienced the visceral impact and transformative potential of crowds at first hand, leaving him deeply fearful of what crowds were capable of. He'd trained as a doctor in Paris in the 1860s, and led a military ambulance division after the outbreak of the Franco-Prussian War in 1870. The humiliation of the French army, followed by the rise of the socialist Paris Commune in the summer of 1871, contributed to Le Bon's deeply conservative political leanings, and his intuition that France had been let down by a spirit of pacifism which socialist ideas had sanctioned. Democratic and socialist trust in "the people" represented an abnegation of military strength and national pride that he believed should be fiercely resisted. Inspired by new theories of evolution, Le Bon married his antipathy to socialism to some profoundly racist and sexist ideas regarding threats to national culture and military prowess, some of which he anchored in the voguish theory of his day, craniology. He spent much of the 1880s traveling in Asia and North Africa, which granted him ample new anthropological material to typecast.

In 1895, Le Bon wrote his most famous book, *The Psychology of Crowds*, which offered a comprehensive if deeply pessimistic view of the mechanics of crowd psychology. What characterized a crowd, Le Bon argued, was its replacement of multiple individual selves (with all the reasonable scientific qualities philosophers had associated with human minds) with a single mass psychology, which potentially subverted individual common sense or morality. "There are certain ideas and feelings," he argued, "which do not come into being, or do not transform themselves into acts except in the case of individuals forming a crowd."[3] As this occurs, "the faculty of observation and the critical spirit possessed by each of them individually at once disappears."[4] Anticipating the later ideas of Sigmund Freud, Le Bon argued that crowds revealed civilization's more dangerous underbelly which was otherwise repressed by individual self-restraint.

As the evidence of republican France seemed to Le Bon to demonstrate, crowds are a constant threat to principles of reason and truth. "When the structure of a civilization is rotten, it is always the masses that bring about its downfall," he declared.[5] They do so thanks to a variety of mechanisms that *The Psychology of Crowds* sought to uncover. The first is the sheer feeling of power that sizeable congregations of people generate, which encourages individuals to engage in activities that they'd otherwise see as foolhardy, immoral, or embarrassing. The size of a crowd matters tremendously, but it matters on an emotional level and not as a matter of official statistical calculation. This was Trump's "sea of love." It is the size of the crowd that allows people to suspend their individual judgment and their inhibitions and give way to their feelings.

Le Bon's militarism and bigotry should make us cautious of how we handle his ideas. His view of the Parisian masses was laced with disgust regarding their ill discipline and stupidity, and his broader cultural pessimism was bleak. But his work provides us with a starting point for thinking through the politics of crowds. To understand how a crowd behaves, one has to view it as a kind of distinctive organism, with its own quirks and behaviors—not unlike how Le Bon had sought to understand the horse that threw him. To participate in a crowd, Le Bon tells us, is to throw off

one's individuality and become immersed in a body larger than the self.
What this points to is a style of politics which is less about policy and
debate and more about being physically present in a certain space at a
certain time.

In what sense is this different from participating in, say, a market or a
democratic system? After all, individuals are constantly engaging in social
institutions that bring people together, creating more than the sum of
their parts. The difference, Le Bon's work would suggest, is that the essence
of a crowd is the intimacy it produces between human bodies. Whereas
the market allows us to interact via the medium of money, and democracy
allows us to do so using votes, text, and speech, the crowd is first and foremost a physical phenomenon. It creates a proximity of flesh to flesh, allowing a range of feelings to emerge and spread. Individual bodies are wired
up into a single nervous system.

Those who gathered in the National Mall on 20 January 2017, forming Trump's "sea of love," could have watched the event on television.
They could have limited their involvement to casting a vote on November
8, 2016, then waiting to see the policies which emerged from the White
House. But instead, they chose to bring their feeling, corporeal selves to
the Mall. Equally, the foundational purpose of Occupy was not to criticize Wall Street, debate financial regulation or to lobby for alternative economic policies, but, as the name says, to occupy physical space—to use
human bodies to render a political movement unavoidable. Activists in
other contemporary protest movements, such as Black Lives Matter and
Greenpeace, jam strategically important infrastructure (airports and high-
ways for example) with their bodies. Mass silence, such as the monthly
silent walks organized to mourn those lost in London's Grenfell Tower fire,
makes a powerful statement of compassion simply through being physically together. Contrary to Le Bon's fears, there are countless examples
from history of crowds peacefully resisting oppression. It's not that these
are less emotional than angry mobs, just that the emotions are different.

Crowds are never the same as audiences, readerships, or electorates.
They don't simply receive information, then respond. What is different
about crowds, Le Bon believed, is that they are influenced via processes
of contagion. Here we can see further evidence of the influence of biology
on Le Bon's thinking: he believed that ideas and emotions spread through

crowds like infectious diseases. "In a crowd every sentiment and act is contagious," he argued, "and contagious to such a degree that an individual readily sacrifices his personal interest to the collective interest."[6] Whereas a reasonable public dialogue might involve the use of evidence and arguments to persuade another person, contagions permeate crowds through a range of conscious, unconscious and bodily messages. In crowds, individuals do not choose to accept the ideas and activities of their peers, but become swept up by them. "Contagion is so powerful," Le Bon wrote, "that it forces upon individuals not only certain opinions, but certain modes of feeling as well."[7] The crowd becomes one vast neural network through which sentiment travels from body to body, at ultra-high speed.

Le Bon believed that crowds are especially susceptible to the sentiments unleashed by orators, particularly those who appear domineering and physically threatening. "An orator wishing to move a crowd must make an abusive use of violent affirmations," he wrote. "To exaggerate, to affirm, to resort to repetitions, and never to attempt to prove anything by reasoning are methods of argument well known to speakers at public meetings."[8] In the presence of such a demagogue, crowds become remarkably obedient, allowing all their darkest and most primitive urges to be channeled into the leader. This popular cult of the leader resembles military culture in its hierarchy and its violent disposition, but crucially—for Le Bon—lacks the norms of discipline and organization that wins wars. It grants a dangerous power to rhetorically gifted but reckless individuals.

There is something paradoxical in Le Bon's assessment. On the one hand, he believed modern crowds had become excessively pacified and weakened by socialist and democratic ideas, an indication that the people were no longer cut out for battle. But on the other hand, he saw a potential for violence lurking in crowd psychology, that could erupt through the veneer of civilian life at any moment. The riddle of the crowd was that it was both dangerous and cowardly at the same time, with an appetite for both too much violence and not enough. Fear and aggression often arise in tandem. Le Bon pessimistically concluded that crowds could neither fight wars *nor* sustain peace. But a better view of this ambiguity would hold that crowds can be actively mobilized for purposes other than just fighting—specifically, they can take private feelings of fear and pain, and render them public. Bodies can be assembled en masse to make a threat;

but they can also be assembled to demonstrate (or express solidarity with) what is under threat. This distinction is key to how political alliances are formed, contradicting those who insist that all populist movements and crowd dynamics are "the same."

Le Bon was right to see crowd psychology as a distinctive entity, rooted in our common corporeal existence, but his assumptions about where this must lead were too bleak. The human body and its nervous system are not, after all, a source only of danger and of fear, but also of compassion. The capacity to feel pain can provoke paranoia and hostility, but also empathy and a recognition of shared humanity. If, as Le Bon argued, crowd psychology reveals aspects of human life that civilization represses, then crowds can also perform valuable therapeutic work in excavating pains and fears that otherwise go unacknowledged. It is indeed risky to unlock those features of humanity that have long been denigrated as "irrational." But they need to go somewhere.

Politics as virus

This fascination with the sentiments of crowds might seem alien, especially to anyone who understands politics more in terms of party organization, policymaking, and legislation. In an age of representative democracy, the physical mobilization of vast numbers of people might seem outdated or irrelevant, a matter that appeals to a minority of unusually passionate political activists. But the processes that Le Bon was analyzing can be traced well beyond the limits of political congregations—indeed they shape our lives today in far more ways than Le Bon could have imagined.

Our contemporary notion of "viral marketing" (which subtly targets influential people, rather than communicating to the public all at once) is an example of systematically employed contagions. As more of our behavior and communication is digitally captured, and with rapid advances in "emotional artificial intelligence" (or "affective computing"), it is becoming possible to study the movement of emotions and sentiments through crowds with increasing scientific precision. Techniques of digital "sentiment analysis," algorithmically trained upon social media content, facial movements, and other bodily cues, is taking Le Bon's biological approach to psychology, and turning it into a whole industry of market research. The emotional content of a tweet, eye movement, or tone of voice can now be captured and analyzed. Faces in crowds can be recognized by smart cameras, which have been put to work in a pilot surveillance project by security services in Chongqing, China. In April 2018, police in Nanchang used facial recognition technology to identify a crime suspect from a crowd of 60,000 people at a pop concert.

Modern political campaigners understand that public opinion and sentiment can often best be swayed through small-scale and seemingly marginal interventions, rather than big formal announcements or information. Electoral systems which employ "first past the post," such as the United States and Britain, have a particular vulnerability to viral campaign tactics and crowd surges, as it is only ever a small number of people in pivotal regions that need persuading in order to sway the overall outcome. A focus on small-scale but influential triggers is also a feature of "nudge" techniques, through which policymakers seek to influence our decision making in areas such as nutrition and personal finance by subtly redesigning how choices are presented to us. In all these respects, the logic of the crowd (as Le Bon characterized it) already permeates our everyday lives, even those of us who would never think to attend a rally or occupation.

Most of us would accept that we are susceptible to emotional contagions in everyday social interactions. Indeed, it is a relief to become swept away by social cues, and not have to judge every situation on its objective merits. It would be odd to spend an evening with friends, constantly watching them with a critical eye, fact-checking their every claim, and resisting any instinctive agreement or shared mood. We know how physically responsive we are to social cues such as body language, and even bio-rhythms like heart rate. In the private and intimate sphere, none of this is cause for concern. But Le Bon's anxiety derived from the belief that democratic movements emerge from the same set of emotional and suggestible dimensions of the human psyche, to the point where it really doesn't matter to the crowd what is said, but merely how it makes them feel. Contagions are in fact less a matter of verbal communication than one of graphical and physical communication. When ideas are converted into images, and those images change the way we feel, then they start to travel through the crowd in the form of "sentiments," passing from person to person. The role of brands and logos today, which manage to communicate an idea or mood without using words, is testimony to the power of visual icons in influencing behavior.

Advertising first converted these insights into a specialist industry around the same time that Le Bon was developing them himself. Studies of human attention carried out by psychologists in the 1880s measured eye movements in order to understand how the mind responded to different stimuli. Early advertising experts adopted these techniques to understand how imagery and branding could attract consumer attention. In his 1928 work *Propaganda*, the Austrian-American Edward Bernays (Sigmund Freud's nephew) suggested that a similarly scientific approach should be used in the political realm. Bernays warned that politics had been left behind by business when it came to analyzing the emotional dimensions of communication. While corporations were busily harnessing the power of imagery and sound, politicians naively continued to fixate on words as the main means of influencing public sentiment. Bernays believed that democracy could only survive if politicians stopped worrying about trying to satisfy public demands, and focused more on trying to influence public sentiment, such that people were content with the status quo.

Bernays saw no contradiction between propaganda and democracy, indeed he believed his vision of a science of public relations was necessary to *save* democracy. "Ours must be a leadership democracy administered by the intelligent minority who know how to regiment and guide the masses," he argued. "Is this government by propaganda? Call it, if you prefer, government by education."[9] He assumed that what the public wants in a democracy is a sense of intimacy with their rulers—not to be listened to or represented, but to gain a *feeling* of proximity to power. It followed that "democratic" governments would be those that understood how to elicit such a sense of intimacy. The alternative was to risk a growing mismatch between the desires of the people, many of which he believed were unconscious, and the policies of the day. In the new context of mass suffrage, propaganda would be an indispensable tool if democracy was to avoid spiraling into chaos.

Whether elections or representative mechanisms are even necessary to produce this mass psychological outcome is unclear. One of the obstacles politicians face, Bernays believed, is that their public status makes it *too easy* for them to attract attention and get reported in the media, meaning they scarcely have to think more strategically about their messaging. They are slow to learn the techniques of public relations, because outdated assumptions about representative democracy and the public sphere prevent them from having to do so. The question politicians *should* be asking, Bernays argued, is how best to use imagery, sound, and speech in combination, so as to produce the right form of popular sentiment. The election of Ronald Reagan, a former film star, to the office of American president would have made perfect sense to Bernays. The arrival of a reality TV star in the Oval Office in January 2017 took things a stage further.

The Internet has given new forms to the multimedia aspect of crowd dynamics, including what some might call "propaganda." The fact that the Internet is as much a visual medium as a textual one is crucial to the power it offers to mobilize and influence crowds. The white supremacist "alt-right" movement began in online forums as a community of libertarians and ethno-nationalists, whose messages and sentiments were spread via pictorial memes, in contrast to the pamphlets, books, and articles that have provided the soil for political movements to grow in the past. One study of online propaganda identifies thirty states around the world, including Russia and China, that are engaged in deliberate use of social media to manipulate public opinion and voting behavior.[10]

The contemporary fear of propaganda really points to a more endemic problem, of how speedily information can circulate if it looks and feels true on a visual and emotional level. Researchers have shown that lies travel faster on Twitter than established facts.[11] Here again, we are all inhabitants of Le Bon's crowd, for whom "the unreal has almost as much influence on them as the real." The reader of the *Financial Times* may believe they are influenced only by facts, and never just by appearances. But if they share a *Financial Times* infographic on Facebook, are they actually doing so because of their attention to data and methodology, or because the logo and the pink background look credible? It's become increasingly clear that the discerning, educated public exist in their own cultural bubbles of content-sharing. Numerical evidence also has certain emotional resonances that attract and repel different people in different ways. The threat of "fake" digital content is getting worse, as artificial intelligence grows capable of generating artificial video footage.

As the power of contagion works its magic through an assembly of bodies, so basic Western assumptions about individual autonomy ("free will") get suspended. Le Bon is no longer read so much for his physiological analysis, but his speculation on the mind/body question is nevertheless suggestive. The actions of the person in a crowd "are far more under the influence of the spinal cord than the brain," he proposed.[12] The nervous system, which produces pain, arousal, stress, excitement, becomes the main organ of political activity. It is as feeling creatures that we become susceptible to contagions of sentiment, and not as intellectuals, critics, scientists, or even as citizens. This flies in the face of the political ideal of an informed, rational electorate. But for a figure such as Edward Bernays, it was a far more realistic basis on which to manage democracy in an age of mass suffrage and mass media than to place trust in public argument. The question was whether the lessons of crowd psychology (and the science of "propaganda") would be best learnt by leaders who still believed in democracy, as Bernays optimistically hoped, or by their opponents.

As crowd dynamics penetrate mass democracy, parties and leaders must strive to mobilize and engage the public, not simply at the level of policy preferences, but by provoking enthusiasm and deep commitment. Populist movements on both left and right disrupt the status quo by channeling a wider, deeper variety of feelings, fears, and physical needs into the political process. Populism may be frightening if it starts to take on the qualities of a violent "mob" as Le Bon warned. But it also potentially expands the appeal and vitality of democracy, beyond the limitations of existing parliamentary and party systems. Crowd dynamics help to reconnect politics to deep human needs, bringing shared feelings—including shared vulnerability—directly into the public domain, rather than waiting for journalists or professional politicians to represent them. Populist surges in Europe and the United States have drawn attention to the lives and experiences of marginalized people who were hitherto ignored. There is certainly risk attached to this, but that is the nature of democracy.

The politics of feeling doesn't automatically lend itself to support for autocratic "strong man" leaders. That threat arises in relation to one particular emotion, namely fear, which can become a danger in its own right. For all the reasons identified by Le Bon, crowds are liable to a vicious circle of fear, in which the perception of threats is amplified and anxiety grows, until the mere feeling of violence produces actual violence. Nervous states can then teeter on the edge of conflict. The mere sense of danger produces a rising desire for safety, which autocrats satisfy through making threats towards others. Much of the nervousness that influences democracy today is not simply because feelings have invaded a space previously occupied by reason, but because the likely sources and nature of violence have become harder to specify.

Weapons of everyday life

When two civilian airliners collided with the World Trade Center on the morning of September 11, 2001, it marked a new era in the use of violence in civil society. The resulting mood has since infected the activities of governments, civilians, and terrorists themselves. Terrorists had previously sought or threatened to destroy buildings and airplanes, for maximum public impact, but they had done so using tools that were purpose-built for violence: guns and explosives. One thing that was different about September 11 was that it involved no purpose-built weapon at all. A civilian jet plane was repurposed as a missile.

In the years that followed, terrorists employed other civilian vehicles as weapons, namely cars and trucks. The tactic of driving cars into crowds of people was first used by terrorists in Israel, and was subsequently repeated in numerous cities, including London, New York, Nice, and Stockholm. This is profoundly disturbing to social peace for several reasons. First, such an attack often involves very little planning on the part of the perpetrators, which lowers the bar for an otherwise powerless individual to launch an assault. Some vehicle-ramming attacks were swiftly named as "terrorism," before later being recognized as the actions of mentally unstable individuals or simple road accidents. Second, such events produce the unconscious feeling that violence could arise from anywhere, attaching risk to ordinary activities such as shopping or sightseeing. Entirely innocent behaviors can also provoke paranoia, if they become viewed in a certain way.

These types of events have the primary effect of highlighting the acute vulnerability of citizens, no matter how rich or strong their governments might be. Where terrorists lack orthodox weaponry or political power, specialist security services find them paradoxically harder to combat. By far the most devastating terrorist attacks still occur in less prosperous societies, using more conventional weaponry of guns and bombs. But the effect of terrorist attacks in Europe has been primarily psychological, as it undermines the authority of governments as a source of protection. When violence no longer uses conventional weapons and becomes aimed at ordinary crowds, the power of the security services shrinks significantly. Vicious circles of fear and knee-jerk reaction become more likely, and sensitivity to danger is heightened.

The notion of "weaponizing" everyday tools has become a familiar part of the political lexicon. The Kremlin has been accused of seeking to *weaponize* social media so as to disrupt democratic elections and spread confusion in the media. As with cars or planes, Facebook and Twitter can be treated as tools of disruption or even violence, as they have the capacity to destabilize and spread fear. Internet "trolls" seek out convivial online discussions and activities, and find innovative ways to disrupt them for no real reason other than because they can. The key to weaponizing an otherwise peaceful tool is simply to see it with a different aspect, not in terms of its intended function, but in terms of its full range of possible impacts. Equally, with the right mind-set, all manner of peaceful activities can be viewed as possible opportunities for disruption and harm, especially where they involve a crowd of people. It is impossible for security services to anticipate every new weaponization, as its main resource is the infinite creativity of human imagination.

Media technologies play an important role here. The attacks of September 11, 2001, were planned to be televised, with a fifteen-minute gap between the two strikes on the World Trade Center. Smartphones and social media massively expand the range of activities that can be videoed and shared globally, allowing small-scale attacks and acts of sabotage to be carried out anywhere in the hope of achieving heroic status. Disruption and gratuitous harm achieve a new allure, where there is the possibility for the entire world to witness it. The same problem afflicts public dialogue, where a party intervenes simply to draw attention to themselves, no matter what harm is done in the process. Conversely, the accusation that a speaker is seeking to weaponize an issue implies they are acting in bad faith (that is, they don't really mean what they say), the habitual accusation that dogs so many online political discussions.

Weaponization of everyday things weakens the distinction between war and peace, injecting fear into politics as it does so. It casts fresh uncertainty upon the possible sources and nature of violence, divorcing them from recognized institutions and groups. Hannah Arendt made a useful distinction between "power" and "violence," which illuminates the way weaponry has become increasingly detached from organization. Power, she argued, means the capacity to organize large numbers of people, using rules, infrastructures, and leaders. It has a constructive quality. It involves bureaucracies, plans, agreements and policies, costing time and money to maintain. Power may not necessarily work toward a desirable goal, but it does involve the careful assembly of political associations and hierarchies, most prominently the state itself. A military force can exercise power, if it seeks to occupy and pacify a territory, or to introduce peacekeeping measures. Power is both predictable and visible in its operation, creating a shared sense of reality and normality in the process.

Violence, on the other hand, is purely "instrumental": it uses weapons to force someone to do something against their will. It doesn't build anything, but simply exploits whatever opportunities are at hand. Aerial bombing is an example of pure violence, seeking to destroy without any ambition to rule. "Violence can always destroy power," Arendt wrote, "out of the barrel of a gun grows the most effective command, resulting in the most instant and perfect obedience. What can never grow out of it is power." This is an important insight as we struggle to understand present political afflictions. In many ways we have become far better at disseminating opportunities for violence (with or without conventional weapons) than at distributing power. The opportunities are not always seized, but they exist nevertheless, and shape the political mood.

Arendt argued that, in practice, power and violence are almost always combined. Governments seek legitimacy through laws, procedures, and elections ("power"), but also rely on prisons, secret services, and riot vans ("violence"). Terrorists achieve notoriety for violence, but usually also have strategies, leaders, and funders with which to achieve their political goals. But the implication of things being "weaponized" is that violence starts to arise independently of power. Tools, such as cars and social media platforms, become subverted as weapons, purely because they can be. Computer hacking and trolling can have a gratuitous dimension to them, being carried out purely to demonstrate the weakness of the target, as with a vehicle-ramming attack. As people become more disempowered—and especially as they start to feel humiliated for some reason—the temptation to weaponize peaceful equipment becomes all the greater. Disruption is an alternative to control.

The effect of such tactics is primarily psychological, but that doesn't mean that it shouldn't count as violence. What it damages are the feelings of security and trust that allow diverse societies to function, and it replaces them with nervousness. The power of democratic and civic institutions is eroded, without anything else being put in its place. Acts of violence may not be the cause of declining trust in government, but they—often intentionally—encourage and accelerate it.

The question is, what do we *do* with a feeling of physical vulnerability? What kind of crowd dynamics and politics does it produce? Le Bon assumed that crowds would quickly resort to violence, especially when mobilized by a reckless charismatic leader. He feared that, in a crowd, a person's feelings of weakness can suddenly flip into a "sentiment of invincible power which allows him to yield to instincts which, had he been alone, he would perforce have kept under restraint."[13] A sense of collective victimhood can be cultivated until it triggers aggression. Political rallies *can* take on the feeling of military or mob-like assemblies, serving to showcase the potential physical muscle available. Far-right groups in Poland and Hungary have used mass public rallies as a thinly veiled threat of violence to come, although support for autocracy in those countries is no higher than average and lower than in the UK.[14] The death of Heather Heyer in Charlottesville, Virginia, in August 2017, after being hit by a speeding car while protesting a white supremacist rally, was a shocking demonstration of the violence that can be deliberately unleashed where large numbers of people are assembled.

The mood of the mob can quickly spiral into a desire for and celebration of conflict, as a means of collective invigoration and purification. Le Bon himself saw war as a positive antidote to socialism and excessive democracy. Nationalists have long bemoaned the influence of pacifists, "liberal elites" and (more recently) "political correctness" for neutering the unity and fighting spirit of the people. Media executive, outspoken nationalist, and former Trump adviser Steve Bannon holds a dim view of the moral fiber of American society, which he believes has been weakened by globalization and can only be repaired with war. "Is that grit still there," he asks, "that tenacity, that we've seen on the battlefield?"[15] The only way to rediscover it, in Bannon's view, is to take to the battlefield once again.

And yet the feeling of vulnerability often has wildly different consequences. In recent history, what has mobilized crowds has more often been opposition to violence than desire for it. Civil rights and anti-war movements have produced many of the largest marches of the postwar era. The 2018 March For Our Lives rallies, held to protest against weak gun laws following the attack at a high school in Parkland, Florida, drew hundreds of thousands of people into the streets. In the face of violence, these crowds channel a different emotion, defiant but unwarlike, bringing a mass of bodies together as evidence of shared humanity rather than of collective threat. Physical vulnerability cannot be eliminated, so the question is how we learn to live with that. The great strength of the crowd that mobilizes against violence is that it is nonexclusive: the sentiment it draws on is a potentially universal human one, and not of some unique or exotic victimhood.

There is no absolute way of distinguishing the "violent" from the "nonviolent" crowd. As Martin Luther King Jr. said, a "riot is the language of the unheard." Transgression possesses a particular type of power, when it comes to engaging with a crowd and drawing attention. Especially online, anger and rage have a particular capacity to move people and coordinate them. In the "attention economy" in which all media outlets are now competing, the expression of outrage attracts more eyeballs than calmness and rationality. Studies of online networks show that text can spread more virally when it contains a high degree of "moral emotion."[16] The quest for attention is also the motivating force of all trolls. Civil rights movements, environmental campaigns, and nonviolent protests in general cannot entirely forgo the use of disruptive tactics that are likely to mobilize people behind them. The question we *can* ask, however, is whether a crowd exists primarily to highlight suffering or to showcase a threat. Does it aim to increase fear or alleviate it? These distinctions have decisive implications for the kinds of democratic movements and political demands that might follow.

The sense that language itself is being weaponized, so as to undermine trust and provoke fear, has become prevalent with the spread of social media and the trolling practices that go with it. Part of the problem consists in our never quite knowing where the boundary between speech and violence lies. This is particularly difficult to establish online, where metaphors of violence are common, but where threats of violence can still be a criminal offence. University students have attracted scorn from older generations and conservatives for practices such as "no-platforming" of speakers deemed offensive, the use of "trigger warnings" to identify certain cultural content as containing violence, and the creation of "safe spaces" where certain political views are unwelcome. To many critics, these practices are pure censorship, and there is never any justification for reducing freedom of speech. They make more sense when viewed as tactics of engagement, through which groups choose who to share space and attention with.

The reframing of public debate along the lines of "war" has often been driven by chauvinistic ideologues eager to intimidate and marginalize their opponents in the first place. Figures such as Milo Yiannopoulos and James Delingpole of Breitbart choose to view democracy and mass culture as a space of combat, in which the strong must overwhelm the weak. They may fall back on more pacifist notions of "free speech" when it suits them, but the reframing of intellectual debate as a form of violence has been advanced by the aggressors as much as by the "snowflakes" whom they so despise. Leaked emails from Bannon, then of Breitbart, to Yiannopoulos sent in late 2016 included lines such as this: "Dude—we r in a global existentialist war where our enemy EXISTS in social media. . . . Drop your toys, pick up your tools and go help save western civilization."[17] Who is to say with any certainty that metaphors of violence have nothing to do with actual violence?

These are uncomfortable realities to confront. The anger, intimidation, and lies that have crept into the media and civil society, destabilizing institutions without constructing alternatives, can generate a downward spiral of fear and mutual suspicion. Politicians of the far right, often loosely allied to online and offline crowds using intimidation, are successfully mobilizing people who are and feel disempowered. Across Europe, the European Union provides a target for nationalists seeking to explain why their society isn't safer and richer. In Arendt's terms, violence becomes attractive when power doesn't seem available, because the "elites" have apparently hoarded it all. Resistance to these nationalist sentiments cannot simply involve a rejection of crowds out of hand. It needs to identify a different set of feelings, to generate a different type of crowd.

Not in my name!

Three months after Trump's inauguration, another crowd descended on Washington, DC. The "March for Science" was billed as "the first step of a global movement to defend the vital role science plays in our health, safety, economies, and governments." As its slogan put it, "it's time to get off the sidelines and make a difference." The march was partly a response to a series of alarming appointments and policy decisions made by the Trump administration that appeared to threaten the public status and financing of scientific research in a range of fields. The appointment of Robert Kennedy Jr., a prominent vaccine conspiracy theorist, to chair a commission on "vaccination safety and scientific integrity" was one of these. Cuts to climate-science budgets of NASA and the Environmental Protection Agency were another.

More diffusely, the march provided an outlet for widespread disgust that the new administration seemed content to allow established scientific truths to become matters of perspective and opinion. US conservatives have challenged the influence of modern science on a range of fronts, especially in areas such as biology where evolution undermines religious beliefs. But the ascent of Trump seemed to have amplified the problem, not simply sowing doubt where scientists saw fact, but injecting chaos into political discourse, as if "reality" had ceased to provide any constraints at all.

Against this backdrop, the March for Science offered an opportunity to demonstrate that experts also command popular support. In an age of crowd-based politics, in which emotions trump evidence, the march arguably fought fire with fire. A similar rationale informed the "Unite for Europe" march that had taken place a month earlier in London, in which pro-EU voices and sentiments gathered to demonstrate their own popularity, at a time when nationalist and pro-Brexit movements seemed to be dominating Britain's political agenda. The March for Science was not without its critics. What was unusual was that many of them came from the very community it was intended to defend.

One such critic was physicist Professor Jim Gates, a leading string theorist and a former adviser to Barack Obama. "To have science represented as this political force I think is just extraordinarily dangerous," he said. There was a risk that the whole event could be perceived as "science against Trump." What purpose was it seeking to serve? This question was frequently put to movements such as Occupy, which was accused of having no positive agenda. But scientists were arguably more damaged by a perception that they were behaving obstructively, rather than rationally. The science-policy scholar Roger Pielke Jr. argued that scientists needed to be more scientific in their adoption of campaigning tools, and while a march was a legitimate form of democratic expression, there was scant evidence that it would work in achieving any goals, whatever these might be.

The March for Science was open to all, and took place across several cities at once. It wasn't just an assembly of scientists and technocrats, although something of that nature had already occurred in Boston in February 2017, following the annual meeting of the American Association for the Advancement of Science. Defenders of the March for Science could argue, reasonably enough, that it provided a rallying point for those concerned about the climate, school curricula, vaccination, not to mention the steady stream of lies that kept pouring out of the White House. If it felt obstructive at all, then maybe that was a good thing.

The immediate risk with an event of this nature is that it turns reason and objectivity into political values like any others—things that need justifying, fighting for, assembling a coalition around. By entering the fray of marches and polemical argument, scientists risk turning 'facts' into precisely the type of hot political issues that religious conservatives, climate skeptics and conspiracy theorists already deem them to be. The worry is that support for science becomes just another form of shared identity or emotional tendency, clustered in certain cultural communities and regions but not others. As Le Bon might have warned the March for Science, you tap the emotional power of the crowd at your peril, for once you've switched gears into a politics of sentiment and suggestion, you can't suddenly switch back and appeal to objectivity and reason. If crowds are where feeling is substituted for reason, perhaps a "march for science" is ultimately self-defeating.

According to the ideal of modern science, scientists are unlike members of a crowd or political figures, because they are able to separate their feelings from their observations. They are able to distinguish that which is a matter of "fact," from that which is one of perspective, ethics, or emotion. They can do so because they are able to park their own identities when they enter the laboratory or field, and act merely as neutral mediators between the data that they collect and the documents that end up in journals. Unlike digital media networks, scientists slow things down: the expert collects data carefully, analyzes it critically, then represents it in a standardized form, rather than trusting and sharing every sensory impression as it arrives. In a similar fashion, when acting as advisers they should aspire to be what Pielke terms "honest brokers," neutral intermediaries between those with the evidence and those designing policies. They are swayed only by the evidence in front of them, rather than the sentiments of those around them. The ability of experts to regulate—and often disregard—their own feelings is crucial to their authority.

To put that another way, scientists seek our trust and respect because they promise to represent things accurately. Their data is a valid representation of nature. Their publications are a valid representation of that data. Their policy advice is a valid response to those publications. To trust in science is to trust in the capacity of people to report and record things in an adequate fashion, and to leave their own biases and emotions at the door. When they tell us how things are, we are willing to "take their word for it," rather than constantly refer back to the thing itself. It is the same kind of trust as that which we might place in a professional journalist, accountant, or a doctor, that they will provide accurate (albeit specialist) reports on what they encounter. And it mirrors the trust we might place in a government official or police officer, that the records they keep are a valid representation of what has happened. This capacity to use language and paperwork in a rigid, reliable fashion is precisely what Le Bon saw evaporating as soon as people entered crowds. It is also what is slipping away today, as trust in the basic institutions of representative democracy and the professional media goes into decline.

Journalists, judges, experts, and various other "elites" are under fire today. Fewer and fewer people believe they are independent. Their capacity to reflect the truth in a neutral fashion, whether as scientists, professionals, journalists or policy advisers, is now attacked on the grounds that it is more self-interested and emotional than the protagonists are willing to let on. From the perspective of many populists, elite journalists project independence, but clearly favor politicians from their own cultural and educational background, and refuse to confront their own privileges. Climate scientists profess to be presenting the "facts" but then—it seems to their critics—get into bed with environmental NGOs. Economists purport to be "scientific," but behave scornfully towards anyone who fails to grasp that free trade is an obvious good. The accusation is that they have in a sense "weaponized" their public status, so as to serve particular interests. In short, all of them are deemed guilty of hypocrisy. And, as Arendt observed, if there is one thing most likely to convert engagement into enragement— more even than injustice—it is hypocrisy.[18]

It is sometimes questioned why antipathy to "elites" rarely manifests itself in scapegoating of the very rich. How can men as wealthy as Beppe Grillo, Aaron Banks, Andrej Babis, or Peter Thiel claim to be leading a movement against *elites*? To which the answer is: unlike a journalist, a government statistician, a member of parliament, or a lawyer, the rich never claim to be speaking for anyone other than themselves. They make no claim to public status, and therefore they cannot be accused of hypocrisy. The perceived arrogance of the expert or professional politician is in claiming some disembodied, dispassionate perspective, not available to the ordinary businessman, consumer, Twitter-user or crowd-member. And so the minute any of these figures forms a crowd of their own or shows emotion, their antagonists have proved a point.

Populism across left and right is really a rebellion against systems of representation of one kind or another—an unmasking of our "representatives" as nothing but self-interested cynics and hypocrites. The relationships between political representatives and the people, between "mainstream media" and actual events, between science and reality, all become viewed as a scam. When trust in one of these elite groups disintegrates, it tends to impact upon trust in all of them. Once people stop trusting systems of representation in general, and especially in the political system, they become less interested in what counts as "true" and what as "false."[19] Liars can become tolerated or even admired, once the very foundations of a political system are no longer viewed as credible.

"Not in my name" has become one of the most popular slogans of anti-war protests, suggesting that our so-called elected representatives are not in fact representative at all. Marine Le Pen has made great play out of the cultural intimacy of French politicians and leading newspapers, referring to them as the "media-political system" or simply as "*la caste*." "The Clinton media" is how Trump supporters would routinely describe East Coast news agencies such as CNN and the *New York Times* when their reporters arrived at his campaign rallies. It is revealing that 61% of those who voted for Trump in 2016 express distrust in the media, compared to 27% of Clinton voters.[20] The term "political correctness" can now be used to mock and debase virtually anyone who believes that how one speaks in public should be different from how one does so in private.

The disintegrating technical division between public and private is making it ever harder to maintain the "disinterested" ideal of representatives. Ad hominem attacks on scientists are just as effective in discrediting their research as criticisms of their research methods.[21] An effect of ubiquitous digital media is to capture the private whims and foibles of public figures, providing a gift to would-be whistle-blowers and leakers, and rendering scandal a virtually constant feature of public life. These vivid details all have the effect of dismantling the claim that it is possible to act in "the public interest" and put one's own feelings and desires to one side. In contrast to all this apparent posturing, the crowd is just what it claims to be: a swarm of human bodies, congregating around a shared feeling, cause, or leader. There is no representation, just mobilization, with an authenticity of emotion that technocrats and elites apparently lack.

The dilemma represented by the March for Science is one faced by many experts and professionals as they confront their contemporary foes: retain a demeanor of rationality and get accused of being "cold," "arrogant," or "distant," or show some passion and then be accused of being no better than your critics. It is the impossible dilemma that trolls seek to contrive online, as they escalate their offensiveness in search of a reaction, and then mock their victim for reacting. It is a trap with no simple means of escape.

Much of the time it is wisest to refuse engagement altogether. That does, however, signal that the public sphere and the public status of experts is no longer the same as it used to be. It demonstrates that the politics of crowds and mobilization described here is now unavoidable, even for those who would prefer to operate exclusively in the currency of objective "facts." Experts cannot help but recognize which "platform" they have chosen to stand on, who they are sharing it with, and whether it is wise to be doing so. But maybe this is a long-overdue wake-up call for those who scarcely ever considered the politics of the knowledge they produce, then share with the public. If even independent experts are having to defend their public status by mobilizing popular support, it is clear that we are undergoing a major historic shift.

Many wish normal politics might survive simply through a reassertion of existing centers of expertise and technocratic government. This is not an option. Scientists may not see themselves as activists, but they need to start, and the March for Science gave a glimpse of what this might look like. The very possibility of a "neutral" perspective has been thrown into doubt by various technological and economic forces that need to be carefully traced and understood. The isolation of reason from feeling is no longer clear-cut. The politics of crowds is creeping into spaces that were once reserved for experts and official representatives with many frightening consequences, but perhaps some welcome ones too.

The modern dream of objective, technocratic government is in very serious trouble. But if we're to understand why, we need first of all to pay much closer attention to the origins and authority of expertise, and the ideal of an objective "apolitical" perspective that accompanies it. One benefit of the current turbulence is that it forces us to look afresh at institutions and traditions we had taken for granted. The attempt to elevate fact over feeling has a long history that is fraught with politics. If there is anything to be saved or resuscitated from the ideal of dispassionate expertise, then we need to understand its genesis. In doing so, we will also discover that "the facts" have never appeared out of nowhere, but are a product of careful institutional design, which might now need refreshing or reforming.

2

KNOWLEDGE FOR PEACE

The birth of expertise

In December 2009, Britain's National Audit Office (NAO) published a report offering an evaluation of a piece of government spending. There is nothing remarkable about that. Assessing the efficiency and effectiveness of public-sector projects is what the NAO exists to do, much like the Government Accountability Office in the United States. This is important work but it's not glamorous and only rarely attracts much media interest. But the December 2009 report in question was more eye-catching, touching on the most foundational functions of the modern state. The report was an evaluation and cost analysis of the government's decision to bail out banks in autumn 2008, but the implications reached much further. It also provided a window through which to inspect the political power of experts, which, as will become clear, has as much to do with the quest for peace as for truth. Reactions against expertise may seem like an irrational rejection of truth itself, yet they are more often a rejection of the broader political edifice from which society is governed. It's not just truth that is at stake but the manner in which feelings of security and trust are generated.

The NAO put the cost of the bank rescue package at £850 billion, over half of Britain's GDP at the time. This sum covered the purchase of shares in RBS, Lloyds, and Northern Rock banks, plus the provision of guarantees, insurance of assets, liquidity provisions, and loans to the financial sector. The government was able to do this thanks to a vast increase in public borrowing, which saw the UK's national debt roughly double between 2007 and 2011. The rescue of the financial sector was dramatic and unprecedented, occurring through a series of rapid decisions made among a small group of senior politicians and advisers, often late at night or over weekends while the banks were closed. In its tremendous scale and pace, this was no ordinary public-spending project. Nevertheless, the NAO concluded on the basis of all the evidence that it was "justified."

Eight hundred and fifty billion pounds was enough to cover the cost of the National Health Service for around eight years, so it is reassuring to know that it was money well spent. On the other hand, what could it possibly mean for experts to carry out an *audit* on this type of epoch-shaping emergency measure? How could they have reached any other conclusion, given what was at stake? The NAO recognized that it was operating at the outer limits of what an auditor could scientifically demonstrate. "It is difficult to imagine the scale of the consequences for the economy and society if major banks had been allowed to collapse," the report admitted. Difficult for an auditor to demonstrate scientifically on the basis of public accounts and paper trails, perhaps—but not impossible for anyone who reflected a little bit on the role banks play in sustaining society as we know it. Let's try to imagine it for a moment.

The banking crisis of autumn 2008 came after a year in which banks had been increasingly reluctant to lend to each other, or what was known as the "credit crunch." If banks were allowed to collapse, confidence in the overall banking system would likely evaporate, producing bank runs, which could only be averted if banks remained closed, withdrawing all credit-making facilities in the process. The sensible thing for customers to do would be to extract as much cash from ATMs as possible until they were empty. Banks would not fill them up again, and payment processing facilities would be suspended. Without banks to provide society with cash or credit, the capacity of consumers and businesses to purchase things from each other would last only a few days.

Suddenly, so-called "advanced" capitalist societies could be dominated by problems of individual survival: in our age of just-in-time inventories, supermarkets only stock enough food to feed the population for a few days. Some peaceful relations of barter might be feasible, but these take a while to emerge, and are scarcely able to mediate the types of complex supply chains and industrialized production methods that allow modern societies to keep people fed and warm. In the meantime, dystopian fantasies of people foraging for survival would become more plausible. Primitive forms of self-defense and sustenance would emerge. Maintaining order could become a job for the army, if civil society were not to be stretched to a breaking point.

All this, presumably, was what the NAO was nodding toward when it referred to the consequences for "society," and not just for the "economy," had the government not done what it did. The emergency of the financial crisis was a reminder of the fragility of social peace and the centrality of money in sustaining trust. Money is really nothing other than a type of promise ("I promise to pay the bearer on demand . . . ," as it says on a British banknote), which depends on trust in order to work. Thanks to the intricate workings of the banking system and the underwriting of the state, it has become a type of promise that strangers are willing to accept from one another. If the monetary system collapses, the possibility of civil and peaceful exchange can disintegrate with it. For example, the choice that the Greek government was presented with by the European Union in the summer of 2015 was between agreeing to a financial bailout, but with heavy obligations attached, or—if they declined that—receiving humanitarian aid to assist with the social catastrophe that would result from a financial collapse. Money performs a basic peacekeeping function.

But as the emergency of the financial crisis receded, it also cast a new light on the technocrats at the heart of our financial system, who were emerging from the crisis with considerably more power than they'd had at the outset. Total civil meltdown had been averted, but the circulation of money remained on the brink of seizing up even several years later. As one recurrent metaphor had it, the financial system had suffered the equivalent of a heart attack, and the recuperation was slow, as the mechanisms responsible for pumping money around—namely the banks—remained in a critical state.[1] The recovery was overseen by central banks, staffed by unelected experts, whose task it was to prevent the system collapsing all over again.

The technique that came to be deployed in Britain and the United States, then later in the eurozone, was "quantitative easing." This saw central banks purchasing hundreds of billions of pounds' worth of assets from pension funds. This strategy pushes money through the banking system (where pension funds keep their cash), which is intended to revive bank lending in the process. But the mystery at the heart of this practice is that central banks don't actually have all that money in the first place: they create it by adding numbers to the bank accounts of the pension companies and adding the same amount as a liability on their own balance sheet.

Sublime sums of money were created this way: $4.5 trillion in the United States, $2.4 trillion in the eurozone and £400 billion in the UK. If the aim was to prevent another financial heart attack, it worked, but the benefits to the broader economy were vague at best. The aftermath of the banking meltdown was still felt in drastic loss of output and productivity, especially in Europe. The language of economics seemed somehow ill-equipped to capture the enormity of the shock that had occurred, and metaphors of life and death recurred. Andy Haldane, chief economist at the Bank of England, explained that this was the type of national economic shock that had only previously been witnessed during wartime.[2] But it was economists in central banks and treasury departments who had ended up with much of the power to steer us through this treacherous situation. They were being tasked with making quick-fire decisions, of the greatest possible consequence, with little possibility for consultation or public debate. Was that really what experts were *for*?

These events are typical of some of the confusions and controversies that now surround the political power of experts, which can incite suspicion and resentment. The appearance of quantitative easing coincided with that of the Tea Party movement in the United States, which fixated on the policy as the definitive example of establishment corruption, through which financial and government elites could rip off the public in secret. The sheer complexity of the policy didn't help, and few of the economists involved in delivering it expressed much confidence in what the outcome was likely to be. After the policy was finished, the Bank of England's own website admitted that "it is difficult to tell if [quantitative easing] has worked, and how well." One of the few indisputable features of quantitative easing is that it benefits the wealthy, as it inflates the price of assets (including real estate), adding to the feeling that this was a conspiracy by elites against ordinary people.[3] In what sense were economic technocrats really being objective or apolitical any longer?

What is even more bewildering about this whole story is how it combines matters of economic expertise, such as model-building and risk analysis, with matters of the greatest national urgency. One moment we were trusting experts to provide an objective analysis of the world; the next, we were trusting them to act decisively to stave off threats to the basic fabric of civil society. Financial regulators and central banks hire people on the basis of their economic and mathematical skills, but have ended up with far weightier responsibilities.

The increased number of politically appointed experts within the state (what are known in Britain as "special advisors") together with politically aligned think tanks in civil society means that the pursuit of facts and the pursuit of power are now often overlapping. The career path linking technical policy or communications expertise to the highest offices of state (exemplified by Emmanuel Macron and David Cameron) demolishes the image of experts as "apolitical" in many eyes. Right-wing populists have taken aim at central banks, with a 2016 Trump campaign video suggesting that Janet Yellen, then chair of the Federal Reserve, was in league with Wall Street bosses, and Europhobic British politician Jacob Rees-Mogg naming Mark Carney, governor of the Bank of England, an "enemy of Brexit." The insulation of technocrats from politics is over, and any claims to dispassionate objectivity have lost credibility.

To understand the co-evolution of expertise and modern government, the place to start is when war and peace were far more fatally entangled than they are today, when questions of truth were matters of life or death. A condition of constant physical threats and nervousness eventually elevated peace to being the overriding political priority in Europe. Just fifty years saw the development of the ingredients that would come to make up technocracy, indeed the main ingredients of modern government itself. In the UK these include a bureaucratic Civil Service, a professional salaried military, expert economic advisers, publicly funded science, and the foundation of the Bank of England. Within this comparatively small historical window are compressed the origins of contemporary elites and expertise. And what this history demonstrates is that many of the expectations we hold for "truth" are fueled as much by a fear of violence as they are by a passion for knowledge.

The escape from war

As the English Civil War was raging between 1642 and 1651, the philosopher Thomas Hobbes was living in France, working on a series of philosophical works that would lead up to his 1651 masterpiece, *Leviathan*, the book that has defined the landscape of modern political philosophy ever since. Hobbes was already in his sixties by the time he wrote the book, and had enjoyed a varied life, working for a while as a tutor to the Earl of Devonshire, which granted him a privileged perspective on English politics of the day. This association took him on a grand tour of Europe as a young man, through which he met a number of scientific pioneers, including Francis Bacon, for whom he later worked as a secretary. During the 1630s he became acquainted with the anatomist William Harvey, who had discovered the circulation of the blood, and it's possible that Hobbes may even have been treated by him in later life.

Hobbes's life coincided with the bloodiest and most protracted religious wars that Europe has ever seen. The Thirty Years War, which began in 1618, erupted over religious conflicts between Catholic and Protestant states in regions now belonging to Germany, but drew in armies from Sweden, Denmark, Spain, Italy, and Poland. The armies that fought these wars were unpredictable and ruthless, terrorizing and plundering civilian villages as they marched. Religious differences were the catalyst, but the wars escalated into matters of territorial and dynastic power. By the time peace was declared with the famous Treaty of Westphalia of 1648, which established the basic idea of national sovereignty that we still recognize today, 8 million people had died.

What had led Hobbes to France was a simple and universal emotion: fear. Thanks to his political connections, he'd been well placed to observe the tensions that were mounting in England between Parliament and the king during the 1630s. While he attempted to avoid taking any side in the conflict, a work of his published in 1640 was interpreted as a defense of the king. He had close connections to the monarchy, which led him to a job working as math tutor to the future Charles II, while he was in exile in France. Furthermore, Hobbes was increasingly concerned that he was being read as an atheist, and feared that he might be arrested on those grounds. He fled the country in 1640.

The political and religious conditions in Europe in the mid-seventeenth century meant that risks were attached to a wide range of intellectual and philosophical positions. To challenge the political authority of the church (as Hobbes did) was to leave one open to the charge of atheism. The dominant philosophical schools of the time, derived from the ideas of Aristotle, were themselves implicated in violent theological conflicts concerning the nature of morality and the basic substance of reality. Battles were being fought in the name of one truth versus another. Hobbes held nothing but scorn for the "schoolmen" who fueled these retrograde disputes. Above all, he believed that philosophy and science ought to provide a basis of peaceful consensus rather than of violent conflict. This is one reason to take his ideas seriously today.

Hobbes was deeply impressed by the advances of anatomists such as Harvey and of astronomers such as Johannes Kepler and Galileo. What underpinned this scientific progress, as Hobbes saw it, was an emphasis on mathematics and geometry, and not on idle and often moralistic speculation as the basis of all truth. Whether it be the circulation of the planets or of the blood (or, as we will see, of money), the underlying reality was always the same, namely the mathematical laws that governed bodies in motion. Geometry revealed the basic rules of physical existence.

This is not to say that the study of mathematics and geometry had no religious dimensions. Scientific pioneers, including Sir Isaac Newton and Bacon, believed that the study of nature's physical mechanics was a way of getting closer to God. For many Protestant sects and for Calvinists in particular, the study of mathematics represented the type of ascetic "good work" that could gain God's approval.[4] According to this philosophy, God produced the world as a machine for human beings to use, and it is our moral duty to understand how it functions. Hobbes concurred with this up to a point, arguing that geometry was "the onely Science that it hath pleased God hitherto to bestow on mankind;" however, he had no intention of grounding his understanding of mathematics or physics in theology.[5] Reason could operate along purely secular lines.

By committing to reason, Hobbes believed philosophy could guide scientific enquiry. Science, as we now know it, was known as "natural philosophy," and not yet separated from philosophical questions, such as the nature of causality and freedom. Philosophers could therefore reveal how nature works, Hobbes argued, as long as they employed strict rational thinking, which he understood as a type of mathematical "computation," not necessarily in a numerical sense, but in the sense of carefully adding one concept on top of another.[6] This was necessarily a slow and painstaking process. To reason was to think in a deliberate way, as if using building blocks, such that every proposition was strong enough to ground the next one. A chain of mathematical arithmetic breaks down if one link is not correctly calculated. Likewise, you cannot understand the motions of the planets or the human body if there isn't careful attention to the cause and effect linking each physical movement to the next. The universe was like a vast billiard table, in which objects traveled around, occasionally ricocheting off one another in predictable directions. Hobbes was sufficiently optimistic that his quasi-mathematical method was correct that he believed that questions of natural philosophy could be answered in ways on which everyone could (or should) agree. If consensus could be achieved on the most basic questions of truth, conflict would be over.

Picturing the world

If reality is ultimately a matter of geometric, mechanical movements, to be discerned by a form of mental computation, what can we learn from our physical impressions of the world? What do our *senses*—our eyes, ears, nose, and so on—contribute to scientific progress? During the 1630s, this question had provoked one of the most decisive existential crises in the history of Western thought, as the French philosopher René Descartes dramatically cast doubt on the images that his eyes presented to him. How can I know that what I see is actually real, and not simply an illusion as experienced in a dream? Given the way a stick appears to bend when it is placed in water, why should I trust the data that I receive via my eyes? In fact, how can I know that *I* even exist at all?

Descartes' famous escape from this doom-loop of doubt was to consider that the very fact of him having these doubts is enough to demonstrate that he existed, at least as a thinking being, if not as a bodily one: "I think therefore I am." However, the realm of the thinking, metaphysical mind (of which I can be certain) and that of the feeling, physical body (of which I am uncertain) would become split into parallel spheres of reality. I, understood as a mind or self, exist completely independently of the body I happen to be physically located in, and could equally exist without it—hence Descartes' belief in the immortality of the soul. From his perspective, rational thought can achieve certainty, but anything that reaches us via our physical feelings—such as images, sounds, or pain—is to be treated with the utmost suspicion. "Nothing is easier for the mind to know but itself," but everything else is dubious.[7]

Descartes was, however, somewhat obsessed with the state of his own body. Minds and bodies might be made of different stuff, but the former depend on the latter. He was neurotic about his physical health and the prospect of death, fixating on strategies for extending longevity. The tragedy of humankind was to have an immortal substance (mind) housed in a mortal one (body). Despite believing animals had no moral value, he was a committed vegetarian, living off plants from his own garden which he believed would add to his vitality. He saw a hundred years as a realistic lifespan to aim for, though reluctantly gave up on that goal for himself when he saw how slowly medical advances were moving. Pneumonia took his life at the age of fifty-three.

Descartes may not have invented our current ideal of a rational scientific mind, but he gave it its most important philosophical definition. The mind becomes an observatory, through which the physical world—from which it is separate and different—can be inspected, criticized, and finally replicated in the form of scientific models that can be committed to paper and shared. The scientific ideal of an objective, neutral perspective on nature derives from this premise, that human beings can look down on things from a position of exteriority, and communicate what they see via facts and figures. The mind is like a camera, creating visual snapshots of things, which (in the form of diagrams, statistics, and so on) can then be used as evidence. As that metaphor suggests, Descartes' philosophy privileged a visual relationship to the world, asking how it is that *images* of a candle or a stick can be trusted as real. It is less clear how other human senses, such as smell or touch or "gut feeling," could generate reliable knowledge.

This philosophy has been critical to the development of modern science and expertise. It opens up the possibility of an authoritative, rational perspective on things. But that comes at a cost. The vision of the self outlined by Descartes is also of an isolated, bloodless entity, cut off from the physical world as a pure observer. Feelings are bracketed as things that afflict the body, and are not really fundamental to who we are. (Part of the appeal of a crowd, as Gustave Le Bon understood it, is that it promises to relieve us of this lonely, external position on the world, and allows us to reunite with our bodily and emotional selves.) Descartes' philosophy makes for a retreat from everyday experience, and a downgrading of appearances and sensations.

Hobbes largely followed Descartes in this split between mind and body. To experience a sensation (such as a change in temperature or color) is not really to achieve *knowledge* so much as to be afflicted by movements of matter. Our sensations of the outside world are simply a reminder that the human body is itself a physical object, which is subject to the same laws of geometry as the rest of nature. Light hits my eye, and my eye is changed in the process, producing the experience we call sight. Pleasure and pain are properties of the nervous system, allowing the body to react mechanically to different stimuli. We can study these laws—as Harvey did in his analysis of the circulation of the blood—but we shouldn't treat the sensations as entirely reliable or certain in themselves. Armed with a good understanding of mathematics and a rational notion of cause and effect, it is possible for scientists to bring fundamental laws of nature to light. But Hobbes thought they could only do so if they placed a heavy emphasis on intellectual reasoning, and less on how things appeared. Reason shunts feeling to the margins.

But what if people didn't listen to reason? What if they would rather trust appearances and gut instinct? It was this fear that pushed Hobbes beyond the philosophy of nature, and into questions of politics. The answers he came up with would be among the most compelling in the history of political thought, and remind us that the problem of truth has always been irredeemably tied up with questions of politics. They cast light on the most basic functions of the state itself: *why*, for example, did governments believe there was no alternative than to bail out the banks? What was there to be so afraid of? The answer, if Hobbes is any guide, is a great deal.

A threat hovering over all human communities, he realized, is that people don't necessarily use language in a consistent and reliable way. People may *think* in a rational and credible fashion, but their words are liable to be misinterpreted. Individual minds can have access to scientific and philosophical certainty (as Descartes said), but they cannot share such thoughts by telepathy. If you ask me what color the sky is, I can strive to answer honestly, but still produce a different description from the one you would use. Feelings are especially problematic, Hobbes argued, because we have no way of knowing if we are all using emotional language in the same way. Mathematics has the advantage of being explicit in its language, avoiding misunderstanding, and sciences (such as astronomy) that rest on math are more liable to develop in a steady and consensual fashion. This has long been recognized as one of the great advantages of a monetary market economy, that it facilitates social interaction without misunderstanding: $5 is a universal and unambiguous symbol. But it is risky to treat any human utterance as entirely dependable. "Words are wise mens counters, they do but reckon by them," Hobbes wrote in *Leviathan*, "but they are the mony of fooles."[8] Somewhat pessimistically he went on, "No Discourse whatsoever, can End in absolute knowledge of Fact."[9]

In his reflections on human psychology, Hobbes spotted an even greater danger: arrogance. Because people can only really know their own thoughts and how they arrived at them, they tend inevitably to place greater value on their own idea of truth than on anybody else's. "They will hardly believe there be many so wise as themselves: for they see their own wit at hand, and other mens at a distance," he argued.[10] Human beings suffer from an innate problem of excessive self-confidence, which makes trust and peaceful exchange harder to achieve. The threat that we all face from one another, as Hobbes saw it, is not that some of us are superior to others, and will therefore oppress them—it's that *everyone* is liable to believe that they are the best, or the smartest, or the most deserving. The difficulty we humans confront is that, at least in our natural abilities and traits, we are all too alike. Throw in weaponry, and anyone can become the aggressor and anyone a victim. The strong are as vulnerable to attack as the weak.

Moral rulebooks are useless in the face of this problem, a claim that was especially provocative to the religious "schoolmen" of Hobbes's day. Words like "good" and "bad" have developed to refer to experiences that cause us pleasure and pain, but there's nothing about the language of morality (such as promises and duties) that actually binds us to do as we say. After all, I may be trustworthy—but if I suspect that you're not, it makes sense for me to break off whatever commitment we might have made to each other. When I give my word about something, I know that I really mean it, but how am I ever to know the same about you? The essence of the problem is that we have no way of knowing if promises will be honored. This is the same problem that the authorities were implicitly grappling with when they imagined the banking system seizing up in 2008: without money, how would trust work?

What makes violence inevitable, Hobbes reasoned, is not so much that certain people are strong and aggressive, but that most people are weak and fearful. If you and I are both afraid of each other, it makes sense for me to attack you, or else risk being attacked first. The weak are as dangerous as the strong, and possibly more so, as they have more reason to be afraid in the first place. This underlying pattern occasionally surfaces in civil society, in the way that violence appears in the hands of fringe conspiracy theorists, terrorists, and trolls, who believe their lives or lifestyles are under threat. The lesson is simple, that violence is very often a product of fear. The way to avert conflict is first to alleviate feelings of fear.

Regardless of people's virtue, Hobbes saw this condition of mutual suspicion as one that constantly threatened to tip into violence. What he realized is that violence is a state of mind (primarily of paranoia) as much as a physical act: "the nature of Warre, consisteth not in actuall fighting; but in the known disposition thereto."[11] A lack of safety is felt as much as known. It is this grim depiction of a barbaric "state of nature" dominated by mutual distrust, false promises, and the constant possibility of violence that we now recognize as "Hobbesian"—a state that Hobbes famously described as a "warre of all against all," in which life would be "nasty, brutish and short." Hobbes's solution to this nightmarish condition represents a turning point in the history of political philosophy.

Peace at all costs

Hobbes declared that there is only one possible way to avoid this condition of constant fear: the people must "appoint one Man, or Assembly of men, to beare their Person; and therein to submit their Wills, every one to his Will, and their Judgments, to his judgment."[12] In plainer language, we must create some kind of institution that we will all obey, on the basis that it will deliver the one outcome we all definitely desire, namely peace. No matter what else this person or body might do, so long as they offer us protection from each other, we must obey them. We must take those thorny, divisive questions of "right" and "wrong," and hand them over to a third party to decide. That third party is what Hobbes termed the "sovereign" and what we otherwise call the state.

We now know that only 30% of the human brain is dedicated to rational cognition, while the other 70% deals with basic matters of physical protection and management of the rest of the body. When a sense of danger arises, we become understandably more focused upon physical response and survival than on calm scientific observation. This is how panics spread through crowds, as manifest in the stampede at Oxford Circus in November 2017 or at JFK airport in August 2016. The challenge, for anyone wanting a society based around reason, is how to prevent this triggering of physical alarm. Bodily impulses and threats have to be kept out of politics. Nerves must be calmed, so that reactions are slower and more considered.

Hobbes saw mortal fear as the one feeling that we all are guaranteed to experience, and all want rescuing from. Nobody really benefits from living in a state of physical, emotional uncertainty. Everybody fears their own physical destruction above all else, and will do anything possible to avert it. Until this fear is alleviated, Hobbes reasoned, no other forms of civilization or progress are possible, be they scientific, economic, or cultural. Everybody has an interest in escaping this vicious circle, for their own sake as much as anybody else's. This basic, stripped-down idea of self-interest, as little more than the preservation of life, becomes the basis for Hobbes's ideas of law, government, and justice.

How can the state save us from the curse of mutual suspicion? Why would our promises suddenly become trustworthy, simply because a government exists? Hobbes's answer is that, unlike informal agreements such as a handshake, the law comes backed with fearsome punishments. And while I cannot be entirely certain that you will keep your promises or behave honorably toward me, I can be entirely certain that you will fear the force of the law, because fear of violence is universal. Fear, that primitive human emotion—the same one that had led Hobbes to flee to

France—becomes the one certainty on which the institutions of law and civil society could be built. Our common mortality provides the basis of a common political system, and binding promises become possible as a result. Rather than fear one another, we fear a common power. A mood of paranoia gives way to one of deference.

For this argument to work, the state must possess absolute power, for how else could we all be sure that every other member of society will fear it as we do? This is a discomforting argument that might now summon up visions of totalitarianism, but it also indicates the devastating logic running through Hobbes's political thinking. After everything he had argued about the vulnerability of verbal promises and mutual trust, he effectively offered his reader a simple binary choice. Either you can have a society in which all rights to violence are centralized in a single body, and used to secure peace for everybody else; or you can have a society in which the people retain some right to violence, but where every interaction is potentially risky. There's no middle ground. It's all or nothing. Only the creation of a single, absolute sovereign power can rescue all of us from a far worse prospect, namely of constantly looking over our shoulders for would-be attackers, and wondering who we can really trust.

The brutal binary at the heart of Hobbes's argument can be used to sanction all manner of extraordinary and exceptional measures, simply on the basis that they are necessary to uphold peace. As new risks and threats emerge, the state must seek new techniques for maintaining its monopoly on violence. The bailout of the banks, in the face of a potentially catastrophic fallout of the alternative, was ultimately an example of this. How else would people have created reliable promises, if the ATMs were empty and bank cards stopped working? In the age of terrorism, the state has mobilized a widening range of emergency powers simply to secure civil society. The appearance of so-called "failed states," such as Somalia and Sudan, which lie somewhere between Hobbes's two poles of "civil society" on the one hand and a "warre of all against all" on the other, represent one of the most awkward challenges to the Hobbesian worldview. New and less tangible categories of violence, such as "cyberattack" or "hate speech," stretch the responsibilities of a Hobbesian sovereign into more and more areas of life. The lengths the state has to go to in guaranteeing protection extend further in response, often beyond the legal definition of its powers.

One of the legal aspirations that follows from this political ideal is that we can achieve clear separation between situations of "war" and those of "peace." States divide their means of force into two categories: those they use to keep the peace within their borders (a police force, prisons, probation and parole, etc.), and those they use to pursue war across borders (a military, spies, prisoner-of-war camps, etc.). Establishing this division, and creating parallel legal systems to govern civilian activity and military activity, was one of the crucial achievements of the treaties that brought peace to Europe in the second half of the seventeenth century. Recognition of civilian noncombatants serves to maintain the separation, at least in traditional combat situations.

The distinction between military and civic violence carries tremendous symbolic power. The prison hunger strikes that killed IRA member Bobby Sands in 1981 began over a dispute as to whether the prisoners were to be treated as ordinary criminals (as the British government insisted) or had a "special category" status closer to prisoners of war (as the IRA demanded). In ordinary circumstances, there is a crucial and highly symbolic moment in the initiation of warfare when political leaders make a *declaration* of war, before handing over responsibility to generals to plan an attack.

Today, however, the distinction between civilian and military interventions has slipped thanks to various developments. Targeted drone strikes, for example, involve individuals being closely watched for several months to gather evidence of their activities in the manner of a police force, before being killed in the manner of a military strike. They are closer to assassinations than conventional acts of war. The Russian government exploits the "full spectrum" of hostile interventions to disrupt enemies both within and beyond its borders. These might be illegal, such as the use of a nerve agent in Britain in March 2018, but fall short of being spoken of as "war." Then there are the various so-called "wars" that don't involve military combat, such as the "war on drugs," "cyberwar" or "information war." States are made increasingly nervous by the difficulty of establishing where war begins and ends, and how to define an enemy. The ambiguity cuts both ways, with military units also being used overseas for peacekeeping and law enforcement, as if they were civilian governments.

Despite Hobbes's case for absolutism, there is one right that none of us can ever relinquish, no matter what orders we receive. While the state may commit various acts of harm upon us, some fairly, others perhaps less fairly, nobody can be ordered to commit an act of harm upon himself. There is a simple reason for this: the only reason why we have a state in the first place is because we all fear violence and seek to avoid it. Self-interest, in the most animalistic, physical sense of that idea, is the starting point for all ideas of justice and authority, and it would be paradoxical to imagine that the law could demand an act of self-harm. There are numerous contemporary legal manifestations of this right, such as the American 5th Amendment (which protects suspects from self-incrimination) or the "right to remain silent" granted to suspects upon arrest.

That Hobbes starts with the concept of a selfish, fearful individual, then reasons outward from there, provides a rough template for the liberal tradition of thought that followed. This includes economics, with its assumption that each of us is seeking to maximize our own satisfaction. But if evidence were to arise that individuals are *not* quite so self-interested and afraid—if, on the contrary, it turned out that we often do ourselves harm and actively seek out danger, sometimes behaving altruistically to the point of self-sacrifice—then one of the main foundations of Hobbes's argument would be instantly weakened. Should our sense of our own mortality *not* lead us to favor protection, but on the contrary lead to seemingly irrational obsessions, rituals, and desires—as Sigmund Freud and others later observed—the argument for sovereignty cannot work quite as Hobbes imagined. A phenomenon such as suicide bombing represents one such difficulty for those viewing politics from a Hobbesian perspective, demonstrating that people are capable of willing their own physical destruction. The claim that Brexit is an act of collective "self-harm," for example, implies that it is entirely senseless. But what if people deem certain things worth suffering for?

In prioritizing the protection of human life at all costs, Hobbes's argument leaves a philosophical vacuum where the *purpose* of life might be addressed. By viewing death merely as something to be avoided and delayed, it fails to connect with the deep-rooted human need to render death meaningful and memorable. Crucially, it offers no place for heroism, which may (for better or worse) hold just as important a place in our psyche as the desire for protection.[13] Hobbes's pacifism is entirely understandable given the devastations of civil and religious conflict that he lived through. But his ambition to eliminate violence from all civil and political relations, save for those prosecuted by the state, arguably excludes certain aspects of the human condition, which leads us to seek out conflict, in some vain search for glory or a deeper sense of security. Who is to say for sure that delaying death is always better than confronting it?

On the surface, Hobbes appears like a deeply pessimistic thinker. After all, here was a man who had so little confidence in people to keep their promises to each other that he believed they needed a terrifying third party to impose rules upon them. The choice he offered was a grim one: obey an all-powerful sovereign, or prepare for carnage. The civil war in England and lengthy religious wars on the continent provided plenty of evidence that religious and moral ideals provoked violence as much as they alleviated it. The authority of the church and of Protestant sects seemed to divide people more than it united them.

On the other hand, Hobbes was gripped by a fiercely modern and optimistic ideal of how reason (specifically, reason in the hands of philosophers such as himself) could provide a way out of this relentless violence. His argument suggests that it is possible for the state to act for all of us, without favoritism, prejudice, or bias, so long as we all agree to respect it. Humans may be condemned to mutual distrust and dishonesty, but we have it in our power to establish the set of institutions that will save us from war. He signed off *Leviathan* with a boast: "Truth, as opposeth no mans profit, nor pleasure, is to all men welcome." He was defying anyone to disagree with him. The ultimate achievement of reason is consensus.

This is not a democratic vision. And yet, unlike many of the political thinkers who had come before him, Hobbes endeavoured to take every member of society's interests into account. The fearsome state that he had in mind would not represent the people in the way that we now expect parliaments and leaders to do, in the age of universal suffrage. A somewhat different form of representation is involved instead: we all agree to let the state decide on matters of right and wrong, instead of us. It's closer to the representation a lawyer offers a client or a parent offers a child, namely, that someone else can be trusted to pursue our real interests, better even than we can. Trust is absolutely essential, if people are to go along with it. But is trust really so dependent on force? Many would argue not.

The civility of facts

Consider some examples of trust in action. A business informs its shareholders that it will be paying them a reduced dividend this quarter, because its sales are down. The shareholders accept this. A scientist announces that they have made some breakthrough in the understanding of cancer, which is likely to improve treatment in years to come. The papers report the discovery and the public celebrates. A house burns down and the owner goes to their insurance company and asks for a payout. They receive one. All of these involve a high degree of trust in the truth of what is being said. Promises are made, accepted, and honored. Peace reigns. What makes this possible?

The answer in each case is that certain recording instruments and techniques have been invented to bolster the mere words of those involved. Businesses keep accounts, using specialized bookkeeping methods that allow them to be checked. Scientists carry out experiments using instruments and witnesses, which are then reported via peer-reviewed journals and which should, in principle, be replicable. An insurance company keeps detailed records, which allow them to calculate risk profiles of certain unexpected events. Many of these tools and recording devices also originated in the seventeenth century, offering a different vision of how peaceful social interaction might occur, not on the basis of law, but on the basis of *facts*. So long as an individual is willing to observe and record things fairly, the facts will speak for themselves. People might lie, but facts don't.

If we take Hobbes's argument at face value, trust should only be possible thanks to the laws issued by an all-powerful state. His objective, in making this argument, was to challenge the religious sects whose conflicting ideas of truth and sin had generated so much violence across Europe. However, his argument also threatened an emerging class who believed that they *could* be trusted to behave honorably and to tell the truth, but for reasons that had little to do with their religious beliefs. While philosophers like Descartes treated the evidence of one's own eyes as unreliable, there were small pockets of innovators who believed they had developed techniques to record their day-to-day experiences in a dependable fashion. These were people who privileged *experience* over abstract issues of geometry and philosophy, and would therefore become known as *experts*.

Trust was possible, they argued, without it necessarily being the work of the state. Instead, specialized instruments and artifacts could do the job instead. Pen, paper, and money were enough to secure promises.

A fact is simply a type of report that is free from distortion by the person making it.[14] The reporter of a fact becomes a mere conduit between how things really are and how they are then known by everyone else. Contrary to Hobbes's worst fears, the reliability of facts implies that human beings *are* able to trust their own eyes and that they *are* able to report what they see in a reliable and consistent fashion, albeit with the help of standardized techniques for writing it down. Hobbes's great worry was that humans are endemically arrogant, always placing greater faith in their own perspective than in anyone else's. They also break their promises. But with facts, I can give just as much credit to your version of events as to my own. Of course facts also demand we exercise humility and decency. Whether in journalism, science, or official statistics, statements of fact are all always implicitly a type of pledge, namely "I promise you that this happened." Facts possess many of the same qualities as banknotes, circulating freely among strangers without their integrity being doubted, and cementing trust in the process.

As the religious wars of the seventeenth century subsided, a number of developments appeared to endorse the idea that trust could be sustained between specialist record-keepers. The ability of merchants to interact peacefully and reliably (often with complete strangers) was a testimony to the power of bookkeeping techniques. The spread of commercial practices, underpinned by an emerging class of insurance brokers and accounting experts, was celebrated as a new way of life that avoided both violence and state control.[15] These individuals exhibited a different way of seeing the world, by collecting and recording information in as standardized and precise a way as possible. Merchants were able to operate across vast distances, and interact across cultural and religious boundaries, without their honesty being doubted. It wasn't his word that a merchant offered, but his books. By attending primarily to the mundane facts and figures of accountancy, these traveling individuals pointed to a mind-set and lifestyle that was transparent, reliable, and peaceful, albeit somewhat empty of any deeper metaphysical purpose.

These merchants provided much of the original readership for newspapers, which had emerged in northern Europe over the first half of the seventeenth century. Many early newspapers were based in Holland, the center of world trade, before becoming established in cities including London and Boston in the second half of the seventeenth century. The printing of weekly and then daily news provided another example of facts at work, showing how text could be used to hold up an objective and dispassionate mirror to reality, as opposed to the more theological and ritualistic uses of writing. News was one more way in which the world was amenable to representation of a sort that was agreeable to all.

As pamphlets on monetary matters appeared in the 1660s and 1670s, signaling the origins of economics as a science, it is telling that the majority of them were published anonymously.[16] This was an indication of the moral opprobrium that surrounded monetary expertise throughout the seventeenth century, but it was also symptomatic of the type of factual analysis being offered, the credibility of which depended on the quality of numerical calculations and not on its author's name. Mechanisms for separating an argument from the person making it were crucial to this emerging style of objective expertise. The contemporary system of "blind" peer review, in which scholarly articles are assessed prior to publication without their author's name attached, is a legacy of early norms of anonymity.

Meanwhile the "Scientific Revolution" gathered pace. In England, the foundation of the Royal Society in 1660 set out to institutionalize experimental methods of natural science. This was effectively a private members' club, founded by the physicist Robert Boyle with the aim of gaining public legitimacy (including royal approval) for the natural experiments that Boyle and his associates were doing. In order for experiments to be accepted as a means of producing truth, it was important that institutions existed through which they could be formally witnessed, recorded, and then reported for the general public. At the very first meeting of the Royal Society, it was agreed that all deliberations would be noted and saved as records, which would be open to other scientific communities across Europe.[17] This was a radical move, effectively banning the use of secret communication channels and private record-keeping that had been common among scholars during medieval times. Openness, at least within this new expert elite, became viewed as the facilitator of progress, allowing one finding to be added to another.

The principle that knowledge belongs in public serves an important political function that is becoming increasingly apparent today, now that there are various forces threatening it. It is only if knowledge is committed to record, and that record is made public, that there can ever be consensus on the nature of truth. Truth is not unaffected by its storage system. If data is hoarded, privatized, and kept secret, as is the case with so much data collected by digital platforms such as Facebook and Uber today, it will not then have the political benefit of supporting agreement on truth. The term "truth," after all, has a common root with the word "trust." The Scientific Revolution was as much a revolution in how people agreed to trust each other, on the basis of openly available records, as it was in methods for probing nature.

Just as bookkeeping allowed merchants to produce objective facts about what they were up to, experimental societies (and subsequently, journals) did the same for the new scientific elite. Boyle recognized the similarity between the type of reports that the Royal Society was producing and those of merchants, and recommended that the latter be employed to store and distribute the data produced by the Society, including the transportation of documents overseas.[18] The merchants' very lack of philosophical or theological concerns meant that they possessed exactly the right mindsets to serve as collectors of scientific facts as well as commercial ones. An eye for the mundane dimensions of experience, and a willingness to write them down methodically, was a rare capability.

The central scientific principle of the Royal Society was the inverse of Hobbes's.[19] Hobbes argued that the evidence of our senses was unreliable and disputable, but that the underlying laws governing the universe—namely geometry—were matters on which we could be certain. By contrast, Boyle believed that questions of underlying cause and effect were philosophical matters that were open to dispute, but on matters of observation there could be only firm consensus. As long as people all witness an event in a certain way, they should agree on what has taken place. Not only that, but their testimony can be treated as reliable for anyone who didn't witness it, assuming it has been recorded and published in the appropriate manner. This way, scientists are able to convince us of things concerning bacteria, nutrition, climate, and pharmaceutical safety, despite most of us never witnessing the corroborating evidence ourselves.

The caveats here are important. Conventions had to be imposed to ensure that experiments followed a certain method and witnesses observed in a certain way. A standard method for reporting on experiments was invented. Royal Society members were permitted to argue over theoretical issues, but were obliged to respect the rigors and routines of experimental work itself. They were not permitted to dispute what another member said he had witnessed. And yet Hobbes was scornful of Boyle's Society (which he was notably barred from joining), arguing that it achieved consensus on its experimental findings only because membership was so tightly restricted. Not *anyone* could serve as a witness to these experiments, thus truth was being produced via a narrow scientific oligarchy of fifty-five carefully chosen men. The experimenters had seized the right to describe nature behind closed doors, and then expected the rest of society to accept their description. It was, in Hobbes's view, a system of representation (both of nature and of the public interest) without any legal underpinnings.

Many contemporary attacks on scientific expertise share certain elements of Hobbes's suspicion of the Royal Society. The sense that experts are a privileged "elite" who then instruct the rest of us what to believe is prevalent in many reactionary and populist movements such as the Tea Party and the alt-right. Dominic Cummings, campaign director of Vote Leave which campaigned for Britain to leave the European Union, is routinely dismissive of "cargo-cult science," a charge that compares established scientific circles to religious cults, impervious to the critiques of outsiders. Climate-change denialism depends on the idea that climate scientists are an inward-looking community, who only seek evidence that reinforces what they've already declared true. And yet when climate scientists *don't* offer consensus, they are attacked on the opposite grounds, that their facts are fraught with politics and nothing is agreed. These attacks cast doubt on the ability of scientists to separate their opinions and tastes from their observations, and treat disciplines merely as private clubs.

To rebuff these kinds of charges, scientists have always had to convincingly separate their powers of observation from their private ambitions and egos. That is, they specifically have to refute Hobbes's suspicion, that human beings are arrogant creatures who invariably rate their own views more highly than others'. The Royal Society placed a slightly phony ethical emphasis on humility, and avoided overt attention-seeking. In a dour puritanical rejection of elegance, its founding constitution stipulated that "in all reports of experiments . . . the matter of fact shall be barely stated, without any preface, apologies and rhetorical flourishes."[20] This allowed

scientists to sustain the idea that they were merely observing and reporting what nature presented to them, and were not seeking glory for themselves. Boyle described his project in religious terms, as a humble effort to
get closer to God: "the knowledge of the Works of God proportions our
Admiration of them . . . our utmost Science can but give us a juster ven-
eration of his Omniscience."[21] By this account, a scientist merely wants to
bear witness to the wondrous machine in front of him.

But while scientists were not expected to celebrate themselves, they
were obliged to treat each other with the utmost respect. The renunciation
of violence was essential. The scientific community of seventeenth-century
England drew heavily on the norms of "gentility" that emerged from the
Elizabethan era.[22] To be a "gentleman" carried heavy moral responsibilities, especially when it came to being truthful. When a gentleman gave his
word, he would do anything within his powers to keep it, regardless of the
costs to himself. Exaggeration and implausible stories were anathema to
gentlemanly conduct, as was going back on a promise. Most importantly,
to accuse another gentleman of lying was the most serious moral breach
imaginable—a norm that survives in the British Parliament, where parliamentarians are banned from accusing each other of lying.

This rhetorical style of civil and—crucially—peaceful disagreement
became adopted within the Royal Society, where it was used to allow
members (many of whom came from the gentry) to politely debate scientific questions without coming to blows. A style of speaking and arguing
emerged which allowed one scientist to challenge the theoretical statements and reasoning of another, without seeming to challenge his character or intentions. These modes of etiquette, which have evolved into
contemporary norms of scientific speech, serve to keep personal identities
and feelings *out* of the space of disagreement. Throwing them back in,
for instance by suggesting that an expert is motivated by some personal
ambition or grudge, is the main strategy of those wanting to discredit the
scientific establishment. The spread of digital media, and the email leaks
that inevitably occur, has been a gift to them, stretching the "gentlemanly"
ideal of impersonal, objective criticism often to breaking point.

Hobbes disagreed virulently with what Boyle stood for. But in many
respects, their projects were similar and help us pinpoint something that is
under threat today. In the aftermath of violent, religiously fueled conflicts,

both were seeking some neutral and dependable basis for secular society on which all could agree, regardless of opinion or feelings. For Hobbes this meant the modern state, whose lawmaking power would eliminate fear and violence from politics. For experts such as Boyle or the merchant class, it meant the techniques of dispassionate observation, measurement, and classification. In either case, the objective was the same: to achieve peaceful agreement and avoid the devastating consequences of moral and theological dispute. The quest was for something that was beyond dispute, but which wasn't God.

They also employed a common political device: both required the public to authorize a small elite to make judgments on their behalf. The Hobbesian sovereign would represent the public by defining justice, while the scientific community would do so by defining reality. The rest of us depend on these elites for the production of a common social and natural world, that we can all (in principle) accept. Implicit in this is a faith in language as a neutral and impersonal tool, through which agreements can be reached if used in the right way. Specialists in law, economics, and science are trained to use the language of each in a strict, independent fashion, that is supposedly immune to political or cultural influence. From these perspectives, what distinguishes lawyers and experts is they possess a way of speaking that is unbiased and free of politics. This gambit has been the basis of social peace.

The intellectual legacy of the seventeenth century was a suspicion and regulation of human feeling. Descartes' philosophical breakthrough occurred when he cast doubt upon the images received by his eyes. Hobbes's great fear was (as Franklin D. Roosevelt later put it) "fear itself": that fear and suspicion escalate, until violence is entirely sensible. The nascent expert communities developed techniques to turn their fleeting subjective impressions into objective evidence, that others could check. All this rests on the premise that what we see, feel, and desire is liable to lead us astray. On this basis, government elites and experts promise to keep their feelings and personal wishes separate from their duties.

The resentment of elites that we see around us today is fueled by a sense that this promise is now bogus. The special status granted to judges, civil servants, and scientists is viewed as illegitimate. Revelations of their personal moral failings, via media exposés, leaks, and social media searches, make the distinction of these figures ever harder to sustain. Their claim to represent our interests becomes nothing but a shroud for their own political agendas. A purportedly objective stance comes to appear emotionally cold and uncaring. The crucial seventeenth-century expectation, that language and numbers could be a neutral tool for the formation of a general public consensus, is dashed once elite culture is viewed as just another closed community, like a glorified golf club or—worse—a conspiracy.

Was it inevitable that this backlash had to occur? Not necessarily. A central weakness of both government and expertise is the confluence between the two, which arouses cynicism. As Hannah Arendt wrote, "there is hardly a political figure more likely to arouse justified suspicion than the professional truth-teller who has discovered some happy coincidence between truth and [political] interest."[23] Certain forms of knowledge have gained considerable political power, while others have not. Politicians frequently duck moral questions by couching their arguments in the language of "evidence" and "what works." As the case of the central bankers and the global financial crisis demonstrates, lawmaking and fact-reporting are no longer clearly distinguishable. The longer-term effect is that it becomes impossible to specify who is a dispassionate observer, and who a judge and decision maker. The name for this convergence of political and scientific authority is "technocracy."

The first technocrats

The English Civil War ended in 1651, three years after the Peace of Westphalia had brought the Thirty Years War to a close. A remarkable feature of the decades that followed is the speed with which the modern state emerged, displaying many of the characteristics that distinguish it today. The Peace of Westphalia produced the basic principle of modern interstate relations: that each state would be recognized as having complete and unchallenged sovereignty within its own recognized borders. To transgress this was to shift from a state of "peace" to a separate one of "war," with no legal scope for ambiguity between the two. A clear sense of where it was legitimate to use force (and where it wasn't) emerged, and the Hobbesian vision of clear, legally mandated concentrations of power became the norm.

Up until this point, armies had typically been made up of acolytes and contractors of the monarch, collected and financed in an ad hoc fashion, and used at the discretion of their royal patron, both at home and abroad. The military had been put to various uses that did not respect any clear division between "war" and "peace." Soldiers, meanwhile, used the means at their disposal to demand lodging and food from civilian populations (including their compatriots), spreading fear as they traveled. But in England by the 1680s, the Crown had become dependent on Parliament for permission to raise and fund an army, and soldiers were housed in state-funded housing. The army acquired new and distinctive peacetime responsibilities—maintaining public order, preventing riots, and cracking down on smuggling—of the sort that would later be associated with a police force. The means of violence were being brought within the bounds of the law and control of Parliament. Hobbes's vision of peace guaranteed by power was becoming realized.

What Hobbes did not foresee was the tremendous opportunity these developments also offered to the new communities of expertise, many of whom he'd been suspicious of. In particular, various techniques associated with mercantile bookkeeping became indispensable to this new type of state, as it set about collecting, storing, and publishing data in an organized and expert fashion. For example, in 1660 the English government employed a mere 1,200 officials for purposes of administration.[24] By 1688, more than 2,500 were employed in tax collection alone, and by 1720 there were more than 12,000 permanent civil servants working for the British government. All public-spending decisions became concentrated within the administration of the Treasury during the 1670s, and recorded carefully for benefit of Parliament. Tax collection, which had been carried out in an unreliable fashion by private contractors spread all over the country until the mid-seventeenth century, became centralized around the same time. In short, the state was becoming the bureaucracy of administrators, record keepers, and calculators we now recognize.

The main catalyst for this rapid accumulation of administrative capabilities was the continued desire of the monarch to wage war, only now subject to various legal constraints and parliamentary scrutiny. Where the Crown had previously been able to raise and finance an army on a contingent basis, often promising certain spoils to the army and its financiers in return, warfare was now subject to more systematic fiscal and parliamentary oversight. It required a transparent tax system and professional army. Parliamentarians demanded to see evidence of how money was being spent and a proper public balance sheet. If the state was to borrow large sums of money in order to go to war, this sum needed formal recording, using the same sorts of technique that the merchants had invented—the sum we now recognize as the national debt.

In 1694, the Bank of England was founded to enable the state to raise further money for purposes of war with France, creating a trusted intermediary between the merchants in the City of London and William III. This co-evolution of the military state and mercantile capitalism saw the former developing a growing array of record-keeping techniques, in order to convince financiers that it could be trusted to honor its debts. Primitive forms of economics and public accounting enabled the state to carry on waging war, only now in a more analyzed, accountable, *matter-of-fact* way.

Yet the rise of the government expert wasn't only about finding new ways of administering and justifying war. Interest in the public uses and benefits of mathematics blossomed through the 1670s and 1680s, not least because of all the new jobs in public finance and taxation that the government was creating at the time. Outside the state, often among the recently established coffee houses of the financial class, a new intellectual culture was developing, centered around a commitment to solving problems using mathematics. Like today's Silicon Valley entrepreneurs, poring over the latest techniques of data analytics in search of the next big business idea, this nerdish culture had world-changing implications. It built on the example of mercantile accounting, which demonstrated the new social possibilities of using numbers to depict social life, while combining it with faith in mathematics. By the early eighteenth century, this had developed to the point where gentlemen and their clubs were building up whole libraries of "useful knowledge," reference books and periodicals of official facts and figures that were kept as much as status symbols as for consultation.

The new intellectual style was embodied by William Petty, a man whose remarkable career spanned the merchant navy, scholarship, and government consultancy, and saw him rise from humble origins to a position of great wealth and political influence. His constant restlessness led him to apply his mind to medicine, cartography, and economics, lifting metaphors from one into the other, and on again. Moving from one country to another, and one elite circle to another, he was the consummate political and intellectual entrepreneur. He never settled on a single area long enough to produce any great works, but played a crucial role in narrowing the gap between the new intellectual clubs and the state, laying the foundations for a form of social science in the process.

Petty was born in 1623, and his first job was as a cabin boy aged fourteen traveling back and forth between the south coast of England and the west coast of France. Showing an early mercantile instinct, he exploited this position to start trading his own goods, building up a profit in the process. Two years later, he moved to London and joined the navy. Aged twenty, he moved to Holland where he studied mathematics and anatomy, a technical training which he then took to Paris, where he was introduced to Hobbes. The two men had precious little in common: one young, excitable, and eagerly devouring new research techniques, the other in his late fifties with a somber skepticism toward many of the latest experimental fads. But Hobbes had grown interested in the mechanics of vision, and Petty was able to perform oracular dissections. In 1645 he became Hobbes's assistant and secretary, providing him with diagrams of the human eye, which Hobbes used to develop geometric theories of sight.

Petty's time in Holland exposed him to the world's most advanced financial and technical culture of its day. The wealth that trade had bestowed on Holland made a deep impression, and provoked in him the question that would later underlie economics and economic policymaking: what are the ingredients of such prosperity, and how can they be actively inculcated by government? Much of Europe in the seventeenth century was beset by constant economic downturns, often linked to plagues and crop failures, which frequently spilled into civil unrest. The struggle to achieve greater levels of prosperity in England was a threat to peace as much as anything else. Achieving a more expert perspective on this, as Petty intended to do, was both a political and a scientific priority. His was not the abstract mind-set of the pure academic, nor the purely practical one of the merchant, but carved a path between the two—the mind-set of the progressive and the technocrat, who seek to employ knowledge toward the transformation of society.

Petty returned to England in 1646 to study at Oxford, and later became a founder member of the Royal Society. His practical and methodological innovations were aimed at reimagining government as a technical enterprise, and never at producing new knowledge for the sake of it. In 1647, for example, he produced a report suggesting hospitals maintain systematic, centrally administered patient records. Not only would this allow doctors to "see the history of the patient most exactly and constantly kept," it would also allow public officials to spot trends in public health and their correlations to weather.[25] Facts would become a basis for progress.

In 1655, while working as physician to Cromwell's army in Ireland, he won a contract to carry out a piece of work estimating the size of the recently reconquered territory, which the English government could use as a basis to distribute land to settlers and soldiers fairly. This was known as the Downs Survey and was a landmark in the political application of mathematical technique. The survey was pathbreaking not only because of its speed (thirteen months) but also because his methodology was comprehensible by soldiers themselves, who were consequently willing to accept the findings. Petty was rewarded with copious lands in Ireland, and remained in Dublin until 1665.

Both mathematics and anatomy remained Petty's touchstones throughout his life. Combining the two, he made advances toward economics. A lesson he took from Hobbes was that reality was fundamentally constituted by physical bodies moving around in space according to geometric patterns. His innovation was to apply this same philosophy to the study of society, a practice he referred to as "political anatomy." An analogy between the human body and the "social body" enabled him to conceive of economic prosperity as analogous to health, where a healthy society would see each unit functioning properly, with money circulating between them, as blood moves around the body. The metaphor of the financial "heart attack" that struck the financial system in 2008 would have made perfect sense to Petty. Advances made by physicians and anatomists, such as Harvey, needed replicating in the arena of society, to understand how prosperity might be nurtured. A healthy body politic required "political medicine."

This implied that mathematics was not only a means of grasping the essential mechanics of the natural world, as it was for Hobbes and Descartes. Combined with an entrepreneurial zeal and an inventive mindset, it could also be a new technique for governing and improving society. Like the technicians of the twenty-first century, offering to solve all manner of social problems using "data analytics," Petty's technocratic exuberance pushed the political and administrative uses of mathematics and data collection into ever more domains. As with today's data evangelism, this was partly because it was fashionable: much of Petty's work argues for governments to consult facts and figures in areas where such data wasn't even available at the time. There is also some evidence that he made mathematically unfounded leaps to make up for the giant holes in the evidence at his disposal, while singing the praises of exactitude and certainty.

Yet the vision he laid out has remained the guide for every expert who has worked for governments since. His major work, *Political Arithmetick*, was written in 1672, but first published anonymously in 1683. In it he defined his method as follows:

> instead of using only comparative and superlative words, and intellectual arguments, I have taken the course to express myself in terms of Number, Weight and Measure; to use only arguments of sense, and to consider only such causes as have visible foundations in nature.[26]

This now strikes us as an obvious approach to take to matters of public policy. During the 1990s, it became known as "evidence-based policy." But in the 1670s, the suggestion that political questions be settled on the basis of numerical facts was radical. Even if Petty's ambitions sometimes exceeded his own technical abilities, he offered the template for a new type of modern political adviser, able to evaluate and criticize on the basis of quantitative methods and facts, rather than on the basis of their own political ambitions or religious beliefs. He was the original technocrat.

The practice of "political arithmetic" and the pursuit of peace are in principle mutually reinforcing. The mathematical approach to society is only possible if a certain level of social stability has been achieved, which allows society to be subjected to a measured and mathematical analysis, in contrast to the upheavals of war where the objective "facts" are hard to discern. Experts such as Petty were beneficiaries of a more stable civil society, while also contributing to that stability. As war became something with its own separate legal status, and the military a more professional and formally administered institution, the politics of physical force—with all the horrors that Hobbes feared—became increasingly distant from everyday experiences. Why, then, would technocrats ever attract hostility? It is, after all, Petty's intellectual heirs that are now routinely reviled as a self-satisfied liberal elite.

The violence of experts?

William Petty's "political arithmetic" was the beginning of a scientific program, that would eventually turn into political economy, and later into what we now recognize as economics. The idea that numbers can represent society just as effectively as they can represent nature has delivered considerable benefits to society over the past three centuries, in terms of health and prosperity. But there is also a somewhat darker lineage here. The project for which Petty won greatest public renown and economic reward was in the service of violent political oppression. The Downs Survey was carried out immediately after Cromwell had put down an Irish rebellion with great brutality, resulting in the deaths of half a million people.

The history of expertise, of the sort pioneered by Petty, is closely entwined with the history of colonialism and of slavery. For while states and experts may have an interest in creating maps and portraits of their own society for purposes of tax collection or social improvement, they have an even greater need to gather knowledge of foreign lands and peoples they seek to dominate. The application of geometry to cartography was an indispensable tool in the discovery and genocidal colonization of the New World. London's insurance sector, which contributed to the City's prominence in global finance, was born out of the coffee shops frequented by the likes of Petty in the 1670s and 1680s. Its main customers were those seeking underwriters for slave ships. Censuses, surveys, and maps have always been a priority for powers wanting to govern a people they don't otherwise know or understand. The need to create a picture of the world can also be born out of a desire to own it.

The technocratic state may indeed be dedicated to peace within its own territory, but it looks less benign when it involves extremities of political inequality. The civil and gentlemanly dimension of expert knowledge never includes everyone as a participant, and can be actively oppressive. This exclusion may not have been recognized as a flaw by those at the center of such clubs and networks, but for colonized territories and peoples, the potential violence of expert research, experimentation, and measurement has always been clear. Colonies were governed without regard for the distinction between "military" and "civil" tools of power, and the difference between civil policing and military conflict was not clear-cut. Developing societies have been used as test beds for economic policy experiments and drug trials, which produce knowledge to be brought back to centers of learning. Political opposition to expert knowledge has been with us all along, merely pushed out of the eyeline of many Westerners.

The thing that *has* changed in recent years, however, is that large swaths of *Western* populations appear to now view expertise in a similar way. The claims of experts—especially of government technocrats—are viewed with greater suspicion, as if they are quasi-colonial tools of domination. Even if people don't feel violently oppressed, they often feel belittled and irrelevant to the style of knowledge being generated by economists, statisticians, and financial reporters. In keeping with a tradition that originally sought to revel in the glory of God or the sovereign, elite communities focus on abstract objects of knowledge, completely missing the injuries that people experience in their everyday lives. Their lack of emotion, which was originally so crucial to their authority, opens them to attack for being cold and selfish.

The problem is especially acute in the European Union, where the technocrats of the European Commission appear even more distant from ordinary people than those operating at the national level. The nationalism that has bubbled up across Europe in the twenty-first century, becoming especially pronounced in Hungary, Poland, and Austria, mobilizes partly against the EU as a source of undemocratic, technocratic rule. Studies show that European "elites" view the EU in an utterly different light from that of most ordinary European citizens.[27] Elites value the EU primarily for delivering peace—the foundational Hobbesian goal—whereas other members of the public are more prone to see it in terms of the removal of national borders, producing immigration, a refugee crisis, and the single currency. The objective reality of peace has not prevented a rising sense of fear.

The cultural and political divisions separating centers of expertise from other sections of their societies have created a situation with rhetorical echoes of the colonial one, in which the methods of science and expertise seem like an arm of some foreign Leviathan state. Modern bureaucratic government becomes represented as the enemy, with Steve Bannon (while still working in the White House) declaring that Trump's cabinet would seek the "deconstruction of the administrative state," and leading Brexiteer Jacob Rees-Mogg accusing the British Treasury of "fiddling figures" to pursue its own political goals.

The nativist idea that the nation needs *reclaiming* from the elites has echoes of the rhetoric of anti-colonial nationalism. Rural resentment toward universities and metropolitan centers is rooted in a slow-building sense that a narrow class of technocrats is governing the nation in their own interests.[28] Racist and ethno-nationalist groups now borrow the language of minority rights and identity politics, to protest the fact *they* are now the downtrodden.

These proto-fascist developments are shocking, but they succeed by exploiting real economic and political inequalities that have driven a wedge between centers of elite power and the broader populace. This is manifest in deep resentment toward governing institutions such as the European Commission, which is exploited by political parties such as the National Front in France and the Northern League in Italy. But underlying that is a sense that expert knowledge is misleading, self-interested, and possibly even fabricated. Experts and policymakers can talk about things like unemployment or the environment, but they will never know how it *feels* to be unemployed or live in a rural community amidst nature. That, at any rate, is the political pitch.

Technocratic overreach is culpable in this decline of political reason. Examples such as bank bailouts and quantitative easing, which attracted so much ire from Occupy and Tea Party activists, generate confusion over what exactly counts as "politics" and what as "expertise." As party politics becomes more professionalized, it becomes harder to see any clear difference between elected representatives and their expert advisers: to be an expert, claiming to represent the "facts," is now one of the main routes into politics, where one claims to represent the "people." The state looks to many like a game being played by insiders. To these critics, the distinction between the expert and the politician has become an illusion.

3

PROGRESS IN QUESTION

Feeling beyond statistics

It is impossible to imagine a democracy that doesn't feature disagreement. Most of us view the capacity to nurture and sustain peaceful disagreement as a positive attribute of a political system. At the same time, no constitutional settlement can survive if *everything* is a value judgment or a matter of opinion. There must be some commonly agreed starting point, that all are willing to recognize, before democratic politics can begin. Some things must sit outside politics, if peaceful political disputes are to be possible.

Among these things are the basic facts of economics and statistics. These are now such ordinary and unremarkable features of public life that we scarcely notice the important work they do in supporting democratic debate. While everything is working as normal, numbers representing GDP, inflation, population growth, health outcomes, life expectancy, unemployment, and income inequality appear as simple and indisputable facts. While disagreements can continue to rage on "moral" issues, such as animal rights or assisted dying, matters of fact, overseen by experts, are areas of public discourse where consensus is expected. Statistics have the useful effect of delimiting the arena of democratic conflict, describing what an economy and society look like in objective terms, such that citizens and politicians can at least agree on the reality they all inhabit.

This is another of the legacies of the Scientific Revolution that occurred in the seventeenth century. The construction of modern government during that time depended not only on systematic record-keeping by a centralized professional administration, but also on the emergence of amateur economists and number-crunchers. The founding promise of statistics and related disciplines was never just to achieve some esoteric mathematical validity (though that certainly drove some of their protagonists) but to forge a new basis for social consensus and peace.

But there are increasing signs that statistics and economics are losing their capacity to end disputes. Just as experts are finding it harder to maintain an air of detachment, official numbers no longer appear outside the terrain of politics. For large swaths of Western societies, statistics are viewed as serving the interests of elites, offering a version of reality that only privileged cultural groups recognize and benefit from. In the United States, trust in the veracity of statistics maps heavily onto political divisions: 86% of those who voted for Hillary Clinton in 2016 expressed trust in the economic data produced by the federal government, compared to just 13% of those who voted for Donald Trump.[1] In Britain, the emotive issue of immigration provokes widespread suspicion of official data, with 55% of people believing the government is *hiding* the truth about the number of immigrants in the country, a percentage that rises as people get older.[2]

The wounds suffered by technocracy are partly self-inflicted. The rhetorical power of numbers, especially concerning economic issues, is often so seductive that politicians and public figures become over-reliant on statistics, to the point where they stretch and bend them to suit political agendas. Rather than fight a policy battle on moral or political grounds, it is easier to invoke the finding of some expert or economic analysis, and assume that the audience won't bother to go and check the workings. Numbers may well be produced by credible sources, in statistics agencies or universities, but then become more dubious as they travel via the media and the announcements of politicians. In Britain, 90% of people trust the Office for National Statistics, but only 26% trust the government to use and represent statistics in an honest fashion.[3] With confidence in the mainstream media also in decline, the power of numbers to facilitate widespread agreement and trust is in peril, as very few people have the skills or time to rely on original data sources and expert analysis. Fact-checking websites seek to hold a line on this, but exist partly because public life is now so awash with numbers that expert perspectives have become largely impossible to distinguish from spin for most people.

This helps explain why campaigns and agendas that appear devoid of statistical or economic credibility nevertheless achieve political success.

The UK government assumed that the 2016 referendum on EU membership would be decided by which side had the most compelling economic analysis, and that this would inevitably lead to the Remain side winning. Just as they did in the run-up to the referendum on Scottish independence, the Treasury and Bank of England made bleak predictions regarding the economic impact of leaving the EU. Supposedly independent experts were wheeled out from across the political spectrum, to voice their support for Britain remaining in the EU, on grounds of evidence alone. A poster was produced listing the hundreds of experts from around the world who endorsed remaining in the EU. These practices seek to batter people into agreement, thanks to some veneer of objectivity and foresight. Such strategies have been dubbed "project fear" by their nationalist opponents: a supposedly dispassionate analysis is cannily reframed as emotional manipulation.

What mainstream campaigns drastically underestimate is how dulled many people have become to the pronouncements and predictions of experts, and quite how little the distinction between "politician" and "expert" seems to matter any longer. As politics becomes more professionalized, and as highly educated and privileged people move between the spheres of research and of politics (often mediated via networks of think tanks, lobbying, and consultancies), whether someone purports to be speaking from a neutral expert position, or from a committed political one, becomes increasingly irrelevant. In the case of the Brexit issue, "experts" endorsing Remain included Christine Lagarde, director of the IMF, scarcely an institution that lacks any political view of how the world *ought* to be governed. Experts themselves may retain ample credibility when they remain within the confines of their academic department or independent office. But as their voices and their evidence become embroiled in policy disputes, so they become treated with the same suspicion as politicians.

It's unlikely that the influence of statistics on democratic participation has ever been entirely decisive. Voters do not typically study party manifestos with a keenly objective and calculating eye, in order to cast their vote in the most rational economic fashion. But as trust in governments has declined, statistics and economics seem almost to provoke anger on the part of those who disagree with them, as if the very act of introducing aggregates and calculations into political issues is an elitist way of framing them. The assumption that the public will dutifully follow the advice of economic analysts has come to seem patronizing and lacking in empathy. Those who oppose "big government" have often looked for ways to withdraw public funding for statistical research, and some statisticians fear for the future of expensive state-funded censuses in the future.

On the question of immigration, the think tank British Futures has conducted focus groups on how best to make the case for immigration in the UK. They found that arguments couched in statistical terms (for instance, that migration represented a positive contribution to GDP) tended to provoke hostility, with people immediately replying that these numbers were made up by the government to suit their liberal pro-migration agenda. But qualitative, anecdotal, or cultural evidence (for instance, stories of individual migrants settling down in Britain) provoked the opposite, much warmer reaction. When Nigel Farage, sometime leader of Britain's anti-immigration UK Independence Party, said in 2014 that he thought there were more important things in politics than GDP growth, he was treated as deluded. Within a couple of years, this was accepted across the political spectrum.

In any case, statistical predictions have not always fared well in the early twenty-first century. Just as the certainty of predictions becomes exaggerated by politicians and the media, so their subsequent inaccuracies become amplified and replayed to create a sense of scandal. Nevertheless, public trust in numbers has taken a series of hits, as statistical pronouncements and predictions are subsequently found wanting. The global financial crisis began deep within the financial system itself, well beyond the purview of most members of the public, but soon revealed itself as an epic failure of numerical calculation on the part of credit-rating agencies and investment analysts. Opinion polling is another area of mathematical modeling that appears to have gone wrong in recent years, as it failed to adequately detect unexpected surges of support for Donald Trump and Brexit in 2016 and Jeremy Corbyn in 2017.

Do numbers still tell the truth? Do they still adequately represent how things are? The answer depends heavily on how they are produced and by whom. The credibility of statistics and economics has profound political implications for how we achieve consensus on the government of society.

To some extent, a fresh skepticism toward expertise and quantification is democratically healthy, pushing arguments and disagreements into areas previously restricted to economists and technicians. Antipathy toward experts asserts new political possibilities. Democracy is undoubtedly more vital, more exciting, and also more risky, as the authority of statistical evidence declines. When emotions invade a policy issue, this also means opening it up to a wider range of perspectives; experts who complain about this are also seeking to close arguments down again. But it is hard to know where this ends. Could we end up splintering into entirely different narratives regarding social and economic realities, reinforced by social media bubbles of like-minded people sharing only reassuring evidence? In order to understand the various forces waged against statistics today, we need to bring to light some of the underlying purpose and assumptions of statistics, which are too often hidden from view.

Picturing society

If you wanted to represent society in terms of numbers for the first time, where would you start? The initial problem is to identify some moral or political issue that deserves quantifying at all. Moral arguments have long swirled around exactly this question, of *what* should and shouldn't be counted. In France it has been illegal to collect census data on ethnicity since 1978, on the basis that such a statistic could be put to racist political purposes, though this rule has the side effect of making it far harder to detect systemic racism within the economy and society. Feminists have long criticized official economic statistics on the basis that they exclude the crucial work done—historically by women—in sustaining family life. But these are relatively recent controversies. What is the initial step toward representing society in numerical terms?

Benjamin Franklin said that there are only two certainties in life: death and taxes. Both of these have proved fertile territory in the history of modern statistical techniques—but especially the former. One of the founding objectives of statistics was to achieve a science of death. This makes sense once we recognize what a prominent political problem mortality was around the time of the Scientific Revolution.

Thomas Hobbes identified one very basic trait that all human beings hold in common: we all fear for our lives. Whatever else we might value—great art, our religious beliefs, our moral principles—our own physical preservation is what we cherish first and foremost. The job of government, as Hobbes had defined it in 1651, is to minimize violence and conflict within its own borders.

However, violence wasn't the only threat to human life in the mid-seventeenth century, indeed it wasn't even the most significant one. During this time, around 40% of European children failed to reach the age of fifteen due to diseases such as scarlet fever, whooping cough, flu, smallpox, and pneumonia.[4] The recurrence of plagues had significant effects on population size, especially in large cities such as London, which in turn had negative effects on economic activity and on the ability of the government to raise an army when one was needed. Death moved through society in waves and surges, leaving ordinary people and their rulers to only guess as to the patterns or aggregate effects. One popular theory held that plagues were more pronounced in years when there was a change of monarch. Others interpreted their frequency in apocalyptic religious terms, fearing the end of days. It wasn't until the groundbreaking work of a shopkeeper called John Graunt that any effort was made to achieve a scientific perspective on all this.

Graunt was born in 1620 and spent his early career working as a successful draper, dealing in cloth and dry goods. Based near the Royal Exchange, his business was located in the heart of the City of London, among the financial institutions and coffee shops where practical applications of mathematics were being pioneered and debated (he later lost the entire business in the Great Fire of London). Graunt became a successful member of the drapers' guild, through which he forged connections in the worlds of politics and finance. During the 1650s, he got to know William Petty, and was influenced by his belief that perspectives of mathematics and anatomy could be applied to the study of society and government. As a shopkeeper himself, he possessed the mind-set and many of the arithmetical skills prized by the emerging scientific culture.

Graunt's scientific breakthrough, and his landmark contribution to the birth of statistics, was made possible by the fact that there was already a system in place to record deaths, albeit a macabre and haphazard one. Since

1592, London's parishes had collected information about individual deaths by sending out "searchers" to people's homes, typically old women who traveled around inspecting dead bodies and collecting information about the circumstances of death. The searchers would trawl the streets once a week calling "bring out your dead," then face the grim task of assessing the corpses. The records of the cause of death were vague, often being bluntly stated as "aged" or "suddenly," although occasionally offering some amateur medical speculation such as "stoppage in the stomach" or "twisting of the guts." The quality of records was not helped by the fact that searchers were open to bribes, allowing families to hide diseases such as syphilis from the public record.

In the 1650s, Graunt developed a growing fascination with these "bills of mortality" as they were known. He realized that they could potentially lend themselves to a more mathematical and disciplined analysis, if only they could be collected together and studied systematically. Aggregating seventy years' worth of mortality data from across the whole of London, he was able to spot trends that had otherwise been invisible, debunking previous theories as to how plagues travel and what causes them to break out. With basic mathematical modeling, he calculated the probability of different age groups dying, and therefore their life expectancy. In 1662, he presented his findings to the Royal Society, which were then published as *Natural and Political Observations Made upon the Bills of Mortality*. This is one of the founding documents of modern demography.

Like Petty, Graunt occupied an ambiguous position in public life. He wasn't a scholar, an aristocrat, a government official, or a philosopher. Nor was he quite a scientist, although he was soon invited to join the Royal Society after the success of his statistical innovation. He wasn't even just a businessman, although a commercial orientation was an ingredient in the matter-of-fact numerical way in which he set about approaching his topic. Together with Petty, Graunt represents the origins of a culture of policy expertise, in which public-spirited individuals put their mathematical skills to work for the benefit of better government, while simultaneously claiming to be outside "politics."

The threat of plague to London's population had led Charles II to seek out technical ways of predicting an outbreak before it hit, something that Graunt believed his mortality tables could do. While it was never put to quite this use, he did provide the king with expert, factual estimations of London's population, of a sort that had never previously been achieved. This involved estimates of the birth rate, even though evidence on births was far sketchier than that on deaths. What he was doing was applying mathematical method to a fundamental question of human society: who lives, who dies, and why? Hobbes's philosophical question, of how to secure the minimal conditions of life, was morphing into a scientific one.

There are various reasons why states might have an interest in the health, size, and longevity of the population they govern. It affects their capacity to wage war effectively. More intriguingly, it affects the capacity of the nation to create wealth through agriculture and commerce, which can then be taxed. This was the insight that would later become the starting point of economics, but which Petty was already seeking to impress upon people in the 1670s. The operating assumption of Graunt and Petty was that, beneath apparently random accidents and misfortunes affecting individuals and their families, there were underlying laws that could be brought to light, if only enough data could be collected in a sufficiently standardized fashion then plugged in to mathematical models. Both men drew heavily on an analogy between the human body and the "body politic" of society. Graunt, for example, compared London to the nation's head, warning that "this Head grows three times as fast as the Body unto which it belongs."

This project rested *and still rests* on a number of key assumptions. The first is that individuals can be treated as predictable and mechanical bodies within some much larger collection of bodies, obeying mathematical laws like billiard balls bouncing around on a table. This is possible only if some very simple notion of human psychology is adopted that assumes that everyone reacts to their environment in the same way. On this basis, people are subject to laws of cause and effect just like the natural world.

Hobbes had provided a particularly stripped-down version of just such a psychology, namely that humans want safety and life above all else. But he added a brief caveat in passing, hinting at what would later become economics: "by safety here, is not meant a bare Preservation, but also other Contentments of life, which every man by lawfull Industry, without danger, or hurt to the Commonwealth, shall acquire to himselfe."[5] These "other Contentments of life" implied that life should be prosperous, and not merely secure. An economic vision of the individual was forming, as a hard-working, pleasure-seeking entity, who would seek to consume and accumulate in the most effective way possible. This vision is not an unrealistic idea of what it means to be human, but it is a somewhat reduced one. Yet the bare principle of hedonism (that we all seek pleasure and avoid pain) provided experts with a basis to predict and model how people would behave, in a mathematical way.

Viewing mortality from this mathematical perspective brings laws of demography to light. But it offers precious little to the individual who has lost a loved one or is confronting their own death. Each death becomes just one data point in some larger mathematical model, a fact in the service of some grander system of population size. Tables of mortality are useful for rulers seeking to govern a city or deal with a problem such as plague, and may deliver benefits to society if they can inform policy for the better. But they offer nothing when it comes to seeking meaning and purpose in life. As states become more statistical in their outlook, the feeling arises that they don't really care about the people themselves. On the most existential issue of them all, elites take up a different perspective from ordinary people.

As we encounter it every day, social life is replete with moral and cultural nuances that resist arithmetic. Who owes what favor to whom? What do that person's clothes communicate about their identity or cultural background? How do our principles and ideas influence our political commitments? For the most part, statistics and economics ignore all this. Only on the assumption that everybody willingly works for money can we have a statistical concept such as "unemployment." Only on the assumption that all individuals want to pay as little as possible for a good does it make sense to treat market prices as a viable indicator of the value of goods. Anything that messes with this stripped-down vision of human psychology creates trouble for both statistics and economics. The vision of society as a machine, subject to its own internal geometric laws, requires the individual parts to work robotically and predictably.

The measure of progress

This reduction of human existence to mathematics is by definition crude. It's never guaranteed that representing society in terms of statistical indicators—GDP, life expectancy, literacy rates, and so on—is preferable to doing so in more romantic ways, which might emphasize a nation's history and cultural identity, and carries greater emotional resonance. The single most important justification for doing so is that, thanks to this pared-down scientific perspective, government will become more scientific in its policy interventions, improving life for all of us in the process. The pioneering statisticians of the seventeenth century didn't study trends in the death rate or harvests only to impress their peers, but because they believed those numbers might reveal how to improve outcomes in the future. The entire venture of statistical measurement and analysis is tied up with the dream of collective *progress*.

When Graunt developed his tables of mortality, the collective entity in question was London, mainly because it was the parishes of London that had instructed the searchers to produce bills of mortality in the first place. But as statistics became established in the eighteenth century as the definitive science of society, the vehicle of collective progress was increasingly understood to be the nation as a whole. National statistics could reveal whether the nation was getting richer or poorer, whether its population was getting bigger or smaller, whether trade was rising or falling. Together with the growth of national newspapers in the eighteenth century, statistics were a crucial ingredient in producing an idea of national citizenship that included the whole population, and not just noblemen or property-owners.

An ideal of progress was central to the political and philosophical vision of the Enlightenment that swept Europe over the second half of the eighteenth century, reaching its zenith with the French Revolution of 1789. This treated history as an unfolding narrative, which human beings could now bend to their will, thanks to the wonders of modern science, reasoned argument, and political determination. From this perspective, we are on a journey from a past veiled in ignorance and superstition, to a future of freedom and reason, all because we have developed the power to know how things really work. But where is the proof that this is happening? And where is the proof that the whole nation is included? In gauging how long people live, how healthy they are, how rich, how equal, and how educated, statistics provide an answer.

It is no coincidence that post-revolutionary France immediately set about establishing rigorous new statistical frameworks, with the world's first official statistics agency established in Paris in 1800. Producing objective depictions of society was a central ingredient in the republican ideal of governing on behalf of everybody. Statistics were imbued with a quasi-democratic function, allowing the entire populace to be represented. With the international standardization of measurement techniques in the twentieth century, statistics also allowed nations to be compared to each other, showing whether France was progressing faster or slower than Germany. The renewed commitment to social and economic progress that followed 1945 saw a fresh wave of statistical optimism, as various indicators of national progress were promoted by newly formed bodies such as the United Nations and the OECD, with GDP the foremost among these. Once again, the experience of horrifying and protracted violence created a renewed appetite for expertise.

Like any type of collective venture, this ideal of national progress demands a certain level of mutual give and take. If we are to treat "economic growth" or "increased life expectancy" as worthwhile goals at the national level, we have to accept that these might improve *in the aggregate* and *on average*, but will not benefit every single member of society equally. Just because the risk of infant mortality falls to a historically low level does not mean that children will never die. Just because the economy has grown by 3% in the past year does not mean there are not some parts of the country which have got poorer. To live in a modern individualistic society is to live amidst a constant flurry of predictions, averages, and risk assessments, all of which give us an idea of how things are in general, but none of which guarantees how things will turn out for our case in particular.

Most of the time, this is something we are content with. We can trust that the government has improved road safety by studying the accident rate, but accept that we might still die in a car crash. The unemployment figures might reveal that the labor market is in a healthy state, even if personally we are struggling to find work. This is the deal that figures such as Petty and Graunt were initially proposing, that by viewing society in mathematical terms we might be able to improve it overall. But that necessarily involves a certain sidelining of individual perspectives along the way, including feelings that might be felt acutely. Statistics tend to presume that numerical aggregates and averages are what matter politically, but it would be naive to think that there are no other political and moral priorities available to people, or other ways of envisioning or imagining a nation.

The clients for early statistical knowledge were states (hence the term *stat*-istics). Petty's survey of Irish lands was carried out for Cromwell. Graunt hoped to provide a technical solution for Charles II. In France, the Marquis de Vauban sought to flatter king Louis XIV into commissioning an annual census, with the promise that he would be able to "review in an hour's time the present and past condition of a great realm of which he is the head, and be able himself to know with certitude in what consists his grandeur, his wealth and his strengths."[6] From the perspective of early modern governments, statistics also provided a useful means of surveillance, helping to keep tabs on trade and demographic trends, so as to gauge how much tax and customs excise they should be receiving, which could also help crack down on smuggling.

But this is not the whole story of how numbers have transformed our politics over the past 350 years. Over time, statistics and statisticians have also sought to serve the public, painting a picture of society that is available for journalists, academics, and civil society to use, often in ways that rebel against the power of the state. Unlike the data gathered by surveillance or by corporations, statistics have been collected partly to be published. This is another more democratic way in which numbers can assist with the core Hobbesian task of sustaining social peace. They provide a common picture of reality on which strangers might all agree.

Statistics offices, funded by government but independent of government, are an important feature of how official numbers retain some credibility in public debate. These can potentially provide tools for criticizing the state, for example by journalists, and not just reinforcing its power. Once public, the possible uses and interpretations of statistics are an open question. Official statisticians might even voice their own criticisms of the government. As prime minister, David Cameron received numerous letters from Britain's chief statistician, to correct claims he had made regarding policy evidence. The fact that statistical agencies such as the US Bureau of Labor Statistics release data according to a fixed, long-term schedule means that they are impervious to the influence of immediate political pressures of the day.

Over time, states have gradually lost their monopoly over statistical data collection. During the late nineteenth century, reformers such as Charles Booth in London and W. E. B. Du Bois in Philadelphia began to collect and publish their own survey data, so as to cast a more objective light on poverty and social ills. This points to another key dimension of statistics in how progress has been understood. To render something an object of statistical analysis is also to state that it matters; if the government isn't interested in measuring something, then activists and reformers often will be. Various "social indicators" have been constructed since the 1960s, such as "quality of life," to challenge the dominance of economic measures in public policy debate.

The "radical statistics" movement was founded in the 1970s, to channel statistical expertise toward specifically progressive political goals. The French economist Thomas Piketty demonstrated the unrivaled power of statistics to draw public attention to a moral concern, with his best-selling 2015 book *Capital in the Twenty-First Century*, consisting largely of statistical analysis of inequality. And activist movements dedicated to counting things that are otherwise never counted—such as missing migrants around the world or the civilian death toll in Iraq—offer hard facts where there is otherwise just general moral concern. The phenomenon dubbed "statactivism," where data analysis is harnessed to serve and coordinate specific social movements, takes this further.[7]

Despite the confidence with which official statisticians might stand up to government, the relationship between state and independent expert remains finely balanced, and can quite easily go wrong. The stance of the independent expert can appear paradoxical, for on the one hand they are simply providing calculations and facts, free of any personal or political interest; on the other, the entire project of statistical science is bound up in the progressive faith that society can be reformed for the better. The expert culture that was born in the late seventeenth century viewed society as just another physical object to be measured and observed, like human anatomy or the movement of the planets, and yet experts are also inhabitants of society, benefiting from its progress, potentially converting their own influence into money and power. This same problem afflicts expertise today.

Numbers allow us to see the world objectively, but the flip side of that is that they eliminate feeling. In order for Graunt to identify the statistical trends influencing London's demography, he had to ignore the emotional and religious dimensions of death, the personal tragedies and grief attached to each child and adult that died. He also had to leave out the gruesome, noxious details of how plague-ridden corpses actually presented themselves to the searchers who recorded them. To discuss an issue in terms of numbers became a way of signaling that one was being objective and apolitical, focused on facts and immune to sentiment. This bestows a kind of authority on mathematics that it hasn't always earned, as if merely to invoke numbers is to achieve an unchallengeable perspective, to which less expert perspectives must yield if they are not to stand in the way of *progress*. Objectivity itself is thereby weaponized, used as a way of silencing dissenting voices.

It is scarcely any surprise that politicians, businesses, and civil society actors would want to exploit some of the rhetorical magic of numbers for their own purposes, paying consultants to produce statistics to suit their interests. Numbers can be selectively chosen to make a case, then repackaged as eye-catching "infographics," to ram home an argument. Commercial consultants can be paid to build an objective-looking evidence base, and some are more amenable to a client's needs than others. These manipulations go undetected for a while but gradually accumulate into a crisis of expertise. In the 350 years since statistical expertise came into being, it has been a victim of its own rhetorical success. So much trust has been placed in numbers that anyone wishing to be trusted (for good reasons or ill) inevitably cloaks themselves in a veneer of mathematical reason. But it's not clear if this ploy is working any longer.

How social and economic reality falls apart

By 2016, the GDP of the United States was almost three times the size it was in the late 1970s. GDP is calculated by taking the sum total of a nation's spending, government spending, investment, and trade balance (exports minus imports), then representing all that as a single number. Quite a bit of this growth is due to an increase in population, but GDP per person has still grown impressively over this period, more than doubling from around $25,000 a year in 1978 (in today's money) to over $50,000 a year in 2016. Following the "Great Recession" that came immediately after the subprime mortgage and banking crisis of 2007–9, the US economy recovered to grow steadily throughout Barack Obama's second term in office. Inflation has remained low throughout the early twenty-first century, while job creation was positive over the final years of Obama's presidency.

These economic indicators seem at odds with much recent political rhetoric and democratic upheavals in America. Donald Trump's presidential campaign was fueled by a feeling of outrage that America was in decline, suffering the consequences of an open global market, that allowed decent jobs to be shifted overseas. Trump's promise to "Make America Great Again" harked back to a golden age of American economic supremacy, when American manufacturers produced goods for much of the world to buy, and offered steady and respectable long-term employment for the working class. Trump's ascendancy seemed to be a symptom of rage and despair at lost prosperity and self-respect. Given the sunny economic outlook represented by key economic indicators, how was Trump able to channel so much anger toward the state of the American economy? Why did the economic facts not successfully convince people things were fine?

Part of the answer lies in inequality. Indicators such as GDP capture things in the aggregate, while GDP per capita captures what this means for people on average. But the divisive effect of economic inequality is such that aggregates and averages are simply no longer credible representations of how things are. Research has shown that while the income of the American population rose by 58% between 1978 and 2015, the income of the bottom half actually *fell* by 1% over the same period.[8] The gains were clustered heavily among those at the top end of the income distribution: the top 10% of earners experienced a 115% increase over this period, while the top 0.001% saw their incomes rise by an astonishing 685%. The richer one is, the faster one's wealth and income has grown.

The practical implication of this data is that half the American population experienced no form of economic progress in nearly forty years. Every time Ronald Reagan, George Bush, Bill Clinton, George W. Bush, or Barack Obama stood up and shared some good news about "the economy," they were speaking about something that effectively excluded half the population. This is an astonishing state of affairs. Could anyone possibly be surprised if that lower 50% lost interest in statistical economic pronouncements of politicians and experts? Meanwhile, given that inequality grows more extreme the further up the income spectrum you go, everyone in the upper 50% could feel aggrieved that their rate of income growth was not as rapid as those above them.

Dig beneath the surface of these headline indicators, and the story becomes far more complicated and we can see how geographically patchy progress really is in the United States today. For around a century up until the 1980s, rich states and poor states gradually converged economically, reducing geographic inequality. But from 1990 onward, this process went into reverse.[9] The economic fates of rich urban areas on the coast and poor regions in the Midwest and South began to head in opposite directions. This is having some clear political consequences. In the 2016 presidential election, Donald Trump won 2,584 counties to Hillary Clinton's 472, but those counties that voted for Clinton account for 64% of American GDP.[10]

Britain has a similar story to tell, with the most extreme geographic polarization of rich and poor regions of any nation in western Europe, contributing directly to the outcome of the 2016 Brexit referendum. Output per head in West London is *eight times* higher than it is in the Welsh Valleys, which was one of the most pro-Brexit regions.[11] During the coalition government of 2010–15, median household wealth in London rose by 14%, while it fell by 8% in Yorkshire and on the Humber, areas that also featured strongly pro-Brexit votes. Britain's economy is the fifth largest in the world, and yet the majority of regions experience GDP per capita below the European average, something that is concealed by the disproportionate wealth and productivity of London.[12] Most London-based media and politicians have no first-hand experience of what is going on beyond the perimeters of prosperous metropolitan cities, but nor do the dominant statistical indicators help them either. Across the *nation*, averages and aggregates don't look as bad as all that. The real story has been happening at a sub-national level.

To put all this another way, the vision of the nation as the principal and natural vehicle of collective progress no longer necessarily holds. Progress has been accelerating for some but has disappeared for others. Statistics were born at a time when the modern nation-state was becoming established as the ultimate and unchallengeable unit of political geography, but globalization and digital technology has disrupted this assumption, not through rendering location irrelevant so much as through concentrating power and resources in particular cities and city-regions. In many ways, the lives of individuals in Manhattan have far more in common with those in central London, Barcelona, or Paris than they do with other Americans in rural Ohio. National aggregates and averages no longer reflect lived reality to the same extent that they once did. They are failing to represent how things are.

In some instances, statistical frameworks have moved even further away from lived experiences, as the expert worldview has shifted to even larger scales of government. The introduction of the euro meant that monetary policymakers in Europe had to focus on economic indicators (unemployment, growth, and especially inflation) that represent the activities of half a billion people. The abstraction from people's day-to-day lives is all the greater. Multilateral organizations, such as the World Bank and the IMF, look at the world economy as a whole. Again, headline indicators conceal underlying variations. One famous study of income growth around the world found that every segment of the global population got richer between 1998–2008, except for two: the very poorest experienced no growth at all, as did those between the 78th–85th percentiles in the income spectrum.[13] That latter segment includes many people in the bottom half of developed nations. Since the financial crisis, things have been even worse: 70% of the developed world experienced stagnation between 2005 and 2014, while in Italy 97% of households saw no increase in income during that time.[14]

Shifting economic geography is one of the main ingredients in the rise of nationalism in the twenty-first century. Some sort of political reaction against economic technocracy was perhaps inevitable. Economists continue to speak about trade as a positive phenomenon, but once again this is only true in the aggregate. It masks the fact that, for certain workers and certain locations, free trade causes clear economic harm, just as authoritarians such as Trump and Marine Le Pen have argued.[15] Close analysis of the 2016 US presidential election showed how important these localized harms were to the result. Of those decisive counties in the Midwest that swung from Obama to Trump, a majority had experienced an industrial plant closure *during* the election campaign itself.[16] Equally, immigration is viewed as making a positive contribution to wages on average and to GDP, but this doesn't mean there aren't certain small sections of local labor markets (clustered around lower-wage jobs) that suffer from increased competition.[17]

Numerical averages and aggregates assume a natural fluctuation in fortune. One might get worse off this year, but better off next year. This town may lose jobs today, but more than make up for it tomorrow. The difficulty arises if certain regions and population groups are perpetually losing, undermining the authority—we might even say the truth—of statistics. It is even possible for headline indicators to suggest collective progress, while the majority of people are getting worse off. In the UK, the economy grew by an average of 1% a year in 2007–15, while average wages contracted at a rate of –1% over the same period.[18] When individuals feel unrepresented by the pronouncements of economists and statisticians, why should they continue to listen to policy experts? When large swaths of the population are not benefiting from a model of social and economic progress, and are suffering, the entire validity of numerical, expert government is thrown into doubt.

The problem of intensity

There is another problem confronting the use of statistics today. In abstract terms, the problem is as follows: statistics have proved very effective at capturing the number of people who belong in a given category, but far less effective at gauging how *intensely* they are affected by something or feel something. Statistics involve placing people in categories selected by the expert—"employed" or "unemployed," "Republican" or "Democrat," "married" or "unmarried." In the original case that concerned John Graunt this was straightforward. It's relatively simple to decide whether someone deserves a check in the box marked "dead" or in the one marked "alive." But in other cases, cultural and economic changes have conspired to push back against the static, sometimes binary distinctions on which statistical classifications rest. Identities have become more complex and lifestyles less predictable. The scientific vision of society as a physical object, made up of individual bodies moving around predictably like billiard balls on a table, has become harder to sustain. The messier aspects of social life, that statistics necessarily have to eliminate, are intruding.

Consider the case of opinion polling. Over recent years, pollsters have suffered high-profile embarrassing failures, especially in the UK where they got the 2015 and 2017 general elections badly wrong, and the 2016 EU referendum wrong, but slightly less so. The main problem facing pollsters today is trying to work out who will actually go out and vote, something that varies hugely depending on age, cultural identity, and class. To put that another way, the difficulty pollsters face is not gauging what someone's electoral preference is (it's not so hard to find out whether someone favors Labour or Conservatives) but whether they *feel* strongly enough to actually vote at all. As engagement in politics falls, so this issue becomes more critical to the outcome of elections.

The problem is compounded by the growing difficulty in achieving a representative sample of the population. For many years, polling companies depended on randomized telephone interviews, but people have become far less tolerant of this technique and now tend to just hang up. Astonishingly, where 72% of people responded to telephone interviews in 1980, less than 10% did in 2016.[19] Inevitably, it is easier to acquire a sample of people who are more interested in politics per se, and are by definition more likely to vote. Pollsters can look at previous rates of voter turnout among different sections of the population, but these can change in either direction. Political alienation manifests itself in non-voting, but if a leader or campaign can convert this into anger, it can swiftly be channeled into the electoral system. This is precisely what Trump and the Brexit campaigns did in 2016, and what Jeremy Corbyn's Labour Party did in 2017, confounding predictions in the process. On the night of Britain's EU referendum, the first sign that the Leave campaign was doing better than predicted were the reports of higher turnout: anti-EU sentiment is stronger than pro-EU sentiment, and this had led people to the polls who didn't usually vote at all. Strength of feeling was what made the difference, and not just demographic reach. In the case of Corbyn, most polling companies had radically underestimated the proportion of people in their twenties and thirties who would turn out, which jumped significantly from the level set at the 2015 election. Labour's capacity to mobilize supporters, forged by street-level networks and social media channels to which experts were largely oblivious, was something that the model-builders were unable to factor in.

Similar problems confront the measurement of unemployment. The category of unemployment came into being toward the end of the nineteenth century, as it became clear that worklessness was not necessarily a moral failing of individuals, but a consequence of how much demand there was for labor in the nation overall. Just as Graunt started to look at death as something that followed certain mathematically calculable trends, if looked at in the aggregate, early studies of unemployment realized that the chance of someone being without work was a consequence of underlying processes, of which the individual was a passive victim.

From this perspective, the total workforce is a relatively homogeneous mass of labor, waiting to be put to work, with various differences of skill but ultimately subject to the same market forces of supply and demand as any other good. Once again, viewing work in terms of averages and aggregates isn't necessarily much succor to the unfortunate individual who has lost their job. But it captures something real, so long as the nature of work itself can be grasped by expert classifications. The most important ones are simple distinctions between those in work ("employed"), those seeking work ("unemployed"), and those not working or seeking work ("non-employed").

These distinctions are not clear-cut any longer. Women traditionally sat in the third category, working in the home as mothers and housewives, but outside the labor market. For cultural and economic reasons, this is no longer the case. As a result, there are cases of societies reducing "non-employment" (as more women move into work) but still having high "unemployment" (men unable to find work) and vice versa. There is also a major problem afflicting advanced capitalist economies of *under*employment, that is, people who have some work but not enough.

The underemployed are not classed as "unemployed," which allows politicians to claim that jobs data is looking good—but that data doesn't capture how much workers are struggling in the new labor market. They often find the wrong kind of work, being insecure, temporary and inadequately paid to cover costs of housing and raising a family. It is work that offers little dignity, sense of self-worth, or improvement over the course of a life, making individuals increasingly skeptical regarding claims of progress or economic growth. The psychological costs of this kind of work can be high, causing high levels of stress as people slip in and out of work, without much certainty, and one result can be that people withdraw from the labor market citing ill health. Sometimes underemployment manifests itself as individuals being forced into *self*-employment, another often vague category, that can mask the fact that people are not benefiting from the labor market properly.

In the wake of the global financial crisis, many governments went to extraordinary lengths to return their economies to stability and growth. Following the deep recession of 2008–9, many headline indicators suggested they had succeeded. Inflation remained low, employment in northern Europe and the USA recovered and GDP began to grow, albeit slowly. A recovery of a sort had been achieved. But below the surface, things were very different. The quality of jobs was deteriorating, the cost of living was rising, government services were shrinking, and people were borrowing more money to make up the shortfall. With the cost of living rising faster than wages, governments seeking to squeeze more and more efficiency gains out of public-sector employees, the emotional and physical experience of economic life was growing steadily worse. Household debt levels continued to rise, which has very direct implications for social and psychological well-being, but because this was never treated as a principal indicator of economic progress, it was rarely headline news.[20] Governments had succeeded in recovering an economy that *looked* healthy to the objective eye, but certainly didn't feel it for a very large number of people.

In many societies, healthy unemployment statistics have become a kind of illusion, that can prop up a policy regime for a while, but eventually throw the credibility of economic policy into question. According to text-book economic principles, if unemployment is low, then wages ought to start rising as the availability of labor is reduced. But if, in reality, workers are doing worse jobs, on fewer hours, for less money and with less psychological engagement with what they're doing, the headline unemployment indicator is worthless. It becomes a form of propaganda, that works to the extent that it persuades and reassures, but can't claim to represent reality with much validity.

Falling unemployment figures in Europe and North America have allowed politicians to keep announcing good news. In late 2017, the UK recorded its lowest unemployment rate in forty years. But behind these numbers are more painful stories, that vary from nation to nation. In France and Italy, large numbers of young people are overlooked by the unemployment data because they have simply given up looking for work, after prolonged unemployment. Britain avoided unemployment by creating a surge in low-skilled, low-productivity jobs, at the same time experiencing a flat-lining of productivity growth that had not been witnessed in over two hundred years. In the United States, fewer men are looking for work, because there are fewer men in the labor market overall. By 2017, the proportion of adult Americans in the labor market was at its lowest level for over forty years. The retirement of baby boomers partly accounts for this, but so do illness, disability, incarceration, and addiction.

The mirage of low unemployment is one more example of how a statistics-led view of the world can disintegrate. In the emerging expert circles of the seventeenth century, geometry was the final measure of all truth about the world. Economics and other quantitative social sciences are a surviving legacy of this worldview. As lived experiences splinter as a consequence of inequality (especially in a geographic sense, of the rural/urban divide), and as lifestyles and institutions become more fluid and less rigidly governed, the capacity of this seventeenth-century apparatus to provide a convincing and coherent picture of progress is no longer assured. Experts might continue to view society through statistical lenses, but if the categories they are using do not capture anything meaningful, they cannot expect to be trusted by the public. One of the consequences of these shifts is that other, less mathematical perspectives on politics and society acquire more credibility.

Once more with feeling

In the heady days of the 1990s, as the world economy started to hum and globalization became the basis of a free-market policy consensus, economic visionaries offered a new recipe for how individual cities and regions could prosper in this era of open borders. Pointing particularly to examples such as "Silicon Fen" around Cambridge University or North Carolina's "Research Triangle," gurus such as Richard Florida, Michael Porter, and Charles Leadbeater argued that the economic success stories of the future would be cities and business clusters that attracted highly educated, socially liberal workers, who were willing to mingle informally and circulate ideas. These centers of innovation would often emerge around universities. With good social connections between entrepreneurs, academic research, and venture capital, a whole new era of prosperity could be achieved, based upon nothing but ideas and imagination. This was the idea of a "knowledge economy" with a "creative class" of open-minded, highly mobile young graduates at its heart. Cities, universities, and other concentrations of people were key to this.

This vision was not wrong, but its applicability was limited. It is certainly true that cities such as London and New York have grown rapidly since the early 1990s, both in population and in wealth, with a side effect being widespread housing crises. There are also a few ex-industrial cities that have managed to position themselves as "hubs" for creativity and innovation, perhaps most famously Bilbao in northern Spain, which benefited from a famous piece of iconic architecture designed by Frank Gehry. But what the gurus did not anticipate (or were never that concerned by) was how these successes would exacerbate latent cultural and economic divisions which slice many Western societies in two, especially in the English-speaking world. The rising prosperity of many urban graduates was in contrast to the slumping fortunes of many rural, ex-industrial and former mining regions. It was difficult to view multiculturalism or fancy architecture as a viable economic strategy for towns that once relied entirely on mining, shipbuilding, or steel.

As policymakers came to view knowledge and cultural diversity as valuable economic assets, so the conflict between metropolitan and rural values was heightened, adding economic inequality to a set of existing moral controversies. Another way in which this split appears is in terms of graduates versus nongraduates. This conflict has been a feature of American politics since the 1960s, and now more or less determines the shape of the electoral map, with Democrats winning in coastal regions, big cities, and university towns, and Republicans winning more or less everywhere else. But a similar divide has subsequently emerged in numerous European countries in the context of deindustrialization.

The geography of Britain's 2016 EU referendum result made this abundantly clear: outside Scotland and Northern Ireland, the areas that voted "Remain" were major cities (London, Manchester, Leeds, much of Birmingham), the high-tech business cluster along the Thames Valley, and smaller university towns and cities (Norwich, Leicester, Exeter, Oxford, Cambridge), but almost the entire rest of England voted "Leave." What makes the conflict particularly intractable in Britain and the United States is that it cuts society roughly down the middle, now that around 50% of people in these societies go to university and 50% don't. Following years in which all policy attention was paid to boosting the "competitive advantage" of cities, universities, and business clusters, the democratic upheavals and threats of the past few years have led to renewed interest in the experiences of those who are excluded from this largely urban model of progress.

How we relate to expert knowledge, such as statistics, has become a key factor in determining the kinds of lives we lead and how we narrate them. The privileged section of society, for whom social and economic progress is still a realistic expectation, includes many people who make their living from the production of expert knowledge, including public-sector professions, academics, consultants, financiers, and business advisers. The scientific perspective on society, as pioneered by Graunt and Petty, continues to provide a plausible picture of reality for most of these people, mediated by the likes of the *New York Times* or the *Economist*. But what of the others? What kinds of perspectives and analyses are suppressed or sidelined by the expert view of aggregates and averages? And can we understand it as something other than just *false*?

Among those not included in this "knowledge economy" vision of progress, an individual is more likely to be an object of expert scrutiny than an agent of it. As cultural and economic advantage becomes increasingly concentrated around big cities and universities, expert knowledge is something the privileged *do to* the less privileged. Bureaucracy and quantitative research become ways of collecting data about the population, but without actually getting to know people or listen to them. The mathematical, abstract view of the world becomes a way of avoiding any engagement with how it appears and feels to those who dwell outside the centers of expertise. René Descartes had laid the foundations of modern philosophy, by splitting everything into things that think (*res cogitans*) and things that are physical (*res extensa*), with human beings both at once. But the cultural divisions we witness in our societies today are as if one set of people are granted the status of *res cogitans* and the other merely *res extensa*: some of us are thinkers, the others are mere bodies.

Something similar is at work in how we relate to the natural environment. The very idea of "nature" as a type of mechanical object, that can be probed and studied via experimentation in laboratories, requires us to observe it from afar. It is how the natural world is imagined, when one is safely protected from it in a university college, laboratory, or elite institution. But for those whose day-to-day lives are shaped by vagaries of weather, foliage, and animals, the natural world is not some set of theories or facts. The urban–rural split in our politics reiterates that: one part of society learns and reads about nature in books, while another uses and coexists with it. Concern for "the environment" is too often an abstract moral or intellectual commitment to something that one never intends to encounter directly. The political challenge this presents is how to narrow the divide between "nature," as studied and theorized by experts, and everyday rural existence.

Expertise has always involved a tight delineation of whose experience counts as valid objective knowledge, as the Royal Society demonstrated from its origins. But the dawn of knowledge-based capitalism means that this cultural elitism doubles up as an economic elitism, which inevitably translates into political divisions and resentment sooner or later. Under the industrial capitalism of the nineteenth and early twentieth centuries, there were those people who got rich, and there were those who claimed to know best. Today, however, the privilege of knowledge and that of wealth reinforce each other: highly educated consultants, lawyers, and investment analysts are also the main beneficiaries of capitalism.

For those whose lives seem untouched by improvements in GDP or reductions in unemployment, alternative ways of understanding collective identity and history are not only plausible but necessary. One of the most potent is obviously nationalism, which offers a way of understanding the life of society in cultural and mythical terms. The acclaimed theorist of nationalism Benedict Anderson argued that nations are "imagined communities," in which a vast number of people buys into a single fiction of what they all hold in common. Anderson argued that the spread of nationwide media in the eighteenth century enabled disparate people, who would never actually meet, to share the same symbols and stories. Statistics are antagonistic to this collective leap of faith, dashing fantasies of military prowess and economic strength. By confronting the nationalist myth with cold statistical facts, evidence for the macroeconomic benefits of immigration presents a threat to an important source of meaning for many people, and is often ignored or actively resisted.

Ironically nationalism is a far more recent historical development than statistics. An idea of a single national people, bound together by tradition and shared feelings, is something that took hold during the nineteenth century, nearly two centuries after the birth of statistics. As the historian Eric Hobsbawm argued, it wasn't until the French Revolution that there was any recognition that "nations existed as something independent of states."[21] The Napoleonic Wars produced the first national heroes (such as Nelson) and the first mass nationally conscripted armies. The technocratic ideal of the modern state, as a collector of facts, staffed by administrators, is therefore a much older historical relic than the romantic ideals of blood and soil to which figures like Marine Le Pen and Viktor Orbán appeal.

Romantic and statistical views of the nation collide around questions of history, especially the value of the distant past. For those who buy into the expert-led vision of scientific government, the present is objectively better than the past, and the future will be objectively better than the present. This is not just a sentiment or opinion, but usually backed up by facts. Statistics drawn from economics, health research, or attitudinal surveys can confirm this, give or take the recessions or other upheavals that occasionally interrupt progress. By contrast, in the imagination of the nationalist, the best days of the community are likely to be in the past, at a time when wars were fought and cultural identities more secure. For someone who has had no pay raise for forty years, or has a job that is lower status than his father's was, this narrative has a credibility that no quantity of facts and figures can acquire. For this person, appeals to statistical objectivity—with the emphasis on averages and aggregation that that implies—can add insult to injury.

There is nothing natural or especially intuitive about the expert perspective on the economy, and it can often be counterintuitive. The founding claim of economics is that, where everyone is free to look out for themselves in a competitive market, the net effect will be positive. The argument for free trade and flexible markets rests on this scientific proposition, backed up by statistical economic evidence. The expert claim is that the free market is a "positive-sum game" (in contrast to a "zero-sum game"), in which one set of competitors can become extremely rich, without this having any negative effect on everybody else. By this account, there is no reason for the poor to resent the rich, as the fortunes of one party have not caused the misfortunes of another.

While rational to an economist, this argument is psychologically naive. Crucially it ignores the extent to which the economy is also a status game that shapes our self-esteem, and not just a means of sustenance and survival. Experimental and survey evidence shows that interpersonal comparisons are hugely important for human well-being. If my status and wealth remains constant, while yours is constantly growing, this will have a negative impact on my self-esteem.[22] The burgeoning sense of resentment that has grown in the context of "knowledge-based" capitalism, directed at "liberal elites" living in cities, is not simply irrational, but reflects basic realities about how we experience inequality as a moral force. One psychological study of people who'd voted for Trump in 2016 showed that they experienced higher than average "relative deprivation," meaning that they weren't necessarily poor (many were actually quite rich), but *felt* that others had overtaken them.[23] Research on European populism, both on the left and right, finds that it arises in tandem with unemployment *increases*, rather than the total unemployment rate, suggesting that it is the injury of being laid off that is most politically decisive, and not the condition of poverty or unemployment itself.[24] The psychological harm enacted by inequality is indirect: it is channeled via small everyday experiences that undermine a person's self-esteem.

Nor are supposedly more rational "liberal elites" immune to the seductions of resentment and envy either. Why do bankers and CEOs today earn far more than they can possibly need or really enjoy? The answer to this is found in moral psychology, not economics: their sense of self-worth depends on comparing themselves to each other and to their previous earnings, rather than by looking at their money in the aggregate. The hypocrisy of privileged elites on this issue is palpable. In one's own day-to-day life, the economy *feels* like a zero-sum game in which one side wins and the other loses, regardless of what experts might say, a feeling that engulfs the rich just as much as the poor. We are all susceptible to the logic of resentment in our own lives, even those of us who adopt a perspective of cool scientific objectivity toward the lives of others.

There are inevitably times when people care more about justice being visited upon the overprivileged and powerful than about becoming better off themselves. Following the 2010 BP oil spill in the Gulf of Mexico, BP set about compensating local fishermen with out-of-court settlements totaling several billion dollars. But for one shrimp producer from Grand Isle, Louisiana, this wasn't what he wanted. "I want my day in court," he said. "If they can get off with just paying the money—well, they've got plenty of money, they are not really going to learn a lesson."[25] Viewed unkindly, this is a demand for vengeance. More sympathetically, it shows that principles of justice and fair punishment are as valid within the economy as anywhere else, and cannot be balanced using money alone. Either way, this fisherman was expressing something that is incomprehensible from the rationalist perspective of economics. It is a demand that Hobbes would have understood—that the force of the law should apply to all equally—but which an increasingly technocratic governing class often can't.

Numerical expert accounts of the world cannot measure this sentiment. They provide no meaningful explanation as to why one's economic or social fortunes have taken a turn for the worse; they certainly provide nobody to blame. When Graunt applied mathematics to the study of death rates in 1662, he achieved a major scientific breakthrough in the study of mortality, but only by defying the more meaningful, more humane understanding of pain and death which makes loss tolerable. Narratives that can account for suffering, whether those be religious, nationalistic, or militaristic, serve a purpose that the scientific perspective cannot. Economists will argue that free markets are a peaceful way of improving the lives of everybody, but the reality of capitalism can sometimes feel closer to war than to peace.

The blindness of facts

Part of the purpose of statistical expertise is to cleanse government policy-making of moral questions of justice, blame, and punishment, allowing it to be anchored purely in facts. But this requires politicians to deny deeper truths about the human condition and the everyday experience of market forces. These then get dismissed as "emotional." The experience of being laid off feels like a judgment or a punishment, rather than just a fact or an efficiency. If one's income starts to fall to where it was several years ago, the psychological effect will be a feeling of failure, even of punishment, *especially* if politicians and the media keep reporting evidence of progress and prosperity.

Consumer culture, which holds up images of perfectly happy and healthy individuals as the norm, produces feelings of inadequacy and self-recrimination by design. Memories of thriving factory towns, now abandoned, are real and painful, even while they are entangled in other emotions and more personal histories. The decline of coal mining seems to generate an especially painful feeling of lost attachments, evident in the regions of Saxony, Appalachia, Wales, and Alsace, as the resource is finite and never to return once gone. The statistical science of society, overseen by a small coterie of experts, never succeeded in eliminating these moral and emotional realities. But during times when collective national progress is more inclusive, politics is more insulated from basic instincts concerning injustice, punishment, fear, and security. Technocratic politics is a good way of keeping these visceral aspects of political psychology out of sight, but they are never eliminated altogether.

These ulterior narratives and beliefs are resurfacing around us today, unleashed partly by the rise of populist parties and leaders, who oppose the dominance of technocratic politics and its constant resort to statistical evidence. They are not doing so because people are uninterested in "truth" or lack education. There is every reason to believe that the highly educated residents of San Francisco, Paris, and Milan view their own fortunes and misfortunes in similarly moralistic, occasionally militaristic, sometimes resentful terms. The failure to sustain a convincing scientific narrative of progress is as much a reflection on the social and economic conditions that developed from the 1980s onward as it is a rejection of expertise.

But there is one particular trend which has been especially significant for the development of a more combative style of politics, which rejects the claims of statisticians and economists. This trend returns us to the question that preoccupied Descartes and Hobbes, and which is fundamental to the promise of progress: to what extent can we preserve our living, feeling, mortal bodies? The way in which inequality and injustice impacts upon us physically—determining how and when we suffer and die—may be most damaging to the hopes for a scientifically governed society. It is when our bodies become swept along and defined by political and economic forces that feeling really takes hold of politics.

4
THE BODY POLITIC
Feeling beyond medicine

How people feel about the human body, both their own and those of others, is at the center of one of the most decisive political schisms of our times. Rising political polarization can be linked to various cultural divisions, for example urban versus rural or graduate versus nongraduate. But there is something more bewildering going on involving the body. Evidence from across Europe and the United States shows that people who are drawn toward nationalists such as Donald Trump or Marine Le Pen often have significantly lower health prospects and life expectancy than average. Pockets of economic decline in deindustrialized areas are suffering especially on this front. Increases in life expectancy have either stagnated or, in certain instances, started to reverse.

Psychologists have noted that nationalists are also more likely to hold "authoritarian values." Predictably, this involves distrust of elected representatives and the mainstream media. But it also involves a particular perspective on the bodies of others: people with authoritarian values are more likely to support the death penalty, physical punishment of children, and torture. Opinion polls in the UK, for example, have shown that 28% of British people believe "torture works" and 27% think it should be permitted. But among supporters of the UK Independence Party, the figures are 53% and 56% respectively, indicating that some UKIP supporters are skeptical that torture works, but believe it should be permitted anyway.[1] This is a political vision in which the infliction of physical pain, and even death, is how authority *should* work, whether that be in the criminal justice system, school, security services, or the family.

These beliefs ultimately reject several hundred years of progress. The birth of experts in the late seventeenth century was the beginning of the end of gratuitous, vicious forms of punishment, which later became labeled "cruel and unusual" by the American Constitution. As the state became more bureaucratic, the exercise of violence became more cautiously employed for specific purposes. The lure of authoritarianism lies in the ideal of resurrecting a more visceral, less careful form of power, that could settle matters of life and death in public, and gives vent to anger. In this imaginary political arena, everything is simple. Guilt should mean pain, innocence should mean comfort, and then justice is finally done.

This is a troubling phenomenon, but it is not inexplicable. The desire to punish physically arises partly out of a sense of one's own vulnerability, feelings that may have been first experienced when being physically punished as a child. It can also be a symptom of age, both in the sense that older generations have more traditional views about punishment, but are also more acutely aware of their own frailty and mortality. Experiments reveal that authoritarian values can be triggered by a simple reminder of death, meaning that all of us are liable to drift toward a harsher, more punitive viewpoint, whenever we get a sense of how precarious life is.[2] A vicious circle develops, in which fear produces an urge to inflict pain, which produces more fear.

A brighter perspective on this syndrome is also possible, which holds valuable political lessons for the future. At a point in history where trust in politicians, journalists, and—in some countries—the judiciary is falling across most of the Western world, it is useful to note some striking exceptions to this trend: doctors and, above all, nurses are respected and trusted to an extent that cuts across all other political and cultural divides.[3] The referendum campaign for Britain to leave the European Union, Vote Leave, is remembered for having promised to bring back £350 million a week from Brussels, and spend it on the National Health Service. The factual inaccuracy of the "£350 million" attracted the ire of Remain campaigners, but they should also have considered why the NHS above all else carried so much political power and resonance with people. A sense of one's own frailty can be diverted toward tough-man politics. But it can also be channeled toward the professions and institutions that provide care.

Achieving alternatives to authoritarianism depends on the second of these two possibilities. Human mortality and vulnerability is a universal condition, which produces sympathy and common experience, as well as fear and suspicion. But it is worrying that sections of the population feel unusually fearful and vulnerable, elevating questions of health, age, physical care, and physical punishment to a renewed significance in the political arena. Placed within the long arc of medical progress, there is no obvious reason why this should be the case. We currently live in an exceptional era, in which death can be avoided and postponed, and the degradations of the body are processes that can be prevented or managed to a large extent. Thanks to the discovery of penicillin in the mid-twentieth century, entire diseases have been wiped out. The invention of the contraceptive pill soon after meant that the most basic problems of human existence—the giving and the preserving of life itself—are under our conscious control in a way that is unprecedented.

And yet this is not how things feel to many of us, and it is this that is generating much of the uncertainty and turbulence that we see played out in our politics. It is possible to dismiss this feeling as irrational, and to point to the facts of how human life has got longer and more comfortable over centuries. But where the human body is concerned, feelings are never irrelevant: our nerves convey crucial information on which our survival depends. We eat when we feel hungry. We avoid touching things that feel very hot. We've evolved to flee situations that seem instantly dangerous. It is not possible to view one's own pain and death with an air of scientific objectivity. The nervous system has always represented a philosophical problem for anyone who, following Descartes, believes "mind" and "body" are fundamentally distinct. The interplay of physical feeling, psychological emotion, and political engagement renders that philosophical distinction untenable.

Medical progress has been remarkable, especially since the mid-nineteenth century when scientific discoveries first began to really transform medical practice. These gains have been achieved by separating matters of anatomical enquiry from moral or political concerns, allowing scientists to study the human body in much the same way that they might study plants, planets, or rock formations: slowly, objectively, and dispassionately. The entangling of physical ailments, resentments, and fears with politics today suggests that this attempt to keep anatomy and politics apart is not working as well as it once did. Yes, we place great trust in medical professionals, but perhaps this is as much because of the need to be cared for and listened to as because of the facts they have at their disposal.

The body has become one of the key areas where experts wrestle with alternative moral, emotional, and political perspectives. This occurs in familiar disputes that have raged over homeopathy and vaccinations, in which scientific authority is directly challenged by holistic philosophies and conspiracy theories. Those conflicts will continue to rage. But there is something less obvious going on, which may ultimately be more significant for our politics. For all the achievements of scientific progress, there is a lurking unease with the principles on which that progress was built and the way in which the benefits are being shared. Across a number of developed societies, people seem less willing to treat physical health and vitality as problems that belong wholly to the scientific community to solve. To understand what's going on, we need to reflect once more on how the expert perspective was first established.

Under the skin

In the seventeenth century, death struck families and communities with a regularity that is hard to imagine from the vantage point of a prosperous twenty-first-century society. Increased commercial traffic and urbanization of the late seventeenth century meant rising frequency of plagues. It was common for children to be given the names and clothes of deceased siblings. Lacking control over these frequent tragedies, people turned to religious and moral explanations. One popular belief was that disease and loss of family members was a punishment for sins committed in a previous life.

At the dawn of the Scientific Revolution, the English scholar and pioneer of scientific method Francis Bacon had outlined a new vision of what a physician could offer: "First, the preservation of health, second, the cure of disease, and third, the prolongation of life."[4] But at the time, this was little more than science fiction. The ideas of Aristotle still dominated medical thinking, which viewed the human animal as an integrated system of body and soul. The writings of Galen, a Greek physician and philosopher whose work was influential in ancient Rome, took a similarly systemic view of the body. Galen's theories drew connections between the health of different organs and different human temperaments, proposing that there were two parallel systems of blood circulation, one governed by the liver and the other by the heart. Galen's thinking shaped Western views about physical health for around 1,300 years. But what ultimately undermined Galen and Aristotle was a practice that was illegal for most of that time: cutting open dead bodies. The ability to see beneath the skin would revolutionize how the body was known and treated.

Cadaverous research was illegal in Europe for 1,700 years up until the fourteenth century. While ancient theories of physiology and health could be corroborated by research on animals, the human body remained a closed object to scientific scrutiny. Anything that lay beyond the visible exterior of the body was a matter of theoretical speculation. Religious taboos on anatomical research were gradually relaxed from the thirteenth century onward, following the foundation of the first universities, and Bologna became a center of anatomical thinking at this time. But human dissections didn't immediately break the hold of ancient ideas. Dissections were carried out as staged performances to illustrate a set of theories, rather than to learn anything new. The Belgian physician Andreas Vesalius in the late sixteenth century was among the first to take a more exploratory approach.

Thanks to the example of Vesalius, the seventeenth century witnessed rapid advances in anatomical science, aided by the invention of the microscope in 1600. William Harvey fundamentally broke with Galenic physiology, by accurately describing the circulation of the blood in 1628. The work of Thomas Sydenham in the second half of the seventeenth century created the template for the modern understanding of disease, as something to be meticulously studied in its characteristics, independently of the sufferer or broader social meaning. These scientists observed each part of the body as an individual mechanism, whose relationship to the others needed to be discovered, rather than deduced from existing scholarship. Such advances corroborated the view of the body that was developing through the philosophy of René Descartes and Thomas Hobbes at the same time; indeed Hobbes was always keen to learn from the latest anatomical breakthroughs of the day.

Descartes offered a particular philosophy in which the mind and soul are metaphysical and immortal, but the body is just an inert machine, obeying geometrical laws of motion. Our bodies respond positively to pleasure and negatively to pain, but that is simply a feature of their natural constitution, and no more philosophically or morally significant than the fact that water turns to steam when it reaches a certain temperature. What makes us human—what makes us *us*—has nothing to do with our physical bodies at all. In Descartes' words:

> on the one side, I have a clear and distinct idea of myself inasmuch as I am only a thinking and unextended thing, and as, on the other, I possess a distinct idea of body, inasmuch as it is only an extended and unthinking thing, it is certain that this I (that is to say, my soul by which I am what I am), is entirely and absolutely distinct from my body, and can exist without it.[5]

By the same token, the deterioration and ultimate death of the body is of no fundamental significance in itself. Illness and mortality possess no moral or theological significance, once the body is regarded as just another object moving around in the natural world, following the laws of cause and effect. Paradoxically, in order for progress to be achieved in medicine and the prevention of death, the inherent value of the physical body had to be drastically downgraded.

The result of this separation of body from soul was that modern medicine left moral and religious questions well alone. It represented no threat to religious authority, and consequently the church largely tolerated it. But ordinary people were not so relaxed. Despite the lifting of restrictions on cadaverous research, public sentiment was broadly opposed to the idea of dissecting dead bodies, producing ongoing difficulties for medical researchers. Treating the deceased as mere physical objects seemed to violate some strongly felt moral intuition. After publishing his work on the circulation of the blood, William Harvey actually lost clients, who were terrified that they would become test cases for his outlandish new physiological claims. There was scarce public demand for the new medical expertise, and family doctors continued to provide the types of holistic remedies and narratives that their clients demanded until the mid-nineteenth century.

The obvious benefit of anatomical science, including human dissection, is that it prolongs life and enables greater health and vitality—just as Francis Bacon had envisaged. The modern ideal of medicine is founded on a specific model of the relationship between patient and doctor, with which we are now entirely familiar. A patient presents some kind of symptom (a pain or observation that's appeared to them), which the doctor uses to diagnose some disease or other underlying organic cause. The non-expert operates at the level of surfaces and feelings, while the medic deals with what lies underneath, somewhere inside our anatomy. This is what constitutes a diagnosis.

There is a considerable degree of trust at stake here, as the doctor is authorized to decide what underlying disease or organic malfunction is indicated by the symptom. To an extent, the patient must suspend their own sense of what's wrong. Such trust was hard-won over centuries, but eventually it stems from the palpable individual and social benefits that medicine has been able to deliver. A typical life has become longer and less disease-ridden.

But resistance to medical research illustrates an important point regarding the status of experts and the cultural acceptance of progress. The modern medical vision of the body, as an inert and physical specimen, is not intuitively appealing. Even today, this vision often repels us where our own bodies or those of our loved ones are concerned. We still need to offer our consent before our dead bodies can be used for scientific or medical purposes, and that consent is something that receives moral plaudits as an altruistic act, even a civic one. This suggests that we *don't* commonly see the body as just another type of organic equipment, in the way that Descartes and Hobbes proposed. And nor do we view our own deaths (or what happens to us after our deaths) as merely physiological events, to be delayed and managed by whatever expert means are available. To hold a purely scientific view of human anatomy requires that we do some violence to instinctive forms of memory and mourning, that are often difficult to dislodge.

Despite twentieth-century scientific advances in delaying and predicting death, it remains a part of life. It is still a matter of interpretation, a source of ritual and meaning like nothing else. Modern medicine and health policy have been able to isolate the human body—and its demise—from broader questions of morality and politics, but they have done so on the basis of the same progressive bargain that has legitimized other forms of expertise since the time of Hobbes: that even if life becomes no more exciting or meaningful, we will nevertheless be guaranteed *more of it*. Just as Hobbes and, subsequently, economists assumed that a desire for life and pleasures was the one thing that is common to everyone, the premise of medical progress is that we will sacrifice rituals and beliefs, if only we can get more and better life. If today some communities currently demonstrate a yearning for something more symbolic than this, even sometimes more self-destructive, it may be because governments and experts have not been keeping their side of the bargain. This is manifest in political movements which reject the very idea of progress.

Physical progress in question

Following the surprise result of the 2016 American presidential election, the *Economist* magazine published a peculiar analysis of what might have caused it, focusing on a few decisive states:

> The data suggest that the ill may have been particularly susceptible to Mr Trump's message. According to our model, if diabetes were just 7% less prevalent in Michigan, Mr Trump would have gained 0.3 fewer percentage points there, enough to swing the state back to the Democrats. Similarly, if an additional 8% of people in Pennsylvania engaged in regular physical activity, and heavy drinking in Wisconsin were 5% lower, Mrs Clinton would be set to enter the White House.[6]

The report was merely noting some statistical correlations, and offered no theory as to what might cause those suffering with illnesses to support Trump. It was, however, pointing to a trend that was difficult to ignore, for anyone wanting to understand the geography and culture of right-wing populism. The physical condition of Trump supporters was notably inferior to that of Clinton supporters. Before considering what might lurk behind this observation, let's look at some of the evidence on how progress in health has stalled and been reversed.

The divisions cutting America in two, between liberal and conservative, urban and rural, college-educated and non-college-educated, also appear to manifest themselves in terms of physical health. A landmark 2015 study published by health economists Anne Case and Angus Deaton revealed an unexpected rise in the mortality rate of middle-aged white, non-Hispanic Americans, caused by a range of factors including drug overdoses, heart disease, alcoholism, and suicide.[7] Following decades of rising life expectancy across all sections of the American population, the evidence showed that mortality rates had started to rise among this group in the late 1990s. By 2015, average life expectancy in the United States started to fall, then fell again the following year.[8] Subsequent analysis showed that the trends identified by Case and Deaton were heavily clustered in rural areas, especially in those economically struggling regions such as Appalachia, which were being hit by the closure of factories and mines.[9]

No other country in the world has experienced a comparable rise in mortality as the one Case and Deaton discovered in the United States in the twenty-first century. The only precedent for this kind of trend since the Second World War is that of Russia in the early 1990s, where the demise of communism and the rise of mass male unemployment saw a sudden spike in the mortality rate of young men, largely connected to increasing reliance on very cheap and dangerous alcohol. In Russia, life expectancy plummeted from seventy in 1989 to sixty-four in 1995.[10] But there are still alarming trends elsewhere.

In Britain, life expectancy had been rising for over a century until it started to stagnate in 2010.[11] The geographer Danny Dorling discovered that Britain had experienced a rising mortality rate and declining average life expectancy in 2015, largely as a result of cuts to social care for the elderly.[12] This was one of the largest such spikes in the death rate since reliable annual figures were first produced in the 1830s.[13] As Dorling observed, "David Cameron left office in June 2016 with UK life expectancy falling. No other post-war prime minister has achieved such a terrible outcome."[14] Inequalities in life expectancy also began widening in the UK post-2012, after narrowing in the early 2000s.[15] This has produced a situation where a person in Chelsea can expect to live to eighty-three, while someone in Blackpool can expect to live to seventy-four. A particular concern is that, while the mortality rate of young men has fallen steadily in the south of England, it began to rise in the north around 2011.[16]

The effects of public-spending cuts (or "austerity"), enacted in the wake of the financial crisis, have been measured around the world in rising death rates and declining health levels, especially in southern Europe. A 2011 study estimated that 10,000 additional suicides around the world had been caused by the global financial crisis.[17] In Greece, the male suicide rate rose by 20% in 2007–9.[18] Austerity in Europe has had major physiological consequences, impacting on the ability of disabled people to live dignified lives, and manifesting itself in deteriorating rates of nutrition and public health. Increases in French life expectancy leveled off after 2011. In Britain, cuts to spending on health and social care are responsible for an additional 120,000 deaths.[19] The market-based health care system in the United States produces some equally harsh consequences, with 40% more "avoidable" deaths (per capita) each year than in Europe.[20] America is the only country in the world where the rate of maternal deaths in childbirth has been rising over the past thirty years, a trend believed to be linked to a rise of pre-existing chronic conditions.[21]

The unexpected rise of mortality rates in various contexts suggests a breakdown in the basic contract underlying notions of collective progress. In a society governed by a centralized technocratic state, we forgo our rights to violence, we give up our dreams of heroism and existential drama, and in return we expect to become progressively better off, in physical and economic comfort. The experts that shape modern society, on whom we depend for the management of our economy, our public services, and our health, offer little of moral or philosophical substance to cling on to. Like the seventeenth-century merchants whose practices of record keeping inspired the first statisticians and experimental scientists, modern medicine paints the world in prosaic, factual terms, which fails to capture the hopes, fears, and meaning that are tied up in our physical condition. But the wager of progress assumes that safety, health, and welfare are more important than fundamental beliefs or cultural romance. If these goods start to recede, at least for certain significant sections of society, then we shouldn't be surprised if the same sections turn against the progressive modern project more generally.

There is a visceral, bodily dimension to how people engage politically with new populist movements, especially those with an authoritarian streak. Health inequalities are fueling this, a trend that has been found across numerous nationalist movements. In her 2017 presidential bid, for example, Marine Le Pen attracted much younger voters than most other nationalist parties in Europe, but these were still located in regions with lower than average health outcomes and life expectancy.[22] The expectation—or hope—that democracy could be a space in which people participate through reasonable, verbal dialogue is threatened, once we realize that people are as influenced by their physical condition and prospects as by their values or preferences. Yet the rising political significance of ill health, age, and mortality to the reactionary populism of the present day suggests something else is going on as well. The experience of physical deterioration provokes in people a desire for a different type of political rule altogether—one that casts experts and technocrats aside.

Psychosomatic politics

Among the various discoveries made by Case and Deaton in their 2015 article was a rise in the number of Americans living with chronic pain. This was most pronounced in the same population segment that displayed a rising mortality rate, namely middle-aged white non-Hispanics. Unsurprisingly, the prevalence of chronic pain rises as people age, and the aging populations of western Europe display a rising rate of pain overall. In the UK, between a third and a half of all adults report that they live with some kind of regular pain, a level that is closer to two-thirds for the over-seventy-fives.[23] Medical advances in keeping people alive for longer are having the unintended side effect of generating a rising amount of physical pain. The medical and social status of pain takes us to the heart of psychosomatic health, that is, how the mind and the body interact with one another. Where it fuses psychological and physical feeling, pain throws fundamental principles of modern science into question. As the categories of "mind" and "body" dissolve into each other, we become increasingly defined by our nerves.

Pain has always been philosophically and politically problematic. Whereas physical injuries and diseases can be observed by others, pain has an apparently private quality, which potentially cuts the sufferer off from others. By its nature, it can be difficult to adequately communicate, a quality that led the cultural theorist Elaine Scarry to describe intense pain as "world-destroying."[24] The sufferer feels alone with their pain, and depends on the capacity of others to empathize and to believe them. As Scarry puts it, "To have pain is to have *certainty*; to hear about pain is to have *doubt*."[25] This generates its own political strains, as some sufferers are inevitably viewed as more credible than others, while some are assumed to exaggerate their pains. The politics of pain involves differing views of who deserves compassion and how much, a matter that generates its own distinctive political positions. For example, American conservatives have historically taken the harsher view, that those in pain are less deserving of sympathy or pain relief.[26]

Descartes tried to deal with pain by viewing it as an entirely physical matter, with its own specific neurological network. To do otherwise would have been to disrupt the separation of bodily and mental worlds on which his philosophical project depended. In his view, pain was the body's internal communication system, which he compared to a system of pulleys that distributed information around the body so as to help it avoid injury. It is not, therefore, something that afflicts us in our selves or souls.

This is a tenable position for an anatomist to take when inspecting a human body, but it is virtually impossible to maintain when one is experiencing pain oneself. Pain carves a path directly between the realms of mind and body, engulfing us in a psychosomatic fashion. There is copious evidence showing that those living in constant pain have a higher propensity to suffer from mental health problems such as depression.[27] They also have a tendency to develop a broader cultural pessimism regarding the future, both their own and that of society. Many effective treatments for chronic pain (especially of the back and neck) are psychological in nature, often encouraging sufferers to change how they feel about their pain, using positive thinking techniques and activity to try to overcome it or, alternatively, accept it as part of their identity and life story. To recognize how suffering pervades both body and mind (the literal meaning of "psychosomatic") does not in any sense reduce the reality or severity of it; on the contrary, it makes it harder to endure.

The experience and reporting of pain also demonstrates cultural and national variations. A study published in late 2017 found that around a third of Americans and Australians reported that they'd "often" or "very often" suffered bodily aches and pains over the previous month, compared to 19% in China, 11% in South Africa, and just 8.5% in the Czech Republic.[28] There is no simple reason why this should be the case, but it relates to a range of psychological and economic factors, including the expectations people have for health care. A consumerist mentality, which insists on total satisfaction, may make pain harder to ignore and to tolerate. The nervous system is not as insulated from cultural influences as Descartes might have liked.

In principle, pain can serve as a medical symptom that can be used for diagnosis, especially if it arises in combination with some other symptom. However, treating pain in this way is not straightforward. First, it raises the same issue of whose reports of pain are to be trusted and whose to be treated with skepticism. Pain does not "present" in the way that a rash or fever does. Doctors would prefer a symptom to be something more visible and objective, rather than something that required their empathy. Second, while pain might represent some underlying problem, doctors have historically been wary of relieving pain itself, often believing that pain has positive therapeutic properties. Until the second half of the twentieth century, the body's capacity to experience pain was generally viewed as a sign of health, and not something to be disrupted using anaesthetics or painkillers. Interrupting the nervous system with painkillers was therefore viewed as unnatural and unhealthy. The discovery of ether and chloroform in the late 1840s opened up a whole different way for doctors and surgeons to relate to patients, granting a new type of expert control over the nervous system. But for much of the nineteenth century, surgeons resisted using these drugs, even though they were proved to work.[29]

In recent decades, however, as rates of pain have risen and the voice of patients has grown louder in health policy, the status of pain has changed. The cultural transformation of the 1960s saw new attention to the subjective experiences of patients, and not only their physical condition. The question of how a disease affected a patient's "quality of life" became a priority, especially as the logic of consumerism was spreading rapidly through society.[30] This shift inevitably drew doctors into psychosomatic territory, introducing questions of how the patient felt about their treatment, how happy they were, how a given disease reduced their freedom or capacity for pleasure. Researchers invented new patient survey techniques, in an effort to place patient experiences on a scientific footing. The influential McGill Pain Questionnaire arrived in 1971, offering a series of adjectives and scales through which sufferers could give their feelings some objective manifestation. This had the unusual effect of converting verbal expressions of feeling into matters of medical fact.

In the context of post-1960s Western societies, the obligation to relieve pain became framed as a moral duty. This was in clear opposition to the traditionalist and religious orientation, which tacitly assumed that pain had an important regulatory function, in keeping human desires and freedoms in check and maintaining a form of discipline. The pain of cancer sufferers became recognized as needless and inhumane, and led to renewed calls to use the full range of pain relief available, most importantly opiates. Opiates had been viewed with great suspicion by the medical establishment since the invention of heroin and morphine in the late nineteenth century, due to their addictive qualities. Use of opiates during the American Civil War left a legacy of 400,000 addicts, and experts continued to see the drugs as an inherent danger to the moral fabric of society right up until the 1960s.

Opiates first crept back into medical usage when morphine was used to treat late-stage cancer sufferers in the 1970s, initially in hospices in Britain, but on the ethical principle that addiction didn't matter if the afflicted were already dying. Once opiates had been granted a small glimmer of medical respectability, the possibility emerged of a much broader acceptance of prescription painkillers. Encouraged by pharmaceutical companies, pain-relief lobby groups were soon arguing that opiates weren't as addictive as long feared, and that their addictive properties could be tempered in various ways. Over the course of the 1980s, pharma companies and patient groups began to demand opiates be prescribed to patients other than cancer sufferers, such as those who'd suffered back injuries. Between 1980 and 2011, the rate of opiate prescription rose thirty-five-fold, of which 90% occurred in the developed world.[31] The infamous opiate-based painkiller OxyContin was launched with great fanfare and the promise that its slow-release technology made it resistant to addiction, a feature that was quickly circumvented as users discovered it could be crushed and injected. Oxy-Contin prescriptions for chronic pain in the US rose from 670,000 in 1997 to 6.7 million just five years later, accounting for 90% of all profits of its manufacturer, Purdue.[32]

The scientific understanding of pain has also undergone profound changes. Descartes' effort to confine pain to the purely physical realm has been found inadequate, due to a new neurological paradigm that emerged in the mid-1960s, known as the "gate control theory."[33] Scientists began to realize that the pains we designate as "physical" (such as back injury) are not intrinsically any different from those we designate as "psychological" (such as loneliness or the loss of a loved one). The mind and body suffer via the same neurological circuits. This makes it impossible to delineate the terrain of medicine from that of broader political or cultural issues, and it becomes easier to understand why one might cross over into the other. The fact that marginalized social groups report higher levels of chronic pain might be as much a reflection of their disempowerment and isolation as of their objective physiological condition.[34]

The gate control theory offered medical confirmation and explanation of something that pain sufferers and many non-Western cultures had always recognized: the physical and the psychological are not ultimately distinguishable. In 1976, the International Association for the Study of Pain offered the following definition of pain: "an unpleasant sensory and emotional experience associated with actual or potential tissue damage, or described in terms of such damage."[35] This is not an ordinary focus of expert scrutiny. Subjective experience, emotions and descriptions are typically matters for artists, psychoanalysts, or priests to deal with, not doctors or anatomical researchers. What is the role of the expert, where feelings themselves are the problem?

Treating the symptom

On one level, the application of modern science to the understanding and eradication of pain would seem like a brilliant use of medical expertise. What could be more important than relieving people of suffering? This was one more way in which postwar society extended the autonomy of the human species, to control its own physical well-being. But on another level, the new preoccupation with fighting pain (as opposed to disease) greatly disrupts core assumptions about the authority of medical expertise. If pain is both physiological and cultural then it is hard to specify where medicine ends and politics starts. Physical feeling starts to morph into emotional expression.

Moreover, the rising status of pain as a medical concern was not really due to growing appreciation of it as a symptom, despite repeated efforts during the 1990s by the American Pain Relief Society to have it viewed as the fifth "vital sign" of diagnosis.[36] It was due to the belief that pain was bad in and of itself, and that human life *should* be pain-free. This is as much a moral view as anything else, and it was not one that doctors, physiologists, or philosophers had traditionally advanced. The modern, technocratic state promised to protect people from avoidable harm, such as violence, severe poverty, or disease, but it had never sought to guarantee a complete absence of pain.

During the 1960s and 1970s, as pain relief was becoming a politicized issue among patient groups and health care professionals, the expert view of depression was undergoing parallel changes. Since the birth of psychoanalysis in the late nineteenth century, psychoanalysts and psychiatrists had never sought to treat unhappiness as such, but to explore it with a view to understanding and relieving underlying neuroses that might be causing it. The outcome of this was not expected to be happiness: as Freud famously said, the purpose of psychoanalysis was to convert "neurotic misery into ordinary human unhappiness." But the rise of "positive psychology" in the 1960s, followed by a rapid turn in American psychiatry toward medical theories of mental illness, meant that the professional view of depression had completely changed by the early 1980s.

New scales and questionnaires for measuring depression were introduced, to help psychiatrists and medical practitioners assess the severity of different cases, such as the 1961 Beck Depression Inventory, and these started to become the basis of diagnosis. Rather than viewing misery as the surface level representation of some underlying disorder (as Freud had done, and psychiatrists had for most of the twentieth century), the misery *was* the disorder. The task of therapeutic intervention became far more straightforward: to eradicate the unhappiness and introduce happiness.[37] Whether this was achieved via pharmaceuticals or a "talking cure" (such as cognitive behavioral therapy) depended on which was most effective in improving the patient's mood. By the 1990s, a whole industry of consultants, gurus, self-help publications, and management ideas had developed, based upon the idea that unhappiness was unhealthy and debilitating, whereas happiness was a form of physical health and an economic asset.

Just as the physical pain of the patient was becoming a social, psychological, and cultural issue (a matter of the patient's individual and consumer rights), so mental illness was being increasingly understood in physical terms, specifically as a disorder in neurochemistry. In effect, the two phenomena were collapsing into each other. The mind/body distinction on which scientific ideals of knowledge are built had begun to fall apart, with knock-on effects for the meaning of diagnosis. The ideal of diagnosis involves metaphors of depth: the patient reports what's on the surface, whereas the physician can bring knowledge from beneath. The patient who simply demands "stop it hurting" or "make me happy" is not asking for an explanation or diagnosis, but merely a termination of suffering. The boundary separating the inside from the outside of the body starts to become less clear-cut. Where does this leave the professional function of the doctor? Is it simply to attack symptoms and make people *feel* better?

There is a cultural and political problem signified by this new agenda for the relief of pain and unhappiness. Crucially, it strips suffering of any broader meaning or context, including even its scientific one. It renders pain a meaningless, wholly private phenomenon, which leaves the sufferer with the sole hope that it might be eradicated. In previous epochs, pain was considered to have a moral function, a form of religious retribution for sin. The terms "pain" and "punishment" originally meant something similar (as indicated by the archaic expression "on pain of being fined £100"). This placed pain in some broader narrative about society and human life.

Modern medicine undermines such moral and religious narratives, but it did originally provide some kind of explanation for suffering, either in the body (disease) or the mind (neurosis or psychosis). This may not be as comforting as the explanatory stories of religious ethics, but it manages to divert attention away from the pain or misery itself, toward some organ or past experience that might be causing it. Pain demands explanation and justification. A crucial ingredient in the allure of authoritarian leaders is their promise to reinstate shared rules and meaning for how suffering gets allocated in society, based around tradition and premodern principles of punishment.

As pain and depression have fallen into the gray zones between "mind" and "body," "symptom," and "disease," they've come to lack adequate explanation. Neither physiology nor psychology can entirely grasp them any longer. They are purely negative psychosomatic events or phases in an individual's life. The expertise of the doctor, who delves beneath the surface in search of underlying causes, is replaced with the surface-level empathy of the pain manager, who hands out pills to help people get through their daily lives. The result is an acute absence of narrative. Studies show that chronic pain sufferers tend to combat this by placing their pain within a broader autobiographical narrative, describing it as a disruptive force that shakes their sense of themselves.[38] Those struggling with chronic depression may keep a diary of it, partly to try and understand their own mood disorder better, but also to achieve some kind of social and biographical meaning for their affliction. However there is another response altogether, which doesn't just seek meaning through alternatives to modern science— it attacks the very ideals of health and progress, seeking not pleasure, happiness, or health, but control.

Taking back control

The First World War exerted a powerful influence over Sigmund Freud's theory of the unconscious, leading him to question the centrality of pleasure and sexuality in his model of the psyche. For twenty-five years prior to the war, Freud had developed his approach to the mind on the notion that humans are shaped by animalistic drives and desires, with sexuality at their core. He referred to this libidinous force as the "pleasure principle." His more famous theories, such as the Oedipus complex, may not strike us as scientifically grounded, but he viewed them as manifestations of innate biological instincts. However, the devastating effects of the war suggested to him that there is another side to human nature, that cannot be reduced to the pleasure principle.

The phenomenon then known as "shell shock" saw soldiers returning from war with an extreme nervousness, often manifest in muteness or paralysis. Some experienced physical tics, which reflected physical traumas they'd experienced or witnessed. Contemporary attitudes judged them harshly, with thousands being shot during the war for cowardice. Yet the symptoms did not disappear after the war was over. Having endured long periods of bombardment in the trenches, they were unable to adapt to civilian life, and exuded a jumpiness as if they were still living under fire. The symptoms had been observed previously in those who had survived train accidents, which were consequently attributed to physical injury. But these First World War veterans were not necessarily injured. Witnessing such cases led Freud to rethink the drives that shape human life. In 1920, he published a famous essay, "Beyond the Pleasure Principle," in which he outlined a new and darker theory of the unconscious.

In that essay, Freud drew on the example of his infant nephew, who he'd watched playing a game in his cot. The child had a toy attached to a piece of string, which he would repeatedly throw from the cot, say "gone," before pulling it back toward him using the string. As the child did not appear to enjoy losing the toy, Freud wondered what it was that led him to keep playing this game. The "unpleasurable nature of an experience does not always unsuit it for play," Freud noticed.[39] Similarly, adults are often drawn toward theater or artworks that re-enact something painful for them. Freud recognized how his own patients' unconscious minds were constantly returning them to past traumas, via dreams and utterances during analysis. He surmised from these examples that people have a "compulsion to repeat" painful experiences, so that they can switch from the status of passive victims to that of active instigators. Repetition of painful experiences allows us to attain control over them, which can often be more appealing than pleasure.

Freud was describing something he believed operated at an unconscious level. Clearly, the victims of shell shock he encountered in postwar Europe were not in control of their own symptoms. But something seemed to compel them to carry on behaving as if they were still in the trenches, that doctors and psychiatrists were unable to understand. In addition to the "pleasure principle," which drives us to satisfy our desires, Freud proposed a more destructive and self-destructive instinct, which drives us to "restore an earlier state of things," but grants us a sense of greater control in the process.[40] We are willing to forgo our own preservation and pleasure, he argued, even to the point of pursuing our own death, just so long as we can exert our own will upon the course of events. This contradicts one of the foundational principles on which modern societies were built, namely—as argued by Hobbes—that human beings are primarily driven to avoid suffering and prolong their own lives.

Fifty years after Freud published "Beyond the Pleasure Principle," some of the same symptoms seen in First World War veterans were encountered in America, among men returning from Vietnam. It seemed that many of them were constantly reliving their experiences, behaving erratically and violently while being unable to speak about what they were doing or feeling. Minor events in day-to-day civilian life were enough to provoke disproportionate reactions, as if they were still in combat. Psychiatrists in the 1970s were more attuned to exploring and understanding the hormonal and neurological causes of this syndrome, which they named post-traumatic stress disorder (PTSD). This became formally recognized as a psychiatric diagnosis in 1980.

Despite his theory being a highly speculative one, Freud had grasped something important about syndromes such as PTSD: there are certain kinds of suffering that we cannot easily let go of, and which trap us in the past. Our nerves become attuned to a level of constant threat, which we then become adapted to. Contemporary neuroscience and psychiatry of PTSD confirms something like the "compulsion to repeat" hypothesis, only now with an explanation framed in terms of neurochemistry and the hormones secreted into the bloodstream. The science of stress has revealed that, when our survival suddenly seems at stake, the human body becomes flooded with adrenaline that allows us to react rapidly against some impending threat.[41] This is often referred to as entering "fight or flight" mode, and is understood to be a crucial evolutionary development for animals that live with the threat of predators.

After the danger has passed, cortisol is released into the blood, reducing the amount of adrenaline in the body and returning it to its normal state (though this has the side effect of gradually hardening the arteries, which is why stress is bad for the heart). However, if this "fight or flight" mode is provoked too often or too acutely, the body becomes somewhat addicted to it, and fails to release cortisol as usual. Adrenaline levels remain constantly high, and the person lives as if in constant danger. Events that remind the sufferer of previous traumas can immediately trigger a repeat of their reaction to it, overwhelming them with panic. An indication that this behavior should be diagnosed as PTSD is that cortisol levels are lower than average.

PTSD can make it harder to experience ordinary emotional responses to everyday events, to the point where the sufferer may cease to believe they can experience them. While past traumas might be horrific, they also provide a source of feeling and stimulation. The sufferer unconsciously seeks out stressful scenarios, simply to feel something again. The alternative is to experience a sheer emotional vacuum. Neuroscientific analysis of PTSD indicates that sufferers have an overdeveloped capacity to react impulsively and emotionally, but at the cost of their ability to empathize with others. Whether we view things in Freud's more speculative terms or through contemporary neuroscience, the phenomenon of PTSD represents one acute way in which the medical vision of a human being as a health-seeking, pleasure-maximizing body can break down.

It is unsurprising that PTSD was first identified among soldiers and veterans. These are people who have suffered sustained threats on their lives. In combat situations, every noise could be an indication of mortal danger, meaning that stress becomes the norm. As the syndrome has become more widely diagnosed since the 1980s, it's offered a disturbing insight into the violence that many people encounter or perceive in their everyday lives, often having nothing to do with war. This includes survivors of abusive and violent relationships or assaults, who often present similar symptoms as military veterans, being constantly braced for rapid response to danger. But similar behavioral patterns have been discovered even in the absence of trauma, simply where people become over-accustomed to stressful environments. A study of smartphone "withdrawal" discovered that people can become fidgety and anxious without their phones, overreacting to stimuli in similar ways to PTSD sufferers.[42] The problem is the same, namely that they have become over-accustomed to an always-on interactive environment, and struggle to adjust to one that is slower and more predictable. Living amidst constantly updated "real time" information means being always primed to react.

There is a further psychological dimension of PTSD which means it cannot be entirely reduced to physical cause and effect. Certain kinds of trauma are more likely to result in PTSD than others, and what distinguishes them is psychological. As they involve power, one might even say they are political. The key question is whether the victim retained any sense of control over their experience or not. Studies of car-crash survivors show that the experience of being trapped after a car accident makes the victim far more likely to develop PTSD than a similar crash from which the victim was able to escape. The common thread linking various experiences of PTSD is that the survivor felt completely disempowered by a given trauma, and it is this that they constantly replay in their minds, and are constantly on guard against. It is the prolonged feeling of complete vulnerability that causes a steady flow of stress hormones into the body, which the person then becomes almost dependent on.

For these reasons, the symptoms of PTSD can develop even when there is no clearly identifiable trauma causing it. A parent constantly worrying about the safety of their child, a teenage girl aware that all her friends are judging her appearance via social media, or an individual who experiences sustained bullying or discrimination may all start to display the symptoms of PTSD. These are some of the many ways in which economic inequality and political marginalization become imprinted upon the body and its symptoms, creating an almost permanent condition of anxiety. In each case, it is the sustained power inequality that is critical, and the feeling that there is no escape. More diffusely, PTSD has led to concerns about how symptoms might be "triggered" by everyday occurrences, something that has provoked controversies on campuses where the occasional use of "trigger warnings" (in relation to particular texts or topics) has raised concerns about students being unwilling to engage with ideas they find offensive.[43]

PTSD has thrown up dilemmas that extend well beyond the realm of psychiatry, disrupting traditional assumptions about the definition of harm. This diagnostic category has implications for all of us, raising questions about the distinction between language and violence, and whether we can be entirely sure as to where one ends and the other begins.[44] Descartes' vision of the body as a purely mechanical realm, separate from the self, takes yet another hit in the process. But so does the absolutist commitment to "free speech," as numerous critics of "trigger warnings" have argued vociferously. Contemporary neuroscience and psychiatry clearly demonstrate the physical nature of emotional trauma, but precisely how sensitive to people's feelings do we therefore need to be? This has become one of the most bitter moral controversies of our age, which has no simple resolution. What is clear is that those who scoff at "snowflakes," arguing that freedom must permit any level of harm to someone's feelings, employ a caricature of "enlightenment" that flatly ignores copious evidence for how emotional and physical being are unified, quite aside from the practical ways in which threatening speech is implicated in violence.

Partly thanks to such cultural controversies, PTSD has become a syndrome with far broader political and cultural significance. It poses profound questions about the nature of violence and the role of feelings in the public sphere, creating polarization between generations and ideological camps. Yet it also offers a way of understanding and narrating pain and injury in today's world. Recognizing the interplay between disempowerment, memory, stress, and repetitive behavior provides a compelling framework through which to make sense of many forms of unhappiness today. Communities that have suffered traumas in the past, such as those that might now be turning toward authoritarian forms of politics, could even be understood via a similar lens. The demand that feelings and vulnerability be taken seriously, whether or not a medical diagnosis is involved, is really an insistence that narrative and memory matter, with respect to problems that can't simply be solved by experts.

The injury of disempowerment

PTSD is not a very common diagnosis, although its prevalence among particular sections of society—especially teenage girls—is very worrying. Estimates suggest that 70% of Americans experience some kind of "trauma" in their lives (such as an assault or serious car crash), of whom around a fifth later develop PTSD. But the case of PTSD, together with Freud's early speculations about the "compulsion to repeat," teaches us that the essence of trauma is not pain, but the acute disempowerment that leaves one vulnerable to pain, even if just as a possibility. The "compulsion to repeat" or the constant surge of a "fight or flight" hormone are ways in which mind and body unconsciously seek to return to the past, only this time with some sense of control or preparation.

This psychological pattern of seeking control over suffering can be observed in other conditions and behaviors. These may appear to contradict basic assumptions about human rationality and self-interest. Take, for example, bodily self-harm. For around thirty years after the Second World War, the typical forms of self-harm recorded by psychiatrists and doctors were those that involved poisoning and attempted suicide, which resulted in the patient being rushed to hospital for treatment.[45] Rightly or wrongly, this was often interpreted as a "cry for help," that is, a way of using one's own body to communicate despair and to seek care. It was a desperate but nevertheless social thing to do, which used the body to convey a message to others. But in the 1970s and 1980s, psychiatrists began to notice a different form of self-harm, now classified as "non-suicidal self-injury" (usually cutting), which individuals carried out in private, apparently for no communicative purpose.

Actions such as cutting are now generally understood as a means of exerting some kind of emotional self-control, to reduce a feeling of tension or to provide emotional stimulation. In direct contrast to the "cry for help," cutting serves as a kind of pressure gauge or self-regulation of one's feelings, putting the cutter in control of their own pain and staving off a sense of emptiness. As the clinical psychologist Jay Watts has written, "often self-harm occurs when this is the only freedom left."[46] It is a common phenomenon among prisoners, but also among those (especially young women and girls today) who feel trapped by exacting standards of appearance or behavior. By channeling psychological harm into physical harm, a cutter gives their pain a tangible existence, which they themselves can see. It proves that they and their feelings are actually real, and can often become the basis of a routine that makes everyday life manageable again.

The same issue of control is pertinent to the midlife mortality spike noticed by Case and Deaton. What was so disturbing about their research was not just the shrinking life expectancy it revealed, but the active role people played in their own premature deaths. As with the sudden increase in mortality in Russia in the early 1990s, which was heavily linked to alcohol, young and middle-aged Americans have been increasingly victims of their own behavior and decisions. The significance of drug overdoses, alcoholism, and suicide to this rising mortality rate led to it being dubbed "deaths of despair." The prevalence of self-inflicted harm in America is now having major demographic and economic consequences, reducing average life expectancy and shrinking the size of the labor market. These are the sorts of statistical effects that would normally only be witnessed in the context of war or major disease outbreaks.

The launch of OxyContin was the beginning of an epidemic of opiate abuse that swept America from the late 1990s to the present, with
overdoses following inevitably in its wake. Between 1999 and 2017,
over 200,000 Americans died of opiate overdoses.[47] This is more than
three times the number of Americans who died in the Vietnam War.
By 2017, opium overdoses were the leading cause of death among
Americans under the age of fifty. Unlike previous waves of drug addiction, largely concentrated in the inner cities, this one has been clustered
in suburbs and economically depressed rural areas, challenging media
stereotypes about addicts. Among the large number of working-age
men who have withdrawn from the American labor market, around half
are taking prescription painkillers.[48] This was an epidemic in which the
pharmaceutical industry, regulators, and some doctors were originally
complicit, meaning it spread through American society with little of the
violence that was associated with drugs such as crack cocaine. The rate
of overdose death exactly mirrored the rate of prescription, with both
rising by 300% in Ohio between 1999 and 2008.[49] The proportions of
this crisis are quite staggering. The number of people dying from opiate overdoses in Ohio overtook the number dying from car accidents in
2008; the number dying nationally from overdoses exceeded the number dying from guns in 2015.

On one level, America's opiate crisis is a symptom of consumer capitalism. A post-1960s ideology which stated that nobody should have to
endure pain was combined with ruthless profit-seeking by pharmaceutical companies. Many of these prescription painkillers were available to
addicts thanks to the "enterprising" behavior of doctors prepared to act
outside the law. Opiates are of course horrifically addictive, but what
makes addiction so hard to break cannot be entirely reduced to brain
chemistry. What traps people in addictions of various kinds (narcotic or
otherwise) is also the control that a given activity grants them while it
endures, then the return to a feeling of complete disempowerment when
it is over.

It might seem odd to describe addiction as a feeling of *control*, given
how enslaved addicts can become, but for those whose lives seem to lack
any meaningful story, addiction provides a purpose in the world and turns
their own body into a source of comfort. Addiction to machine gambling,

for example, has nothing to do with the outcome (which is dire) and everything to do with the sense of calm the gambler feels while the lights are flashing and they're smacking buttons, a state they describe as being in "the zone."[50] Heroin addicts often report that they find satisfaction in the entire daily ritual of being a junkie, and not simply in the blissful sensation of the drug itself. These are the aspects of addiction that can be hardest to lose, and which rehab programs fight hardest to overcome in the longer term. The recovering addict needs a new biographical story, which they must constantly tell themselves in the hope that it becomes believable.

Much of this gets overlooked in discussions of public health and well-being. A simplistic assumption states that people who are poor and marginalized reach for drugs and alcohol simply to make them feel better. The deeper truth, and sometimes the darker one, is that people don't simply desire more pleasure. Nor do they desire more health, or even more life, even if that choice were available to them. In a society that offers no broader narrative of suffering, other than that it needs eradicating, what some people most yearn for is a means of bringing their pain or trauma within their control—of making it *theirs*. If this means bringing their own death a little closer, so be it. The progressive assumption that everyone must desire a longer, healthier life, may not be as psychologically obvious for those who lack deeper explanation for their suffering.

The majority of people are fortunate enough never to suffer PTSD, drug addiction, or compulsive self-harm. But the logic threaded through these afflictions cannot be completely contained within specific diagnoses or neurochemical processes. Together they tell us something important about the politics of feeling: there is something worse than pain, and that is a total loss of control. Taking control over one's own feelings, even if that means deliberately inflicting pain or anaesthetising them at huge risk, offers relief, in a world that bombards us with stimulations and demands. This desperation for control is also a political syndrome, in which disenfranchised groups might go as far as sabotaging their own prosperity, if only that grants a little more agency over their own future. Better to be the perpetrator of harm than always the victim, even if it is harm to oneself.

In search of empathy

People who are suffering, emotionally and physically, will go in search of explanations for their feelings. But they will also go in search of recognition for them. One of the greatest political assets of populist leaders, spanning both left and right, has been their ability to visit economically depressed regions and convey empathy with people who were otherwise ignored or dismissed. This is not something that more mainstream or professional political figures are able to do with the same perceived authenticity. Political threats to the status quo, led by unlikely figures from the media, business, and political margins, can perform a powerful function, when they give voice to pain that is otherwise mute. Just as physical pain becomes manageable with the aid of narratives, prolonged social and psychological suffering makes people unusually responsive to anyone who is willing simply to name it. Populist leadership becomes more disturbing when it takes distress and disempowerment, and converts those feelings into hatred.

People who seek empathy can be drawn in various political directions, and nationalism is one of the most seductive. Surveys consistently show that supporters of nationalist parties believe their country is getting worse over time, and that things were better in the past. The nationalist leader holds out the promise of restoring things to how they were, including all the forms of brutality—such as capital punishment, back-breaking physical work, patriarchal domination—that social progress had consigned to history. For reasons Freud would have understood, this isn't as simple as wanting life to be more pleasurable, but a deep desire to restore a political order that made sense, in spite of its harshness. It is a rejection of progress in all its forms.

What is equally troubling is that, at least on a rhetorical level, it is also a rejection of peace. As the language of politics grows more violent, and attacks on the "elites" become more vociferous, democracy starts to inch closer to violence, with more instruments and institutions being "weaponized." How could this be desirable? What possible emotional logic could underpin it? At least in the nationalist imagination, war also offers a form of community and emotional empathy that is not found in commerce or democratic politics. War provides recognition, explanation, and commemoration of pain, of the sort that policy experts and professional politicians seem unable to provide. One of the curiosities of nationalism is that, despite appeals to famous battles and heroes, it is often most kindled by moments of defeat and suffering, which shape identity more forcefully than victories. For romantic patriots, Britain was never more truly British than when fleeing Dunkirk or enduring the Blitz. The common identity of the American South is forged out of the experience, then memory, of defeat in civil war, as mourned by the Lost Cause movement of thinkers and writers. On a more literally physiological level, it has long been noted that injuries sustained in battle, where they happen for a *reason* and are *expected* to happen, do not seem to cause as much pain as civilians in peacetime might assume. War helps to narrate pain rather than treat it.

The major achievement of scientific expertise and modern government, dating back to the mid-seventeenth century, was to establish a basis for civic interaction, from which violence had been eliminated. The boundary between war and peace was unambiguous, and a public respect for facts reinforced this. There are various forces at large in the twenty-first century that test this boundary, including technologies and military strategies that blur the distinction between war and peace. But there are also emotional reasons why that line is becoming blurred. Part of the appeal of war, at least as an idea, is that—unlike the civil society designed by the likes of Hobbes—it represents a form of politics where feelings really matter.

PART TWO

The Rise of Feeling

5
KNOWLEDGE FOR WAR
Secrecy, sentiment, and real-time intelligence

In an influential article published in 2013, the Russian general Valery Gerasimov argued that "in the twenty-first century we have seen a tendency toward blurring the lines between the states of war and peace. Wars are no longer declared." The example of the 2011 Arab Spring suggested to Gerasimov that "nonmilitary" means of war could be far more threatening to state powers in the future than traditional military ones. All political regimes have points of acute vulnerability, he argued, of which they themselves may not be aware because they've never considered them in terms of war. Small acts of transgression can have major political effects, if the right tool and target are carefully selected.

The article was widely read as a way of understanding Russian tactics and strategies in the context of cyberwar and other covert hostilities, such as those that have sought to disrupt elections in NATO countries. The "Gerasimov Doctrine," as it became known, has helped to explain why Russia seems to be using a wider range of nonmilitary means, such as online trolling, data breaches, and "fake news," to sow civic and political unrest. If fact-based consensus is becoming harder to establish, this may be partly because there are forces at large on the international stage that are deliberately seeking this outcome.

The Gerasimov Doctrine, if correct, has implications as much for the nature of peace as it does for that of war. For if military strategy is being diverted through traditionally civic and economic mechanisms, "weaponizing" them in the process, then spheres of peaceful exchange will also become more combative, and shrouded in uncertainty. These trends are already possible to discern, in the way trolls and fringe groups treat public argument as a form of warfare, using ad hominem attacks on public figures to discredit and intimidate them. Even without any form of Russian interference, election campaigns use sophisticated digital technologies to identify very small sections of the population who are worth targeting, and can mobilize large numbers of supporters to turn up in particular neighborhoods to knock on doors. Concerns about Russian "propaganda" distract attention from the fact that businesses and political parties already use Facebook to subtly tailor their communications to thousands of different psychological profiles. The secrecy surrounding these new strategies and technologies suggests that they owe as much to traditions of war as to peace.

Warfare requires knowledge, just not of the same variety that we are familiar with in times of peace. The facts provided by economists, statisticians, and academic scientists have a peace-building quality, to the extent that they provide a common reality that can be agreed upon. They remove questions of truth from the domain of politics, rescuing us from the types of conflicts that tore Europe apart over the first half of the seventeenth century. Viewed in that way, we can see facts as akin to contracts, types of promises that experts make to each other and the public, that records are accurate and free from any personal bias or political agenda.

The type of knowledge used in warfare is different. The most valuable knowledge in combat situations (regarding tactics, technologies, movements, and so on) is often shrouded in secrecy, while deliberate efforts are made to mislead the enemy. The goal is victory, not consensus. A key problem in war is making sure that necessary information is available at the right place and at the right time, and isn't intercepted. There isn't the luxury of slow, reasonable, open debate of the sort that scientific progress has been built upon. Science and expertise have a great deal to offer wartime governments and defense agencies, but they sacrifice many of their founding principles when they are co-opted for military purposes. Speed of research and advice becomes all-important. It's no good being right if you've already lost. Reason is accelerated until it is something else altogether.

In addition to intelligence, emotions take on a whole new importance in war. Combat requires aggression, solidarity, and a belief in one's own superiority, sometimes to the point of assuming the enemy's inhumanity. Throughout history, military commanders have paid attention to the morale of their troops, and not just their physical condition and number. Conversely, efforts to undermine the spirit of the enemy become an important weapon in warfare. The Gerasimov Doctrine highlights a long-standing truth of how valuable propaganda and psychological disruption can be in weakening an opponent.

War elevates feeling to a status it doesn't have during times of peace, in two senses. First, our emotions and physical sensations acquire a fundamental value. Courage, stamina, optimism, and aggression are crucial resources in battle. Fear, pain, and pessimism are deliberately triggered in the enemy. All the same things that experts pledge to disregard when they inspect things objectively become instrumental when war breaks out. The natural psychological dynamics that Thomas Hobbes wanted to quell—of arrogance, paranoia, distrust, and aggression—come alive once societies move from a state of peace to one of war. For better or for worse, war can trigger emotions in a way that commerce and rational debate do not.

Second, feeling becomes a navigational aid and source of information, rather as one might feel one's way through a darkened room. Where there is an absence of commonly agreed facts, each side has to rely on a combination of private intelligence and instinct. The quality of information in war isn't always very clear, so gut feeling and other senses play a role: the body becomes a source of valuable data. In fast-moving scenarios, especially with aerial warfare involved, new technologies such as radar need developing to sense incoming threats, before it's too late. The augmentation of the human senses to detect threats is as important a focus for military innovation as the development of new weaponry.

Gerasimov's proposition that the division between war and peace is dissolving therefore carries dramatic implications for the status of knowledge and emotion in society. Ultimately it challenges the ideal of expert knowledge, as something that sits outside the sphere of conflict, putting in its place a different ideal, in which knowledge is used as a weapon. Once this happens, facts become manipulated for maximum emotional impact (either positive or negative), while feelings become a valuable way of navigating a rapidly changing environment. The most serious threat here is not that we lose any respect for truth as such, but that truth becomes a political issue, which heightens disagreement and the potential for conflict rather than resolving them. That may be what Russian defense strategists are seeking.

The Gerasimov Doctrine speaks specifically to the age of social media and "cyberwar." But its underlying proposition is not new. The legal commitment to splitting "war" from "peace" that was established in Europe in the mid-seventeenth century may have survived rhetorically, but the distinction has been muddied by a whole range of technical and administrative innovations, which crisscross between military, government, business, and back to the military again. If we want to understand the forces that are pitted against expertise today, and the new forms of knowledge and feeling that threaten to discredit experts, we will need to consider politics from a different perspective altogether: not as an alternative to war, as Hobbes hoped, but as an ingredient in war. The place to begin is at the zenith of the Enlightenment, when an entirely new mold of political leadership was formed. No sooner had human reason triumphed over superstition and divine rights, than the power of human emotion and feeling would be discovered, as a way of disrupting and dominating the new political order.

Mobilizing the masses

Between 1792 and 1815, Europe experienced virtually uninterrupted warfare, the longest period of conflict since the Thirty Years War which had ended in 1648. The catalyst for this protracted conflict was the French Revolution and the figure at its heart was Napoleon. By more recent standards, or even by those of the Thirty Years War, these wars were not unusually bloody.[1] But their legacy forever altered the nature of warfare, leadership, nationhood, and government. Just as the protracted conflicts of the seventeenth century set the stage for a whole new type of political power—centralized and technocratic, based around the collection of facts and figures—so the Napoleonic Wars ushered in a new era, with its own distinctive approach to knowledge and expertise.

One thing that gave the French an advantage over this period was the ability to convert the popular revolutionary spirit into military fervor. Up until this point, many European armies consisted of aging noblemen supported by a band of "undesirables"—low-level criminals and foreign mercenaries trained and paid to obey the officers in charge. Armies were comparatively small, and conflicts took place in confined spaces for short periods of time. Achieving discipline was a constant struggle for the nobility in charge, and the threat of desertion was high. In comparison to what followed, the stakes and aims were low, often reducible to squabbles between rulers, none of whom could afford to run the risk of serious losses. But in 1793, the new French republic introduced a measure that changed all this forever: conscription. A year later, the French army numbered 800,000, more than three times the size of Louis XIV's largest army.

Conscription vastly increases the potential size of an army, but it also transforms its nature. In place of specialist training or a talent for fighting, conscription channels the public's national sentiment and enthusiasm. It places a new emphasis on shared cultural identity and the feelings of ordinary people. As more men are drafted into the army, women and children become mobilized toward economic production. Once the entire population becomes a potential military resource, each and every member of society is invested with value. In contrast to the view of mortality presented by demographers such as John Graunt, in which death is treated as an object of probabilistic calculation, civilian mobilization grants a purpose to life and a potential meaning for each death. The demographer records your death as a statistic; the military commander will engrave your name on a monument. A grim tragedy of this revolutionary ideal is that, for most combatants, warfare became progressively less heroic as technology advanced thereafter.

Possessing Europe's only conscripted army, the French were able to adopt a new set of tactics for which their opponents were utterly unprepared. In contrast to the rigid, predictable, and small-scale style of eighteenth-century battle, Napoleon's forces advanced as a mass swarm, unleashing small acts of sabotage and engaging in skirmishes from multiple directions. The amateur nature of this new military force was an advantage, especially when confronting the armies of Prussia, which still operated with aristocratic ideals of combat that had been passed down over several generations. Napoleon's army was an early demonstration of a principle that grew in significance over time, to become something of an ideology by the end of the twentieth century: the power of the distributed network. Until the French Revolution, no state had channeled so much of its administrative capacity toward warfare, mobilizing the nation's horses, textile production, and agriculture toward war, and introducing rationing among the civilian population. From this point on, an entirely new style of government and political leadership would be required.

How does one resist such an operation? Between 1804 and 1812, as French armies pushed the length and breadth of Europe, there was no obvious answer to this question. Following the invasion of Spain in 1808, resistance did emerge from among the civilian population, through small-scale acts of sabotage—fighters who were given the name "guerrillas." In 1811, following repeated humiliations at the hands of the French, Prussian generals began to ask if they needed an equivalent popular mobilization. But they had no way to manufacture the nationalist sentiment they believed was needed. The political and technical transformations unleashed by the French Revolution, then coupled to Napoleon's strategic brilliance, represented a riddle that couldn't be solved. Napoleon was able to bend whole states to his will.

For one man, Carl von Clausewitz, the Napoleonic Wars opened up a whole new field of theoretical enquiry. He was a fascinated observer of Napoleon, but he was also much more than that. He'd joined the Prussian army at the age of eleven, had his first taste of combat with the French in 1793 at the age of twelve, and witnessed his country make a (to his mind) humiliating peace with the French a couple of years later. Due to the terms of this peace, Prussia had been forced to stand by as Napoleon conquered Europe, something which this young observer found acutely painful to watch. As he wrote to his wife in 1806, "my Fatherland needs war and—plainly speaking—war alone can lead me to happy goals." So strong was his yearning for combat that he was tempted to join the Austrian army in 1809, and then later joined the Russians, allowing him to witness Napoleon's eventual defeat firsthand.

Clausewitz had been raised by his military father to view the Prussian army as representing the pinnacle of valor. The overwhelming victories of Napoleon struck him as both shameful and awe-inspiring at the same time. While Napoleon's ascent was under way he was a student in the War College in Berlin, of which he would later become director. As a student, he took classes in philosophy, reading the work of Immanuel Kant and the "idealist" thinkers that followed him. But the task that preoccupied him was analyzing the new military machine that had overwhelmed Europe. So transformative was the effect of the French Revolution, so brilliant was

Napoleon's leadership, and so devastating were the consequences for European states from Gibraltar to Moscow, that an entire new theory of warfare was required.

His most important observation concerned the immense power of a conscripted, popular army, especially when fueled by nationalist fervor. This was a discovery he'd made early on, in the traumatic events of his first military encounter: "It was expected that a moderate auxiliary corps would be enough to end a civil war; but the colossal weight of the whole French people, unhinged by political fanaticism, came crashing down on us."[2] He marveled at the capacity to mobilize an entire nation in warfare. Thanks to the French Revolution, "suddenly war again became the business of the people—a people of thirty millions, all of whom considered themselves to be citizens."[3] In this new age, war had become almost democratic. A nation's population was not just a disparate mass to be governed and pacified, but was now a strategic resource. Unless other nations—especially Prussia—could cultivate a similarly popular enthusiasm for war, they would have no answer to Napoleon's threat.

In addition to this unprecedented human resource, Clausewitz was also deeply struck by the new character of war under Napoleon. It wasn't just popular sentiment that Napoleon was able to mobilize, but the full administrative capacities of the modern state. There was something new and scientific about how Napoleon set about conquering Europe, moving at unprecedented speed, avoiding conflict unless there was a decisive probability of victory. The French established lengthy supply lines of food that could serve armies even when hundreds of miles into foreign territory, accompanied by rationing at home. The "chappe system"—an optical telegraphy network that could send simple information over long distances by adjusting signals—had been established across France from 1792 onward, and Napoleon seized upon this new technology to build similar lines into Italy, Prussia, and Holland, to support military coordination.

Tactically, Napoleon placed great emphasis on severing the enemy's lines of communication and food supply, turning the focus of war upon infrastructure. Anticipating the "total" wars of the twentieth century, such tactics turned war into a contest of information and logistics, drawing in civilian government. Napoleon was as much a politician as he was a general, but a politician whose ambition was to build an empire. He didn't

fight only for the glory of it, but to achieve clearly defined objectives, and
continued to fight until he'd achieved them. Reflecting on this led Clausewitz to make the observation for which he is best known: "war is the continuation of politics by other means."

The book in which that quote appears was written as a series of unpub-
lished essays between 1816 and his death from cholera in 1831, later assembled
by his wife to be published as *On War*. A number of his more sympathetic
readers have noticed the influence of Kant over his work, especially in
the method with which *On War* weaves together abstract principles with
practical realities. Less generously, Clausewitz is often judged as some kind
of nihilist who glorified slaughter, and whose strategic advice created the
template for the ghastly gridlock of the First World War (though this claim
is disputed by military historians). His definition of war—"an act of violence intended to compel our opponent to fulfil our will"—was brutal
in its simplicity and he believed that (in contrast to the smaller wars that
came before) modern warfare was only really finished when one side had
been utterly disempowered.[4]

In other respects, Clausewitz can be read like a management con-
sultant, helping decisionmakers to dispassionately weigh the costs and
benefits of different courses of action. In the aftermath of the Vietnam
War, his work became required reading in US military colleges, as the
Pentagon sought to rethink its core principles of defense and attack. To
say that "war is the continuation of politics by other means" is to say that
fighting is just one of various means of achieving some objective, to be
used as and when it is rational to do so. General Gerasimov was arguing
precisely this, leading observers to describe his doctrine as "Clausewitz-
ian." This idea reduces war to something administrative, turning violence into one of many instruments at the state's disposal, to get stuff
done. If there is anything chilling about Clausewitz, it is not so much
his glorification of war as the cold calculating way in which he analyzes
it—and this despite having repeatedly witnessed the physical traumas of
battle from an early age.

Why exactly might we return to Clausewitz's ideas today? How could
this aggrieved Prussian officer, with a passion for combat, possibly help
us understand our present moment? One immediate answer is that, at
least on a rhetorical level, "wars" seem to engulf us with a frightening

regularity and diversity, now penetrating traditionally "civilian" culture and politics. States today are engaged in a range of new wars that are less and less tangible: the "war on terror," the "war on drugs," "cyberwarfare." Civil society and democracy are also framed as "wars," with the "culture wars" splitting American politics down the middle since the 1960s, and Alex Jones, the notorious far-right talk-show host and conspiracy theorist, warning that "there's a war on for your mind." The alt-right accuses left-wingers of being "SJWs" (social justice *warriors*). In the early twenty-first century, it's not so much that "war is a continuation of politics by other means" but that "politics is a continuation of war by other means," although precisely where "peaceful" means end and "violent" ones begin is less and less clear.

Of course most of these "wars" are not really wars at all, but only framed as such so as to mobilize supporters and frighten opponents. But the public and economic sphere is becoming increasingly organized around principles of conflict, attack, and defense, with less trust placed in those voices—such as professional journalists and judges—who purport to stand outside the fray. Mobilizing supporters and sabotaging opponents have become the means through which political and economic competition is conducted. The power of facts and expertise to settle disputes conclusively appears to be in decline. The framing of political, cultural, and economic conflicts as "wars" resonates, and we need to consider why.

If we want to understand how feelings, pains, and nerves are coming to organize the world around us, we need to see this situation from the inside, to understand its appeal and logic as well as its threat. It isn't simply irrational or nihilistic, but possesses a distinctive rationality that overturns many of the core political and philosophical assumptions of seventeenth-century expertise, and introduces others in their place. In place of Hobbes's strict separation of war and peace, there is a creeping militarization of politics. And in place of Descartes' strict separation of mind and body, there is instead an image of a human being possessed of instinct, emotion, and calculation, all fused together. Civil techniques of knowledge collection, such as bookkeeping and scientific publication, are replaced by military techniques of intelligence gathering, real-time decision making, and sensory devices. Truth becomes allied to courage.

From "facts" to "intelligence"

Speaking at a press briefing on Iraq in February 2002, the then US Defense Secretary, Donald Rumsfeld, offered the philosophical analysis which has stuck to him ever since:

> as we know, there are known knowns; there are things we know we know. We also know there are known unknowns; that is to say we know there are some things we do not know. But there are also unknown unknowns—the ones we don't know we don't know. And if one looks throughout the history of our country and other free countries, it is the latter category that tend to be the difficult ones.

Rumsfeld's tripartite classification spawned jokes, astonishment, and even some admiration. However it left out a fourth category essential to war, and which preoccupies security services and the intelligence community: *unknown knowns*. These are things that somebody somewhere knows, but which "we" (whoever we might happen to be) are presently unable to discover. Viewed a little differently, the existence of weapons of mass destruction in Iraq, which Rumsfeld was commenting on, was an "unknown known," inasmuch as *somebody* surely knew the truth about the weapons program (or lack of it), it just wasn't the Pentagon.

It is often said that truth is one of the first casualties of war. If we cling to the standards of seventeenth-century science, in which expert knowledge is something which is open to public scrutiny, and is separate from emotions or politics, then war can indeed inflict tremendous damage upon truth. However, war has also been the catalyst for many of the most significant scientific and technological advances of the past century. The digital computer was a product of the intensification of research during the Second World War, while the field of cybernetics which emerged alongside it was formed out of efforts to produce more-accurate antiaircraft guns. New fields of psychology and economics (such as game theory) took root in the context of the Cold War. And we owe much of our scientific understanding of climate to US military efforts to spy on Russian nuclear weapons stockpiles and assess the fallout of nuclear tests.[5]

In contrast to the seventeenth-century ideal of truth, science and technology became far more intimate with each other in wartime. The same is true in corporate research and development (R&D), where "blue sky" research is often undertaken but only with the expectation that it will yield technical, political, and economic payoff. This is not knowledge for knowledge's sake. The term "scientist" was only first coined in the 1830s in the context of the Industrial Revolution, to distinguish those producing new knowledge from the engineers and entrepreneurs who applied it—the implication being that knowledge was now a tool. The social and behavioral sciences funded during the Cold War offered clear and rationally grounded advice on strategic decision making. Science became as much about manipulating and "weaponizing" nature as about knowing it. In situations of conflict, the goal is not to represent the world but to bring it under control.

But to really grasp the significance of war for the mutations of science, we need to think through the implications of "unknown knowns" as the decisive strategic issue. Amidst his ruminations on the nature of war, Clausewitz admitted that there was one brutally simple issue which did more to determine the outcome of war than any other: war is most often won by the side with the greatest number of soldiers, both on the battlefield and in reserve. Individual battles could sometimes be swayed by tactical genius or sheer luck, but numbers would always eventually overwhelm, where the ratio of one side to the other was large enough. Napoleon was defeated over the course of 1812–15, Clausewitz reasoned, because he finally encountered larger populations, including that of Russia.

War, in Clausewitz's view, is a numbers game. But unlike the market, where accountants and economists produce dispassionate financial information that can be publicly inspected, it is a numbers game without any authoritative sources of data. There is no equivalent of the Office for National Statistics or the Royal Society to offer an objective measurement of how the two sides compare in number. In that regard it is similar to the arguments that surround crowd sizes. In war, numbers matter more than anything, but they are hard to come by and risky to trust. Rather as Hobbes argued of individual psychology in a "state of nature," a general can be quite confident of his own side's capacity and size, but be radically uncertain of what his enemy is up to. However, in contrast to Hobbes's diagnosis (that uncertainty would prompt aggression), Clausewitz feared that the most likely result of this paranoid situation was for both sides to do nothing or to retreat, as rumors circulated that exaggerated the enemy's numbers. The key challenge of strategy is how to take decisions when the facts simply aren't available.

As a soldier himself, Clausewitz had suffered a number of intelligence failures, and become suspicious of the use of intelligence in war. Meanwhile, losses suffered in war are impossible to gauge accurately until much later, and it is crucial that they are downplayed for the sake of morale. "Most reports [during war] are false," he argued, "and the timidity of men acts as a multiplier of lies and untruths."[6] If a general were to wait until he had entirely objective evidence of his own side's advantage, then he would likely be waiting forever. That kind of factual truth simply isn't available during war, so some other spur to action is required. Efforts to calculate the best strategic path take up valuable time, and speed is of the essence.

Clausewitz's suspicion of military intelligence may have been valid during the Napoleonic Wars, before the age of the electrical telegraph or the railway. But as the potential for rapid dissemination of knowledge emerged, so the strategic significance of intelligence became much greater. The first centralized intelligence services were established by European governments in the 1850s. Advances in information and communication technology can be deployed in war, but some are much more useful than others. The most crucial are those which serve to detect what the enemy is up to, and to conceal what one's own side is doing. War is not only a numbers game, but a game of detection and awareness. Speed of knowledge can often be more useful than precise accuracy. War places a huge premium on technologies that can accelerate the acquisition and processing of information. Our present fixation on "real time" data, as provided by screens, "timelines" and "smart devices," is a distant cousin of the military mindset, that cannot trust circumstances to remain the same from one moment to the next.

The nose surpasses the eye

The quest for rapid intelligence has major implications for the status of knowledge in society. Once knowledge becomes valued for its speed, rather than its public credibility, this transforms the status of science and expertise in society. These transformations are twofold. The first is that intelligence becomes a form of monitoring, mining, and sensing. Rather than seeking to hold up a "mirror" to nature or society, in the way that the seventeenth-century expert originally hoped to do (whether it be for the glory of God or the glory of the sovereign state), the assumption is that someone out there *already* knows something and is *already* doing something, and that knowledge needs to be identified and tracked down. This is a similar challenge to what is known as "data mining" in the digital age.

Clausewitz believed that a great general had an instinct for this sort of thing, what he called a "skilled intelligence to scent out the truth."[7] Part of this instinct involves knowing what to pay attention to in a complex and fast-moving environment. Clausewitz's metaphor of "scenting" is a revealing one, suggesting that the nose might be a more useful way of encountering the world than the eye. Unlike sight or sound, scent is not typically seen as a basis for objective knowledge or facts, but more for instantaneous recognition. A witness statement or newspaper report would be unlikely to rest on a *smell* as sufficient confirmation that something had happened. Yet the speed and immediacy of smell makes it an indispensable means of recognizing individual places, foods, and possessions, with a level of certainty that cannot be converted into an objective fact. Our dependence on the nose is certainly different from that on the eye, but not necessarily any lesser. People who lose their sense of smell can experience profound unhappiness, as it becomes harder to develop interest or excitement in various experiences.

In the military arena, "scenting out the truth" would increasingly be viewed as a technological challenge, especially with the dawn of aerial warfare in the twentieth century. Many of the most transformative military technologies of the past hundred years have been those which serve as detection devices. Beyond radar, for example, air-defense systems were developed during the Cold War which pioneered the use of digital computers and satellites to detect enemy movements. Or consider the Pentagon's construction of a worldwide network of seismology centers during the early 1960s, which aimed to sense Soviet underground nuclear missile tests.[8] This infrastructure had its own scientific payoff, subsequently enabling seismologists to confirm geological theories of tectonics. The Cold War was the stuff of copious spy thrillers, listening devices, and occasionally deranged efforts to get inside the heads of the enemy, to the point where psychics were hired in the early

1970s to sense what the Soviet Union and its allies were doing. Satellites and spy planes provide a different form of "objectivity" on the enemy's activities. One of the central technological challenges confronted by the Pentagon during the Vietnam War was finding ways of detecting the presence of enemy soldiers in forests, with various types of "sniffing" devices developed to sense underground tunnels and human activity.

The "war on terror" produced its own distinctive approach to "unknown knowns," euphemistically known as "enhanced interrogation techniques." In January 2002, Alberto Gonzales, legal counsel to President Bush, offered an infamous memo outlining justifications for techniques of torture such as water-boarding. The argument rested on the notion that the threat posed by terrorist networks such as al-Qaeda was entirely unprecedented, and could not be combated by traditional military or intelligence techniques. As Gonzales argued:

> The nature of the new war places a high premium on other factors, such as the ability to quickly obtain information from captured terrorists and their sponsors in order to avoid further atrocities against American civilians.[9]

The fact that Gonzales emphasized *speed* with which information is obtained, rather than the quality of the knowledge, tells us a great deal about what happens to expertise during warfare. It is questionable whether torture is really motivated by a concern for the truth, and the usefulness of the "truth" it yields is rarely clear-cut. But at least at the level of its authorization, the assumption is that the victim holds a piece of information, and that only intense physical and/or psychological suffering will persuade them to reveal it *quickly*. Academically qualified psychologists acted as consultants to the CIA in helping to design torture techniques, offering another chilling example of how scientific expertise can be employed to counter perceived security threats. The promise of mind-reading and lie-detection technologies has always held particular allure in the context of war.

A second way in which war transforms the status of knowledge in society is the flip side of the first. Just as new techniques of detection are needed to uncover the enemy's knowledge, so new techniques of secrecy, encryption, and deception are required to conceal one's own military knowledge. In the first instance, this means classifying military plans and preparations, but as the intellectual resources of war become more diffuse, so the need for secrecy extends further into the realm of science and expertise. Comparative advantages in scientific and technological prowess have to be defended, even if this means concealing them from the rest of the scientific community.

National-security concerns can extend to controlling individual scientists, as occurred at the end of the Second World War when America and Russia fought to capture the German missile experts that had designed the V2 flying bomb. During the McCarthyite era of the 1940s and 1950s, the FBI paid closer attention to the activities of American scientists than any other group. Scientists represented a particular dilemma for the Soviet Union, being pivotal to the Cold War and space race, but also among the loudest voices calling for greater openness, especially during the 1960s. In 1968–9, the Soviet government enacted a purge of the scientific community, firing hundreds and sending thousands of others for political examinations and "re-education."

The American government has progressively expanded the scope of secrecy legislation from the First World War onward, initially classifying secret locations and banning certain kinds of public speech, before then encroaching into academic research during the Second World War and after.[10] An astonishing feature of the development of the atomic bomb was that it occurred without any public awareness, despite it involving 125,000 people over two and a half years, at a cost of over $2 billion.[11] The "war on terror" allowed for even greater infiltration of secrecy into civil society, with the 2001 Patriot Act granting government the right to classify "vulnerabilities or capabilities of systems, installations, infrastructure, projects, plans, or protection services related to the national security."

There is a palpable conflict between the seventeenth-century ideal of scientific progress and the paranoid scientific requirements of the wartime (and quasi-wartime) state. The aspiration of the former is to provide a basis for public consensus, in the form of facts, statistics, and rules, and therefore a basis for peace. Agreement on truth is impossible unless facts are made public, even if the bodies responsible for producing and publishing them (such as the Royal Society, statistics offices, or newspapers) remain closed. The publicity of statistics, economics, experimental findings, and philosophical arguments is crucial to their authority, for it is precisely the sense that they *could* be criticized or tested further that allows them to hold sway. Facts of this nature are "known knowns," extracted from the larger "known unknown" that we call "nature" or "society." By contrast, secrets ("unknown knowns") may be a necessary ingredient in achieving security or military advantage, but are necessarily a precarious basis for peace. The influence and popularity of conspiracy theories in American public life is partly a signal of the power of the military and intelligence services over the American state and American civil society more broadly.

This is not to deny that statistics have been integral to how modern warfare has been conducted, especially from the Second World War onward. The initial imperative to measure a nation's total economic output (now known as GDP) arose during the Second World War, provoked by the anxiety that the war would ultimately be determined by which side had the greatest productive capacity. Aerial bombing exacerbates this concern, as it can target civilian and industrial infrastructure on which the rest of society depends. Economic statistics reveal something of potentially great urgency. Statistical techniques such as "cost-benefit analysis" also played a central and controversial role in informing decision making during the Vietnam War, including on specific bombing targets and tactics.

But the authority and value of these techniques is significantly altered by the requirements of war. They're not there to produce *facts*, in the sense of publicly available evidence which invite general agreement. They're there to facilitate more rapid decisions on the part of military strategists. During the Second World War, Winston Churchill and his scientific adviser Lord Lindemann assembled their own private source of statistical analysis that cut out the rest of government.[12] Churchill was content to let his cabinet members express grave public concerns about national productive capacity, while receiving top-secret economic analysis that suggested things were better than the public realized. At Potsdam in 1945, he joked to Stalin that Lindemann was his own version of the Gestapo.[13] Often he simply rejected expert statistical analysis, on the basis that he didn't agree with it, and hired scientific advisers whom he had no intention of actually listening to, purely to convince bodies such as the Royal Society that their expertise was valued.

One of the problems with military intelligence and secret research is the difficulty of knowing whether it's any good or not. Public procedures of critique and peer review don't simply help endorse certain expert claims. They also identify and root out bad ones. Scientific experiments purport to be "replicable" by other scientists. Modern science developed in tandem with journals, citation practices, and blind peer review, which underpin academic scholarship and reputations. Take all that away and you have something much more conspiratorial.

Military intelligence is thus quite unlike facts of the sort produced by statisticians, academic researchers or professional journalists. The term "intelligence" derives from the Latin words *inter* (between) and *legere* (choose), implying that intelligence (unlike other forms of knowledge or theory) is something that allows us to *choose between*—to decide or to navigate. The purpose of intelligence is not so much to represent the world faithfully, in the way that experts and natural philosophers originally believed we should do, but to solve dilemmas and aid strategy in situations of the greatest urgency. Like anything else in war, it is valuable to the extent that it facilitates speed of decision making and victory over the enemy; whether it is "true" is something that the public cannot establish, given the secrecy that surrounds it. Intelligence is really a resource to be hoarded, not unlike physical weaponry and equipment, rather than a set of facts to be shared. Above all, it is a source of competitive advantage, which aims for *our* survival and *their* destruction.

The language of the body

By the late nineteenth century, René Descartes' separation of mind and body was being dismantled by wide-ranging scientific, philosophical, and social forces. The birth of modern psychology in the 1870s sought to study mental activity scientifically, by focusing on external indicators of attention such as eye movement. New mental illnesses such as neurasthenia and hysteria prompted new biological perspectives upon the mind, developed in psychiatry by Emil Kraepelin and in psychoanalysis by Sigmund Freud. And the rise of advertising and consumer culture was predicated on the idea that people's choices and desires can be deliberately influenced by outside forces.

The cumulative effect of these changes was to render thinking a scientifically observable phenomenon, not entirely unlike other anatomical processes. Physical movements and symptoms could now be classified in terms of what a person desired or intended. This was an especially enticing prospect for the nascent marketing profession, whose job it was to know and predict what consumers wanted. It would subsequently interest political leaders and parties, who relied on pollsters and psychologists to inform them of what the mass public had in mind. In the age of fMRI and EEG scanners, which produce pictures of brain activity to be used by physicians, psychiatrists, philosophers, and marketers, Descartes' notion of the mind as a fully private and intangible entity is no longer tenable. We can witness someone else's inner life without them expressing it in words.

As Descartes' binary of mind and body dissolves, emotion takes on a whole new significance. From the 1870s onward, various studies began to examine human and animal bodies on the basis that they could reveal mental activity—but the activity in question was emotional, not rational or cognitive. For example, Charles Darwin's 1872 book *The Expression of the Emotions in Man and Animal* focused on photographs of facial and bodily expressions, on the basis that "when our minds are much affected, so are the movement of our bodies."[14] In 1884, the psychologist and philosopher William James published the hugely influential paper "What Is an Emotion?" In it he suggested that the emotions we describe as belonging to our minds are really emanating from our bodies. We are first *physically* moved by something, and only then do we notice how it changes our psychological experience. As James put it, "we feel sorry because we cry, angry because we strike, afraid because we tremble."[15] What we call "feelings" of an emotional variety are ultimately no different from those we associate with touch or taste.

The science of emotion is potentially a powerful tool of political control, as it bridges our "outer" and "inner" lives. Techniques of emotional detection represent a threat to privacy, where companies such as Facebook are able to track social behavior for clues of how people are feeling. A growing industry of market-research companies use "emotional artificial intelligence" to detect signs of emotion in the body, face, eyes, and online activity. Such techniques also represent a threat to (or at least a distortion of) democracy, as they enable crowd psychology to be strategically influenced, or what is otherwise known as propaganda. These anxieties are far from new, although cutting-edge techniques of "emotional AI," "facial analytics," and "affective computing" have understandably amplified them.

The experts who emerged in the late seventeenth century could provide an objective picture of human beings, in terms of statistics and anatomical facts. But they had neither the desire nor the techniques to discover the population's inner emotional states. By the late nineteenth century, this had changed and new questions could be posed scientifically: what do people want, who do they identify with, how are they feeling? Marketers were among the first to seize upon these scientific techniques, but they were not the first to call for them. Once again, the impetus to uncover the "unknown known" of other minds and emotions was forged in war. If Napoleon's advantage lay partly in the enthusiasm of his vast army, then leaders would have to start taking popular feeling far more seriously.

According to Clausewitz's theory, there are three basic factors which determine the outcome of war. There is the governmental element, which shapes the overall strategy, planning, and logistics. Then there is the military element, where everything is determined by a combination of mathematical probability (largely to do with quantity of resources and men) and luck. And finally there is the emotional element: how much courage and animosity toward the enemy can be drawn upon? This was what the French Revolution unleashed in its general population, which no rival nation had any match for. As a set of shared feelings, nationalism began in the context of revolutionary, popular fervor, and was only much later adopted by traditionalists to prop up the political establishment.[16]

The essence of war, Clausewitz believed, is the attempt to physically destroy the enemy, to the point where they cannot then rearm and fight back. "All war supposes human weakness and against that it is directed," he wrote.[17] It has a brute physicality about it, of bodies against bodies, yielding—indeed *seeking*—traumatic injury and pain. Clausewitz had witnessed this firsthand and had no qualms about the visceral horrors that are generated by military combat. A problem that worried him was how a vast army of men might be persuaded to engage in such conflict, against all their better self-interest. He was concerned that the mentality of commerce and civilian life led to a weakening of military sentiments, calling this the "softness and desire for ease which debase the people in times of growing prosperity and increasing trade."[18]

The harrowing bodily demands of war can only be met, Clausewitz reasoned, if men are infused with a certain emotional spirit. This wasn't a challenge that was purely physical or psychological, but straddled the two, as Darwin and others would later articulate. If men lost the desire to fight and to kill, or lost their optimism regarding the outcome, defeat would become inevitable. Pharmacology would later provide part of the solution, with the American Civil War and Franco-Prussian War contributing major advances in anaesthetics, and recent Pentagon investments seeking drugs that might reduce fear. Mastering nerves, both those of the leader and his followers, is a long-standing ambition of military research.

And yet the sources of courage are diffuse, and not simply limited to the body or the battlefield. There are certain things a general can do in the short term to influence the feelings of an army, and Clausewitz believed that the emotions of soldiers should be a factor in selecting tactics. For instance, tactics that demonstrate great optimism might be more likely to trigger bravery and enthusiasm than more defensive ones. Several decades before emotions began to be studied by laboratory psychologists, Clausewitz was proposing a clinical and strategic approach to psychological engagement, which cannily triggered certain physical feelings, so as to alter behavior.

The broader problem of morale (as demonstrated by the aftermath of the French Revolution) was that it really stemmed from the national culture at large. "Moral forces form the spirit which permeates the whole being of War," from the administrative planning through the strategic operations, right down to the individual skirmish. Napoleon had pioneered the use of propaganda, running a government newspaper, *Le Moniteur Universel*, which shared news—factual and fabricated—of his military heroics with the French public back home. "It's not what is true that counts," Napoleon remarked, "but what people think is true." In the wake of the Napoleonic Wars, the central problem of European nation-states—in Clausewitz's eyes—was how they could develop the kind of national sentiments that would unite a whole people and a whole state behind a single political-military program. As the "total" wars of the twentieth century would attest, where nationhood itself is at stake, every man, woman and child is given a part to play. It is this as much as anything that nostalgic nationalism imagines and pines for.

Clausewitz's insights were hugely prescient. As the destructive potential of war grew, so the significance of morale grew with it. With the rise of aerial bombardment in the twentieth century, the scope and damage of war expanded far beyond the limits of the traditional battlefield. Bombing raids target political and economic infrastructure as much as they do military resources, dissolving the distinction between "combatant" and "noncombatant," at least insofar as the victims are concerned. While civilians accounted for only 5% for all the dead in the First World War, this rate had risen to 50% for the wars fought in the 1950s, and reached over 80% by the early twenty-first century.[19] The capacity of aerial bombing to wreak terror in the civilian population has always been part of its point: the expectation that bombing gradually weakens the psychological resolve of civilians is central to its strategic application. From the first time a bomb was dropped out of a plane by the Italian pilot Giulio Gavotti in Libya in 1911, through the Blitz of the Second World War and the carpet-bombing of North Vietnam in 1965–8, this has always been a form of warfare that targets the mind as much as the body.

For the nation being bombed, the morale of civilians is therefore a valuable source of resistance. Politicians began actively measuring and influencing public sentiment in the build-up to the Second World War, as the mood of the civilian population came to be viewed as a crucial resource in the war effort. Propaganda can be seen as the logical extension of advertising techniques into politics, much as Edward Bernays argued. But it also represents the expansion of military techniques of emotional coordination into the civilian sphere.

War demands a science of feelings, which might help manufacture greater morale and reduce the influence of physical pain and fear. Sheer quantity of bodies might be the most important resource to mobilize, as Clausewitz argued. But they need to be energized, aggressive, and as numb as possible to pain. Clausewitz suspected that vanity could play a key part in generating this. "Of all the noble feelings which fill the human heart in the exciting tumult of battle," he argued, "none, we must admit, are so powerful and constant as the soul's thirst for honor and renown."[20] With sufficient shared cultural identity, pain and suffering could be rendered glorious, and not simply fearful.

Collectivizing pain

Clausewitz was calling for a deliberate program of national, cultural activation, such that the Prussians might become able to match the French in their mass enthusiasm for war.[21] Techniques aimed at generating courage and enthusiasm would have to transcend the merely linguistic and employ imagery and sound, not least because close to half of western European populations were illiterate in the first half of the nineteenth century. The task of the state during peacetime was to prepare people physically and psychologically for the next outbreak of war, in the expectation that it would engulf more and more of civilian life. If "war is the continuation of politics by other means," then equally politics is nothing other than the prelude to war.

In an age before mass media, possibilities for propaganda were inevitably limited. Conservative nationalism was virtually an oxymoron during Clausewitz's lifetime, and only really became a plausible proposition with the rise of mass literacy toward the end of the nineteenth century, when mass education and mass media could be used to generate shared national myths and traditions. One of the difficulties faced by states such as Prussia up until that point was that few people had any reason to identify with their own national culture (if such a thing even existed) more than with that of French national culture, and—given the romance surrounding the French Revolution and Napoleon—often they had far less. There was, however, one particular emotional response that an entire people might feel simultaneously, Clausewitz believed, and which could potentially be converted into a fearsome military resource. That emotion was resentment.

Having witnessed battle firsthand, and suffered various defeats to the French, Clausewitz was highly sensitized to the psychological aftermath. He noticed that the experience of defeat had a far more lasting emotional impact than victory. "The vanquished sinks much further below the original line of equilibrium than the conqueror raises himself above it," he noted.[22] On a cultural and psychological level, war is fundamentally a question of who is destroyed, not of who gains. In more prosaic contexts, this is an insight that has been confirmed by behavioral economists. Experiments show that, all else being equal, people place greater value on not losing that which they already have, than on gaining something of equivalent value. As these behavioral economists would say, we are fundamentally "loss-averse" creatures. Where victory is enjoyed and then quickly taken for granted, the experience of loss shapes our identity, forging a melancholic sense of nostalgia.

Paradoxically, this melancholic sense of having lost can have its own mobilizing effect, if it can be triggered in the right way. Clausewitz wondered whether "through the loss of a great battle, forces are not perhaps roused into existence, which otherwise would never have come to life."[23] The pain of defeat produces a feeling of victimhood through which national cohesion starts to emerge. Revisiting past losses—even deliberately refighting the identical battles—has a potency due to the "feeling of rage and revenge" that arise once the reminder is issued.[24]

Political demagogues understand this all too well. Nationalist parties across Europe conjure support by aiming their message directly at those native populations who feel most disenfranchised and marginalized, hammering a message of national indignity to do so. Metropolitan "elites," "globalists," and the European Union are accused of inviting national humiliation, by dissolving sovereign borders and selling out to globalization. Vladimir Putin floods Russian television with messages of how the Russian people have been humiliated at the hands of the West. Donald Trump's 2016 campaign slogan, "Make America Great Again," assumed that America was a nation in decline. Trump extracted maximum political and emotional gains from listing America's apparent defeats on the world stage. China and Mexico had stolen its manufacturing jobs, NATO was a parasite on its military capacity, and immigrants were running riot in American cities.

The paradoxical effect of resentment is to convert power into a feeling of powerlessness, and vice versa. Part of the resentment that right-wing populists speak to today is the feeling that the world has taken rich nations for granted, with migrants and poorer nations exploiting their generosity and "political correctness." Clausewitz complained that the only apparently "peace-loving" countries are those that have already triumphed—and this is also their weakness. On the other hand, being small and weak has its own irresistible potency, if the sole aim is to inflict harm upon the strong. The reason guerrillas, computer hackers, suicide-bombers, or Internet trolls are so difficult to disempower is that they *have* very little power in the first place. All they have is their resentment. Asymmetrical war, in which the powerful struggle to resist sporadic attacks by the powerless, is the result.

What Clausewitz understood, which those of a more commercial and progressive persuasion are often oblivious to, is that there is a political energy in suffering and defeat. This can be far more psychologically powerful than the type of narrow "self-interest" that economists and policymakers conventionally assume we are governed by. Acts of sabotage and—in the business realm—"disruption" take on a heroic quality, where they vent some pent-up resentment toward established powers. Resentment can even be the basis of self-sabotage, if in damaging oneself one is also damaging the other. In certain cases this manifests itself in the fanaticism of the suicide bomber. In others, it may appear like an absurd act of self-harm, a charge frequently made by economists against Brexit and protectionist policies. Hungary, for example, receives subsidies from the EU worth 5% of GDP, yet still its prime minister represents Brussels as some sort of imperial power, dominating a proud people. Global elites fear that, if popular movements start to threaten globalization, all will be worse off. But there is something addictive and mobilizing about the feeling of having lost, that cannot be relieved simply with the offer of more progress.

From consensus to coordination

The Napoleonic ideal of the "great leader," be it personified by a demagogue, military commander, or CEO, possesses a distinctive type of authority, that disrupts comforting visions of an informed democratic public. It's not so much that such figures are uninterested in facts, more that they have the tenacity to stick to their strategy and their beliefs, even in the absence of facts. What Clausewitz admired so much about Napoleon was his capacity to shape political events to his will. Those who thrive in war are those with the clarity and strength to cope with a lack of clear objective knowledge, and carry on regardless. In Clausewitz's words:

if the mind is to emerge unscathed from this relentless struggle with the unforeseen two qualities are indispensable: first, an intellect that, even in the darkest hour, retains some glimmerings of the inner light which leads to truth; and second, the courage to follow this faint light wherever it may lead.

By this reckoning, the mark of a great intellect is the ability to ignore much of what's going on, and focus only on what is deemed important. Intelligence is more about navigation, of steering through a bewildering world, than about knowledge of facts. Leaders must extract coherent truth from the meaningless chaos of sensory impressions and rumors. With the rise of information theory during the Second World War, this would become known as identifying the "signal" from the "noise."

Underlying this vision of leadership, whether embodied by a politician, a military general, or a CEO, is a particular ideal of knowledge, which no longer treats the mind as a means of representing the world, as it had been for Descartes and Hobbes. Instead, it becomes a weapon with which to act on the world, including upon the minds of others. The leader, as exemplified by Napoleon, is not an observer, but a protagonist, operating outside the confines of facts or, for that matter, religion. As Eric Hobsbawm observed, Napoleon was the world's first "secular deity . . . the figure every man who broke with tradition could identify himself with in his dreams."[25]

The crucial psychological attribute of such a figure is not honesty but "resolution," not the capacity to provide accurate reports on the world, but to dominate it. As countless business books on "leadership" have subsequently sought to articulate, the greatest challenge of navigating fast moving strategic situations is how to combine instinct, emotion, and knowledge for rapid decision making. In war or in technological disruption, there are no rules and the job of the leader is to impose them by force of mental strength. In Clausewitz's words, in the turmoil of battle, the great general maintains a psychological serenity "like the needle of the compass in the storm-tossed ship."[26] In that metaphor the leader *becomes* the truth.

The anxiety that surrounds propaganda stems not so much from concerns that people are being lied to, but from the worry that the distinction between "fact" and "fiction" is no longer so relevant. Language becomes more like a set of instructions or military commands than it does a set of facts, albeit instructions and commands with careful attention to the emotional and psychological makeup of the audience. As politics becomes a branch of warfare, words become like weapons, selected for their impact, both on one's own side (who need to be enthused and enraged) and on the other (who need to be demoralized and hurt). Knowledge, meanwhile, is less to be valued for accuracy, and more for how it steers the decision maker through the chaos. The concept of intelligence assumes that we have a choice to make, and must select one path or the other. Doing nothing is not an option.

The seventeenth-century ideal of knowledge was anchored in the Hobbesian problem of how to secure promises. A valid representation of reality, whether provided by merchants, statisticians, or natural philosophers, was one which would facilitate agreements between strangers. Expert knowledge takes the form of a promise: trust me, these are the facts. But what emerges in the context of modern warfare and corporate strategy is less a basis for social consensus than tools for social *coordination*. The basic injunction of any leader is *follow me*. The question is then not whether everybody agrees on the state of affairs, but how everybody's physical, intellectual, and emotional movements can be brought into some kind of alliance with each other. The feeling that the great leader engenders is not trust so much as loyalty.

Achieving this involves a range of psychological, managerial, and rhetorical techniques, that have included marketing, propaganda, flag-waving, and the triggering of deep-lying resentments. Language becomes a tool of domination; for the same reason, it really can wreak emotional harm. Non-verbal symbols and media, aimed squarely at our feelings, become even more important in the battle to mobilize and control people. The knowledge and techniques that were originally demanded in war are now everyday features of civilian life, partly because metaphors of "war" have become adopted by populists, conspiracy theorists, or trolls. But the emphasis on knowledge being fast and strategically useful doesn't only belong to the realm of security and defense any longer. It is also how businesses maintain their advantages and public influence. The cult of Napoleonic leaders, trusting their "nose" and shaping the world around them, now surrounds entrepreneurs more than it does military figures. Driving this cult of entrepreneurship was one of the most influential intellectual movements of the twentieth century.

6

GUESSING GAMES

Market sentiment and the price of knowledge

As the founder of PayPal and an early investor in Facebook, Peter Thiel is one of the most renowned venture capitalists working in Silicon Valley, and was actively involved in seeking to build bridges between US tech companies and the Trump administration. He's known for his outlandish ideas and futuristic schemes, including the notion that death may only be "optional," once the body's natural aging process can be properly understood and halted. To this end he's expressed an interest in "parabiosis," in which the blood of young people is harvested and used as a source of rejuvenation. His deepest political fear is that democratic politics will eventually overwhelm economic freedom, and he believes that this needs resisting by building floating cities in the ocean and extending capitalist development into outer space.[1]

Thiel also holds a distinctive philosophy of knowledge, which shapes his faith in entrepreneurship. "Every great business is built around a secret that's hidden from the outside," he writes in his book *Zero to One*, "A great business is a conspiracy to change the world."[2] The world consists of an infinite number of secrets that are waiting to be discovered and exploited by entrepreneurs, and then guarded jealously as the basis to build future business empires. A really ambitious entrepreneur, or "founder" as Thiel prefers to call them, starts with the same question as the intelligence officer: what is it that someone or something *isn't telling me*?

Traditional scientific research, as conducted in universities, is of limited value from this perspective. Scientists generate plenty of facts that can be shared and built upon, but generally lack the passion to identify or guard secrets. By contrast, Thiel is interested in knowledge that is not publicly accepted, and may even be denied by mainstream experts:

Whenever I interview someone for a job, I like to ask this question: "What important truth do very few people agree with you on?" . . . It's intellectually difficult because the knowledge that everyone is taught in school is by definition agreed upon.[3]

In 2010, he announced he would be funding a new fellowship scheme, offering twenty-four young people $100,000 each to drop out of college and pursue their dreams via other means. Once knowledge is valued for the competitive advantages it provides, the scientific ideal of public consensus on facts evaporates. Instead, truth and intelligence are things to be hoarded and exploited to the maximum.

Business starts to take on the air of a military campaign, in which subterfuge and deception are key weapons, and the aim is to destroy rivals in the field. In Thiel's eyes world-changing founders, such as Jeff Bezos of Amazon or Mark Zuckerberg of Facebook, are willing to exploit their secret to its ultimate conclusion, to the point of destroying all competition. If monopoly seems unfair or threatening, as economists and regulators have traditionally argued, Thiel's answer is brutal: "competition is for losers." The triumphant entrepreneur becomes a Napoleonic figure, who changes the world through sheer force of will. Like a great general, a founder combines instinct, intelligence, and mental fortitude to steer a path that most people cannot, "disrupting" the status quo in the process, and creating a new one.

In some ways, Thiel's philosophy is an aggressive extrapolation of a set of trends that emerged in the mid-nineteenth century. With industrialization, followed by the birth of professionally managed corporations, a need developed to treat engineering knowledge as a private asset, to avoid competitors exploiting it. The phrase "intellectual property" first appeared in an American legal opinion in 1845 and spread to Europe in the 1860s. Trade secrets and brands became legally recognized soon after. With sufficient legal protections and managerial structures, corporations were able to engage in forms of scientific research for private commercial purposes, safe in the knowledge that this would remain their "property." The seventeenth-century ideal of expert knowledge as something that belongs in the public domain was challenged by an industrial alternative, where science becomes a tool for generating profit. Many contemporary anxieties regarding commercial secrecy—for instance, that pharmaceutical patents are blocking affordable medicine, or that digital algorithms lack public transparency—can be traced back to the period at the end of the nineteenth century, when businesses first came to treat knowledge as a unique source of competitive advantage.

But Thiel's worldview extends beyond a robust defense of intellectual property and monopoly. The business that accounts for most of Thiel's estimated $2.6 billion net worth, Palantir, is a data analytics company that was seed-funded by the CIA, and provides security and border-control services for governments around the world including those of the UK and Denmark. Originally founded to offer counterterrorism and counterinsurgency consultancy to the US military, Palantir's expertise lies in sifting through vast quantities of data—any data—to sniff out suspicious patterns. The company has since put these techniques of military intelligence to work in a range of civil contexts: in 2018, it emerged it was secretly providing "predictive policing" analytics to the New Orleans police, calculating the likelihood of citizens being gang members on the basis of behavioral patterns rather than crime detection. In cases such as these, the worlds of business and military strategy really do start to edge closer to each other. The secrecy of world-changing entrepreneurship potentially becomes enmeshed with that of the intelligence agency. In his occasional philosophical musings, Thiel has expressed a deep dislike for pacifism, with a particular disgust for Thomas Hobbes whom he accuses of valuing "cowardly life" over "heroic but meaningless death."[4] Thiel's celebration of "disruption," the guiding ethos of all Silicon Valley start-ups, thus takes on a more threatening geopolitical quality.

Thiel represents a certain extreme of libertarian business thinking. However, his ideas and success pose some unavoidable questions about the status of knowledge and expertise in society: what kind of knowledge do we value, and why do we value it? Since the 1980s, policymakers in many countries have deliberately sought to encourage greater commercial applications of scientific knowledge, to develop a "knowledge economy." Treating knowledge as a private economic asset has led to a vast expansion in consultancy services, such that by the late 1990s, one-sixth of all graduates from American Ivy League universities and Oxford and Cambridge were going into careers in management consultancy.[5] In post-industrial societies "creative industries" became viewed as a gold mine, as long as copyright enforcement was strong enough to protect their assets.

Universities have been encouraged, and often required, to act more like commercial entities, and to pay more attention to the commercial value of research and education. Commensurately, students are pushed to behave more like consumers or investors, seeking an education so as to maximize their own value in the labor market. University rankings allow prospective students to inspect the value of a degree in terms of student satisfaction and future earnings. Legislative changes, such as the landmark 1980 Bayh–Dole Act in the United States, created incentives for scholars to patent more of their findings, rather than merely to share them with the rest of the scientific community as had been the norm for centuries. The marketplace would set the value of knowledge, that is, how it contributes to efficiency, customer satisfaction, and wealth creation. But how far toward the Thiel vision are we prepared to go? Would we go as far as defending scientific secrecy and private "truths"?

Once knowledge is treated primarily as a business instrument, the instinct is to develop ever faster and better-tailored means of acquiring and controlling it. As in war, the goal is not public agreement, but rapid response to a changing environment. Military techniques stray into the business world, blurring the distinction between "war" and "peace" in the process, producing a culture of economic combat. There is a long history of leadership training and team-building crossing backwards and forwards between the corporate world and the military. But newly expanded surveillance infrastructures are providing secretive forms of monitoring of tremendous commercial value. It was discovered in 2017, for example, that spy-plane technology developed for the National Security Agency to monitor mobile phones from the air was being used by Acorn, a private equity company, to collect "commercial intelligence" on shopping habits.[6] Meanwhile the state is increasingly reliant on the technologies and services of private companies like Palantir for its most essential functions, of policing borders and waging war.

The ideal of reasoned facts relies on their being public, in order that they can be validated and added to. This ideal is being challenged by a number of forces today, including populist insurgents who cast doubt on the legitimacy and neutrality of expert knowledge. However, it is also threatened by a rival philosophy, which—not unlike Clausewitz's theory of war—sees knowledge as a weapon to be used against one's rivals, and not as a basis for peace at all. As in war, knowledge of this nature needs to be fast, useful, and secretive, if it is to be acquired before one's rivals. Guesswork and instinct play a role, while success depends on sensing and influencing mass sentiment. The difference, in this case, is that the combatants are in industrial conflict with one another, rather than at literal war. The context for such contests is the market, whose constantly fluctuating prices serve society with its nervous system, transmitting information from one node to another in real time, never sleeping or providing any certainty. The origins of this philosophy, of which Thiel is an advanced standard-bearer, lie in 1920s Vienna.

The warrior-entrepreneur

The First World War placed unprecedented weight upon the management and restructuring of domestic economies. It required governments to divert resources toward munitions production and saw the widespread use of rationing. Women entered the workforce in much larger numbers than before, and into new areas of the economy such as transport and heavy manufacturing. Conscription saw 60 million people mobilized across Europe. This was also the first major war to feature aerial bombing, an innovation which drew additional civilian resources and infrastructure into the war effort. Politicians began to demand faster, more detailed statistical updates on the performance of key industries, presaging the statistical innovations of the Second World War. By necessity, the state was tasked with economic planning, mobilizing whole industries.

Immediately after the First World War, the Austrian philosopher Otto Neurath offered an optimistic analysis entitled "War Economy." Neurath argued that war had had the positive effect of diverting attention away from monetary valuations of goods, and toward the intrinsic needs of the population and the state. Even a nation that had just been defeated in war, such as Austro-Hungary, might end up stronger thanks to the lessons learned for effective management of its economy. Strange as it may sound, war might "even be a kind of salvation." The war economy revealed that states could manage industry more efficiently than private businesses, because they were unaffected by the bubbles and slumps of the market economy. Neurath concluded with the not unreasonable question, "could not the same or even a better result be achieved in a peaceful way?"[7] To put this another way, might the wartime economy demonstrate the superiority of socialism?

In answer to this question, a pamphlet was published the following year containing a resounding "no." It was titled *Economic Calculation in the Socialist Commonwealth*, and its author was the libertarian economist Ludwig von Mises. Mises served in the army during the First World War, and also as an economic adviser to the Austrian War Department. His career in Vienna after the war combined academic appointments with positions in the civil service, and he became renowned as one of the great defenders of the free market, building on the insights of his intellectual inspiration, the economist Carl Menger. Mises was also Jewish, which led him to flee Austria for the United States in 1940.

Mises later became a hero to American libertarians, including to many of the most vehemently anti-government forces in American politics today, such as Ron Paul and the Koch brothers, who studied Mises' work closely during the 1960s. The Ludwig von Mises Institute was founded in Auburn, Alabama, in 1982, to advance anti-government and pro-market thinking. *Economic Calculation in the Socialist Commonwealth* rebutted Neurath's argument, at a time when socialism was gaining rapidly in popularity in so-called "Red Vienna." In the process, it laid the foundations of an entirely new way of understanding the virtues of the free market, that would eventually wind its way into the policy programs of Margaret Thatcher and Ronald Reagan. Like all these subsequent followers, Mises was consumed by a deep animosity toward socialism, to the extent that he initially viewed fascism as an acceptable way of resisting the rising red tide.

While Mises' argument was multifaceted and sophisticated, at its core was a simple claim about the advantages of free markets: they calculate the value of goods *in real time*. It was the speed and sensitivity of markets that were crucial. Governments might be able to work out how many munitions to produce at a given time or place, and they might be able to work out how much bread is needed to feed a wartime population. But first they must collect data, construct mathematical models, then perform calculations. Facts of this nature are slow to produce. By the time experts have worked out what needs producing, the world has changed. Mises argued that a free-market economy can do considerably better than a planned one, because the former features prices constantly rising and falling, in response to a vast number of choices, desires, and expectations of the population.

Mises admitted that if an economy were very simple (such as a small agrarian community) or if human needs never changed from one year to the next, then economic decisions could be successfully centralized among a small group of planners. But given the circumstances of industrial production serving a national population, efficient economic planning would require an impossibly complicated set of calculations to be performed at impossible speed. Throw in technological change, and things become too complex for experts to compute. Socialism, Mises argued, was not so much ethically or politically undesirable (though he thought that as well) as *technically and scientifically* impossible, given the limitations of the human mind. In a centrally planned economy, "every economic change becomes an undertaking whose success can be neither appraised in advance nor later retrospectively determined," he wrote; "There is only groping in the dark."[8] The defining problem of an industrial economy is that it moves too fast and too erratically to be dealt with by the human mind alone.

Speed of calculation wasn't the only advantage of the free market for Mises. Markets are also effective ways of gauging a very large number of tastes and opinions, because they respond to consumer preferences. Mises argued that it was virtually impossible to establish any objective facts about consumer needs and desires. What *I* want or need to consume is really a subjective matter for me; there is no way to prove that my preferences are correct or more valid than yours. In this sense, Mises was a relativist, who believed that there is no objective way of gauging the right amount of goods to produced. A planned economy required experts to establish facts on questions that were really all a matter of personal perspective. Markets, on the other hand, save us from having to all agree on what is needed. Like a successful military operation, markets coordinate people without the need for consensus.

In the context of 1920s "Red Vienna," and in the immediate aftermath of the Russian Revolution, Mises' critique of socialism created an intellectual storm. It provoked a series of responses not only from other Austrian intellectuals, but from across Europe for years afterwards, which subsequently became known as the "socialist calculation debate." Economists with socialist sympathies fought valiantly to prove that an economy *could* in principle be planned in an efficient manner, even without free markets to act as signaling devices, although the economics would indeed be fiendishly difficult. Others accepted some of Mises' argument, and developed a vision of "market socialism," in which key decisions about production were made by government experts, but questions of allocation were left to the market. The debate raged on, and occasionally still reverberates whenever advances in digital computing power seem to render the socialist case more technically plausible.

But Mises wasn't only concerned with demolishing the case for economic planning. He was also clearing the ground for a particular type of economic leadership, that figures like Thiel have built entire belief systems upon: entrepreneurship. Entrepreneurship was still a variety of planning, but operated in the private sector with private capital and private costs. What was so valuable about entrepreneurs, Mises believed, was not that they knew for sure what techniques would work or which products would sell, but that they were prepared to act even when they didn't. They were brave enough to take severe risks and (together with their investors) accept the consequences of failure. This was a strategic and courageous mind-set that had otherwise been encountered in battle—indeed it was very similar to the qualities that Carl von Clausewitz had applauded in great generals.

What allows entrepreneurs to do this is not facts or professional qualifications, so much as impressions and information that others haven't (yet) received. As in war, speed, secrecy, and courage are of the essence. The analogy between great business innovators and military leaders was made explicit by another Viennese economist, with a similar enthusiasm for raw capitalism, Joseph Schumpeter. As he wrote in the early 1930s:

> As military action must be taken in a given strategic position even if all the data potentially procurable are not available, so also in economic life action must be taken without working out all the details of what is to be done. Here the success of everything depends upon intuition.[9]

Anticipating contemporary fascination with the personalities of Steve Jobs or Mark Zuckerberg, Schumpeter was intrigued by the exceptional psychological attributes of these characters. It wasn't just money that motivated them, but "the will to conquer: the impulse to fight, to prove oneself superior to others," he suggested.[10] Austrian economics, as it became known, sought to channel the aristocratic, military ethos into the realm of entrepreneurial combat, and the state needed to stand well back.

The only facts that really count in the heat of entrepreneurial battle are market prices. But a price is a curious kind of fact, that differs starkly from the type of fact that seventeenth-century experts were seeking to defend. For one thing, there *is* no expert in charge of prices in a free-market society. Unlike the facts of statistics, accountancy, anatomy, or the natural world which are deliberated, generated, and validated by experts, prices arise spontaneously. This was precisely what Mises believed was so valuable about them. For another thing, as markets become freer or more liquid, prices move almost constantly. Consider stock prices today, which are always in flux, requiring new technologies such as ticker tapes and digital screens to ensure that the price displayed is current. A price is thus a strange kind of fact. It provides little certainty or common ground, and always offers an advantage to the person who detects it and reacts fastest.

The Austrian free marketeers were not arguing that businessmen always know best. What they were claiming was that only a system of flexible prices could ensure that errors came to light. Under socialism, so the argument went, a bad economic idea or bad product could become firmly established, because it had the full backing of the state. But in a competitive economy, bad strategies or technologies would soon be abandoned, with entrepreneurs and investors losing their money in the process. Capitalism was therefore a form of Darwinism, in which constant disruption leads to an ever stronger system. It is a game of guessing, sensing, and anticipating, in which the winner is the person whose instincts prove most prescient and durable.

For Mises and his allies, Neurath had drawn the wrong conclusions from the example of a wartime economy. Neurath had focused on the extended role of the state in warfare, suggesting that the state could continue to produce and allocate goods during peacetime. Mises, on the other hand, extracted a different lesson altogether: capitalism is already akin to warfare, fought between entrepreneurs, marshalling their courage, innovation, and capital in the field of conflict. As in war, there are few firm facts to rely on, and everything comes down to nerve, strategy, and intuition.

Of course there is no actual physical injury involved, but the stakes should be as high as possible. The key thing for governments to focus on was not production or distribution of goods, but the protection of private property. Given the importance of ideas and invention for such a system, these rights would have to extend forcefully into the intellectual realm as well. Mises was fully aware that this was, at its core, a matter of physical force: "all ownership derives from occupation and violence," he argued.[11] But without this protection, there could be no capitalism; and without capitalism, there could be no economic progress or individual freedom.

In the decades following Mises' death in 1973, libertarians inspired by him have fought increasingly aggressive and often successful campaigns to expand the reach of private economic power. Such campaigns depict virtually all taxation and regulation as socialist conspiracies, hell-bent on destroying individual liberty. As historian Nancy MacLean and investigative journalist Jane Mayer have revealed, American organizations such as the Cato Institute, the Reason Foundation, and the Liberty Fund have worked tirelessly, though with ample support from wealthy donors, to argue against basic social and environmental regulations. The right of corporations to commit acts of harm upon the natural environment and their own employees is defended as a basic principle of liberty, the alternative to which is state socialism. The election of Barack Obama in 2008, with plans to rescue the financial system and provide social health insurance, was the catalyst for fearsome mobilization of economic and intellectual muscle, fueled by libertarian ideology.

Whether Mises won or lost the "socialist calculation debate" is not really the point. What was more important was that, in emphasizing the problem of rapid calculation, he set the terms on which the debate took place. In doing so, as the historian of economics Philip Mirowski has shown, he established the template for how mainstream economics would develop over the second half of the twentieth century, especially in the United States.[12] Following Mises' critique of Neurath, economists increasingly came to view their subject matter in terms of information and to understand markets as information processors. Mirowski notes that economists working on the topic of information came to dominate the list of Nobel Prize recipients from the 1960s onwards, helping to lay the intellectual foundations for the resurrection of free-market policy programs in the 1970s. Many of these were relatively traditional economists, using mathematical formulae to model market forces. But they also included Friedrich von Hayek, the winner of the 1974 Nobel, in whose work we can discover a more original and transformative approach to philosophy of knowledge, that represents arguably the twentieth century's most influential—and consequential—attack on the foundations and authority of public expertise.

Useful knowledge

Growing up in Vienna in the years before the First World War, Hayek acquired an ambivalent view of traditional academic scholarship. His father was a doctor, but had always wanted to be a botanist, and Hayek came to view a university career as something to aspire to. However, there was no particular area of study that held his attention. He developed some interest in biology at school, especially in Darwin's theory of evolution, but was more drawn toward practical activities such as rock climbing and theater. As an adult, Hayek contrasted two types of intellectual, the "master of his subject" who has authority over a certain field of knowledge, and the "puzzler" who toys with problems, but doesn't necessarily know very much. Hayek placed himself firmly in the latter camp.

His ambivalence toward universities and professional knowledge would be integral to his subsequent philosophy. As a theorist, he was fascinated by the role of intellectuals in society, and believed that ideas shaped both policy design and public common sense. On the other hand, he was deeply afraid—paranoid even—about the potential of intellectuals and experts to design and authorize tyrannical political systems. Ultimately, his work amounts to a defense of practical know-how and instinct, such as that possessed by the businessperson, and an attack on the arrogance of experts and theorists, who purport to know how society works.

Hayek served in the Austro-Hungarian army on the Italian front in the second half of the First World War. The vogue for socialist ideas in the immediate postwar period led him to identify briefly as a socialist, and to encounter economic theory for the first time. But Mises' critique of economic planning transformed his ideological worldview. In 1922,

Hayek came across Mises' book *Socialism* (an expansion of the 1920 pamphlet written against Neurath) and he found its logic utterly compelling. As Hayek later recalled, "socialism promised to fulfil our hopes for a more rational, more just world. And then came this book. Our hopes were dashed."[13]

Hayek grew to know Mises during the 1920s, becoming his assistant before taking up a junior lectureship in economics at the University of Vienna in 1929. He was never quite as politically libertarian as Mises, although he also would later receive widespread plaudits from free marketeers, including Ronald Reagan and Margaret Thatcher. Thatcher famously once interrupted a Conservative Party policy discussion, by slamming a copy of Hayek's 1960 work *The Constitution of Liberty* down on the table, with the words "*This* is what we believe." He was a hero to the American free-market thinker Milton Friedman, and spent the 1950s at the University of Chicago, where Friedman led the influential "Chicago School" of economics. Hayek's 1944 classic, *The Road to Serfdom*, made him a cult figure in the United States, at a time when free-market ideas were out of favor the world over, and when Hayek himself was viewed as an ideological crank by much of the economics profession, Chicago notwithstanding.

But the most decisive phase of Hayek's career happened in the interim between his association with Mises in Vienna and with Friedman in Chicago, during the 1930s and 1940s when he was employed at the London School of Economics (LSE). Many of the papers he published while at LSE were within the parameters of the "socialist calculation debate" that was ongoing. Hayek was certainly seeking to buttress the case for the free market, and continue the critical demolition of socialism that Mises had initiated. But in doing so, he also developed a theory of knowledge that had implications extending well beyond economics, to challenge the political status of experts in general. Against the romantic ideal of the intellectual, as a detached truth-seeker, Hayek posed the cynical question of what *use* was knowledge, and who really benefited from it. A fresh suspicion was cast upon experts in the process, as their claim to be apolitical (at least on social and economic matters) was thrown into doubt.

In 1936 he was invited to give his inaugural lecture at LSE, for which he selected the topic "Economics and Knowledge." The lecture contained the kernel of the argument that would appear nine years later in his article "The Use of Knowledge in Society." In that article, clearly mindful of the upset he might be causing, Hayek put forward the following claim:

> Today it is almost heresy to suggest that scientific knowledge is not the sum of all knowledge. But a little reflection will show that there is beyond question a body of very important but unorganized knowledge which cannot possibly be called scientific in the sense of knowledge of general rules: the knowledge of the particular circumstances of time and place.[14]

This latter type of knowledge is the knowledge employed by entrepreneurs and managers, when, for example, they "put to use a machine not fully employed, or somebody's skill which could be better utilized."[15] Hinting at what would later become a resentment toward "liberal elites," Hayek went on to note that "it is fashionable today to minimize the importance of [this] knowledge." Overturning this "fashion" would be one of his main philosophical and political objectives.

As Mises had argued before him, Hayek stressed that the central problem of all economic management is change. New ideas, techniques, and consumer desires appear constantly. Machinery breaks in unexpected ways. Random events, such as energy shortages or freak weather incidents, disrupt our plans in unpredictable ways. This constant uncertainty is a healthy state of affairs, according to Hayek, because it allows diversity and competition to prosper. The only alternative is a quasi-totalitarian scenario, in which everything is organized by centralized diktat.

Uncertainty places far more value upon people who can solve problems and respond to circumstances than upon abstract theorists or experts. Coping with the unknown and unforeseen requires skills of flexibility and resilience, which don't necessarily have much to do with scientific method. Statisticians, for example, might be able to spot "laws" governing how economies work, but they are less useful than the managers, entrepreneurs, and engineers who are actually applying their knowledge in specific, concrete situations. Why do we assume that a statistician's knowledge about the economy is "better" or more "true" than the knowledge that individual businessmen have about what is going on? For Hayek, the answer lay in a kind of snobbery that "intellectuals" had toward practical and local knowledge.

One of the reasons for this snobbery was that practical know-how is challenging to communicate or write down. It is knowledge that sits closely to the person who possesses it, and can't be shared with the public in any straightforward way, by publishing, statistics, or public debate. The knowledge of a successful entrepreneur, like that of a skilled mechanic or military commander, doesn't consist of a set of findings or facts. It isn't a representation of the world, but an ability to manipulate it. It's what is sometimes called "embodied knowledge" or "tacit knowledge"—a knowing *how*, not a knowing *that*. At a time when business schools and vocational qualifications were still almost unknown in universities (especially in Europe), Hayek believed that this type of know-how was denigrated by intellectuals for lacking objectivity. But in its humility and limitations, he deemed it far less politically dangerous than the knowledge of experts seeking to put their factual and theoretical knowledge to public use.

Hayek went further still. It wasn't only that this type of knowledge is *hard* to share or publish; much of its value derives from the fact that it isn't generally available. It is what gives successful entrepreneurs their edge over others. Knowledge needs to be respected as a private asset, or else the competitive game of entrepreneurial capitalism can't carry on. As Mises and Schumpeter had stressed before him, Hayek insisted that entrepreneurs all have slightly different perspectives, advantages, and insights, and the only way of ranking these is to allow the market to sort it out. By the same principle, efforts to establish generally agreed facts, known to all, have a dampening effect on enterprise. To assert consensus is to risk socialism. This starts to cast a new light on experts, as if the very act of seeking a common reality threatens to destroy freedom.

Against experts

During the 1930s and 1940s, Hayek became increasingly perturbed by the socialist sympathies of intellectuals. This he put down to the intellectual proclivity toward "generalization," the assumption that there are laws governing society *as a whole* and history *as a whole*. What starts as merely a "mental scheme for interpretation" of social events becomes, in the hands of intellectuals, a set of objective *facts* about why things happen as they do.[16] This is an entirely unwarranted leap, in Hayek's view. If you want to understand economic and social changes, you're far better off consulting the people who actually make the changes happen—the consumers, entrepreneurs, managers—than experts looking at these events from some presumed position of neutral objectivity.

When experts seek objectivity, Hayek argued, they become oblivious to other perspectives on the world. They convince themselves that they are pursuing their knowledge on behalf of the public, but they have no real interest or understanding of what the public thinks or wants. He believed that the public vocation of experts was a danger, as it translated into a monopoly over how facts were defined. As states invested more public money in scientific research, this produced a dangerous oligarchy in which tacitly or explicitly socialist intellectuals would allow their "objective" perspective to shape how people were governed.

Because of their control over public institutions, intellectuals face minimal competition. Consensus among the knowledge elite concerned Hayek. Ideas and knowledge should only be deemed trustworthy if they were tested in a competitive arena, by rivals. For Hayek, we shouldn't rely on individual scientists to achieve progress, but on the overall competitive system that pits one scientist against another.[17] But what happens when the scientific establishment *does* broadly agree on something, such as climate change or the health effects of smoking? Must the definition of "scientist" be stretched, until a dissenting voice can be found? Many libertarians inspired by Hayek would argue that it must.

On a practical level, Hayek fought the monopoly of experts on various fronts. He was a founding member of the Society for Freedom in Science, established in Britain in 1940 to combat perceived Marxist influence over science policy. In 1947, he formed the Mont Pelerin Society, an international think tank dedicated to resurrecting liberal and libertarian thinking, and resisting the perceived drift toward socialism in the postwar world. This society, whose membership included economists such as Mises and Friedman and renowned philosophers such as Karl Popper and Michael Polanyi, became one of the main networks through which free-market thinking circulated in the decades leading up to the Thatcher and Reagan victories. But it also demonstrated the practical implications of

Hayek's critique of expertise. The sense that dominant academic and government institutions had been corrupted by delusions of "objectivity" and "the public interest" meant that resistance needed to be forged through a whole new infrastructure of knowledge production. The monopoly that intellectuals exerted over the mainstream public sphere could only be broken by establishing a rival one.

Over the following decades, the Mont Pelerin Society became a model for various think tanks of the "New Right," such as the Heritage Foundation in the United States, the World Economic Forum in Switzerland, and the Center for Policy Studies in the UK. Like Hayek, the new think tanks were often fueled by the suspicion that universities and media organizations were irredeemably blinkered by their own commitment to "objectivity" or "impartiality," which in practice just meant socialism. Research institutes backed by private donors became a way to bypass the existing channels of intellectual exchange, often circumventing the public sphere altogether. For intellectuals who view the ideal of public knowledge as a dangerous socialist conceit, private and even secretive networks of political discussion make complete sense. Summits hosted by the Koch brothers, at which big business donors share political ideas, have even featured white-noise-emitting loudspeakers around the perimeter to deter eavesdroppers, taking the commitment to privacy to new extremes.[18]

Today a vast American industry of private philanthropic trusts underwrites this agenda, diverting extraordinary sums of money toward tailored research programs without accountability or public visibility. Their charitable status means that donors can reduce their tax bills, which is succor to those of a libertarian bent such as the Kochs. The growth of these financial entities is astonishing: in 1930, there were 200 private foundations registered in the US, a number that had grown to over 100,000 by the early twenty-first century, with assets of over $800 billion.[19]

Implicit in much of the Hayekian agenda is that traditional universities are a type of cartel, which conspire against the public by asserting their right to control the facts. From the radical free-market perspective, monopoly is not necessarily bad if it has been earned through imagination and risk-taking. But academics are only protected from market competition by erroneous notions of the public interest and historical privilege. They've done nothing to earn this advantage, and it would be in the public interest to break up the cartel with the introduction of more competition. For-profit universities, privately backed think tanks, and consultancies may not have any greater access to the truth than traditional public institutions, but by injecting a greater variety of political ideas and voices, they smash the intellectual cartel of expertise, and replace it with something more like a market.

From a business point of view, this injection of "competition" into the production of research has reaped significant dividends, although at some terrible social costs and potentially catastrophic environmental ones. Oil companies, such as Exxon, had the opportunity—through often opaque funding intermediaries such as Donors Trust—to funnel money toward research institutes and quasi-academics who were willing to contradict the consensus that burning fossil fuels caused climate change.[20] Research has since shown that Exxon first became aware of the scientific link between fossil fuels and climate change in 1977, then spent extravagantly in seeking to conceal and cast doubt on this evidence.[21] Individuals who seemed to be experts could be paraded in public debates to give the "other side" of the argument, where that other side had been effectively concocted for financial gain.

Phony science can be demolished. The problem is, it takes time. Where one side is involved in a project of *representation*, seeking to create the most accurate records and images of climate with immense care, and the other is involved in a project of *mobilization*, seeking to win a battle over public sentiment, the former becomes very vulnerable. The alternative perspective will eventually be shown as phony, but often it is too late. In the case of climate change, it might be far too late. Regardless, knowledge has become a matter of timing and speed, in a way that was inconceivable 350 years ago when our ideals of scientific expertise were established.

Real-time knowing

From the mid-1970s onwards, free-market ideas promoted by Hayek started to attract serious attention from mainstream politicians, as the postwar policy consensus began to break down. Efforts to manage national economies on the basis of Keynesian economic theory stopped working in the early 1970s, due to a combination of technological and political pressures, as well as unforeseeable events such as the sudden increase in the price of oil in autumn 1973. The end of fixed currency exchange rates in 1973, followed by the end of controls on cross-border currency movements, meant that the value of money was set by international markets, rather than politicians. A counter revolution against the ambitions of public economic planners was under way, and the ideas of Mises, Hayek, and Friedman were suddenly coming into vogue. By the early 1980s, surveys showed Americans trusting businesses more highly than government for the first time. The victories of Reagan and Thatcher, which promised renewed respect for enterprise and free markets, were a sign that a new intellectual orthodoxy had emerged.

But it would be wrong to assume that this shift involved a like-for-like replacement of policy frameworks. This wasn't simply about ousting one intellectual orthodoxy and putting another one in its place. Something even more fundamental was going on, which was in keeping with Mises and Hayek's long-term vision. The argument that the Austrian economists had made in favor of the free market was never simply that it would produce the most wealth or the best products, even if they suspected that it would. The more transformative and disconcerting claim was that it could reduce the need for public, centralized experts as such. One might go further still and say that they reduced the need for truth. Dating back to Mises' 1920 pamphlet on economic calculation, an ideal had developed that, so long as markets were relatively unimpaired by government intervention, they could become the organizing principle of an otherwise disorganized, unplanned, even ignorant society. As long as there was a way of coordinating people peacefully, in real time, why the need for experts or facts at all?

Hayek had developed an argument along these lines in *The Road to Serfdom*. If society harnessed the local practical knowledge of entrepreneurs and consumers, and discarded the theories and facts of "intellectuals" working for the state, the question still remained of how to coordinate a large population. If people did not recognize a scientific consensus or *truth*, what would ensure that they interacted peacefully at all? This same question had concerned Thomas Hobbes in the 1640s. But where Hobbes identified the sovereign law as the tool that would perform this job, forcing people to honor their promises by threat of violence, Hayek looked to the market, with the support of the state in defending property rights.

The brilliance of markets, from Hayek's perspective, lies in how little they require people to actually know or understand. In order for the market for soft drinks to work, it isn't necessary for anyone to understand the whole system. No "soft-drink economist" is required. It is only necessary for people to buy a drink if they choose to, and for manufacturers and retailers to seek revenue. Prices do the rest. If experts *really* want to be neutral, they should give up trying to understand what is happening, and simply focus on creating the conditions for competition to take place.

The market is therefore a type of "post-truth" institution, that saves us from having to know what is going on overall. It actually works *better* if we ignore the facts of the system at large, and focus only on the part of it that concerns us. From Hayek's perspective, the market does what intellectual elites refuse to do, namely to factor in the feelings, instincts, and perspective of the mass of ordinary people on the ground. As long as experts or politicians don't interfere, markets have an anti-intellectual populist quality. And this is a good thing.

By this reckoning, the market is a type of mass sensory device, that exists to detect sentiment and changes in public mood. It's like a constant opinion-polling device or survey, only with the advantage that it responds in real time and reflects things as they are *now*. When something happens, such as a policy announcement or natural disaster, one can immediately check how *the markets* have responded. Rumors of impending shortages or regulatory changes can be met with instant reactions from *the markets*. Understood as real-time monitoring devices, markets are not so much tools for producing facts but for gauging our feelings. This is where faith in the market maps onto populism and nationalism, for all these creeds see politics as little other than mass public coordination via shared feeling. Reason becomes sidelined in favor of sentiment.

Men such as William Petty and John Graunt had developed nascent forms of social science by imagining society as a human body, with goods and money circulating like the blood. The study of "political anatomy" would seek the forms of "medicine" that were needed to keep this body healthy. Adapting the same metaphor, we might say that Hayek viewed the market as society's nervous system, an information network of immense complexity and speed, whose genius lay in its distributed nature. Rather than seek knowledge of this network in an effort to govern it, better simply to recognize what a miraculous form of real-time intelligence it provides.

While the market takes responsibility for knowledge, the job of the human being is simply to make choices and act on them. These needn't be founded in objective knowledge or rationality. In Hayek's view, choice is driven by "emotion and impulse," and the distinction between "good" and "bad" decisions, "true" and "false" opinions, is one for the market to sort out.[22] In a society operating along these lines, everything becomes a PR exercise, in which businesses and governments manipulate their image to win the favor of investors and consumers. There are no facts, just trends and feelings. Like military generals, central bankers have to factor in the effect of their statements and decisions on public sentiment, weighing each word of a speech in terms of how the markets might interpret it. CEOs and politicians must take great pains to avoid "talking down" their stock or currency, and nurture "confidence" in the future. Reality is all in the eye of the investor, creditor, or shopper. "Market intelligence" means detecting what desire or sentiment is about to bubble up next.

Starting in the 1970s, banks began to develop complex mathematical models to calculate risks of possible future outcomes, which allowed abstract risks—such as bad weather, a crop failure or a currency depreciation—to be converted into products that could be bought and sold on the open market. These "derivatives" are another example of how markets challenge the authority of experts. The economists and mathematicians who develop these instruments offer no claim about how things actually *are* or what *will* actually happen, but merely calculate the mathematical chance that they *might*, in order to profit from that like bookmakers. With a suitable number placed upon some future eventuality—such as a low-income American mortgage-holder defaulting on their payments—there is no need to know very much more about it. Of course that also places a frightening degree of responsibility in the hands of whoever gets to calculate the risk in question. The economic rewards for the institutions and individuals who construct and sell these insurance products are legion. The stark implication is that there is more money to be made in what cannot be known, namely the future, than in what can.

To inhabit the free-market society that emerged from the upheavals of the 1970s, and which persists today, is to live in a state of constant flexibility and reactivity. Twenty-four-hour news channels display real-time financial market reports. Companies employ futurists, trend-spotters, and horizon-scanners to imagine what might bubble up next. A surging management consultancy industry and outsourcing of research reduce the need for companies to maintain expertise internally. As in war, the intelligence that matters most is that which can be accessed quickly, facilitating the most rapid response possible. High-frequency traders extrapolate this logic to its limit, investing millions in equipment (such as private cables and computer servers that have advantageous geographic positions) that allows them and their algorithms to respond to price movements mere milliseconds before the rest of the market.

In these conditions, individuals must focus less on seeking truth or objectivity, and more on being adaptable. In a society governed by free markets, individuals must consider how to market themselves to potential employers or customers. Education becomes less significant for the knowledge that it provides than for how it contributes to the employability of the recipient, which is as much about attitude, flexibility, and technical skills as it is about traditional intellectual or professional vocations. What is referred to as "networking" in practice means seeking knowledge that others don't have: in a competitive environment, valuable knowledge is knowledge that is specifically *not* in the public domain. Rumor offers far more potential for profit than published fact. The context for every life choice is that of competition, how to distinguish oneself from rivals, by qualifications, image-making, and management of oneself.

As the free-market ethos has infiltrated traditional spheres of scholarship, it has produced some disconcerting results. Academic life is accelerated, with new pressures to publish and/or patent research findings more quickly, so as to claim ownership over a subject area before anyone else. In the competitive rush to establish findings, the quality of what is being patented appears to have deteriorated over time.[23] Universities have to engage in extensive image management and marketing, in a permanent struggle to distinguish themselves as "excellent" in the overall market for education and research. Researchers are measured and rewarded according to conventional productivity indexes, creating an incentive to produce more research at higher speed, regardless of what this means for the quality of the work. The way for universities to retain legitimacy in the age of real-time facts is to be responsive to a constantly changing world, not to seek the causes or structures that might lie beneath the churn.

Hayekian suspicion about public expertise has become a type of self-fulfilling prophecy. University reforms start with the assumption that researchers and teachers are looking out for themselves, using their public status and protection to resist competitive pressures. League tables and metrics are then introduced, so as to get them to focus on indicators such as "student satisfaction" and "graduate employment," which has the intended effect of making them behave more like conventional businesses. As this proceeds, the argument that universities are unlike private businesses becomes harder to sustain, and the case for comparing them—unfavorably—to the commercial sector becomes more intuitively obvious. Researchers are instructed to provide evidence of what economic or other benefit their work has delivered, so as to drag them out of the ivory towers (in Britain this is referred to as "impact"), which entrenches a view that knowledge is really a practical tool for getting things done, and the pursuit of "pure" knowledge just a state-backed indulgence.

The market does not offer or require any consensus as to what is going on, but it does serve to coordinate a complex mass of contradictory perspectives, sentiments, and ideas, relieving governments and experts of the need to take responsibility instead. So long as everyone is plugged into the same information network, namely the market, everyone's perspective can be treated equally, and there is no need to distinguish "truth" from "falsehood," "objectivity" from "subjectivity." As Hayek put it, "knowledge and ignorance are relative concepts."[24] We're all just trying our luck, and the winner will emerge over time. The problem with this radical intellectual egalitarianism is that, in material terms, it is anything but egalitarian.

Survival of the truest

What made Napoleon so remarkable in the eyes of his admirers was that, by sheer willpower and strategic brilliance, he demonstrated that the entire map of Europe could be remade. Here was a leader attacking the very nature of political reality, jeopardizing entire nations, and striving to produce a new reality. The Napoleonic mentality begins with a refusal to accept things as they are, and a refusal to view anything as permanent. Ultimately he was defeated, but failure is one possible outcome of that initial act of refusal. War doesn't simply make facts harder to establish, but introduces a prolonged period of fundamental uncertainty as to what the eventual truth will turn out to be.

A similar pattern of disruption pertains in Darwin's theory of evolution. Evolutionary advance occurs not through predictable and repetitive progress, but through freakish mistakes. In order for biological reality to be transformed, there must be accidents and disruptions, which overturn convention. One might even say that such "falsehoods" become the basis of an entirely different future. The vast majority of these errors lead nowhere. But every so often, one of them transforms reality. What begins as a mistake later becomes the norm, thanks to its superior strength and environmental adaptation. The status quo is reconfigured by abnormality.

It was a similar ideal of disruptive change that our handful of twentieth-century Viennese intellectuals hoped to defend as the basic principle of a free society. Hayek termed competition a "discovery procedure," through which reality was revealed. The philosopher Karl Popper, who was a friend and acolyte of Hayek, argued in his famous book of 1945, *The Open Society and Its Enemies*, that the mark of scientific knowledge was not that it was true as such, but that it was at least open to "falsification" by alternative claims. It was crucial that people were free to say things which are not considered "true," if only because this allows us to discover whether our existing facts can stand up to being challenged. Like a genetic mutation, what looks like a falsehood may turn out to be superior given time. Schumpeter, meanwhile, argued that entrepreneurs unleash "creative destruction" within the economy, overturning one set of established techniques and institutions, and replacing them with another. The real danger facing the West lies in efforts by governments and experts to pacify such processes of disruption.

However, this philosophy respects no clear distinction between the realm of intellectual competition and that of economic competition. Once we are placing our trust in Darwinian processes of mutation and elimination, the pursuit of wealth, of power, and of truth start to gradually blend into one. This presents obvious and immediate threats to the status of facts in society. After all, if the value of knowledge lies primarily in the market, then the question is whether a given claim is marketable, not whether it is a valid description of the world. In the years preceding 2007, investment banks were able to deceive their customers as to the underlying risks attached to the derivatives they were selling. But they were successful only because these derivatives had been analyzed by professional credit raters, who had awarded them an AAA rating, meaning ultra-low risk. Meanwhile, the credit raters were earning money from the investment banks for doing so. As Mises correctly understood, the market is a space of subjective impressions and opinions. "Truth" is whatever has not yet been eliminated by something else.

Furthermore, a pure free-market ideology installs social Darwinism as the organizing principle of society, resulting inevitably in spiraling inequality. The principal "losers" from the economic upheavals that began in the 1970s are the populations and industries that failed to change or to move, such as the shipbuilders of Glasgow or the steel plants of Indiana. It wasn't that Western manufacturing industries made a mistake or suddenly became less productive, it's that they failed to *change* and became inferior by comparison. As with Darwinian evolution, stasis equals vulnerability. From this perspective, those regions, populations, and cultures that were attached to failing industries lost their function in the overall competition. They have been superseded and discarded, and really have no reason to persist as they are.

In the United States, attacks on socialized health insurance have obvious implications for the mortality rate among poor Americans. One estimate in 2017 suggested that, if the Republican Party succeeded in repealing "Obamacare," an additional 208,500 people would die within a decade.[25] The question arises whether libertarians necessarily view this as a bad thing—do they consider those lives worth living? Or are they satisfied with a sort of market-based eugenics where competition determines biological success and failure? The strains on physical and mental health of constant competition, and dwindling chances of "winning," become clearer all the time. The rise of physical pain, in America in particular, is a symptom of overstressed minds and bodies. Among the thousands of tragic stories that make up America's opiate epidemic are many young men who first took painkillers to allow them to cope with the physical demands of playing football, a sport they played because they saw it as their only path into college. On a smaller scale, Ireland has suffered a similar problem with the painkiller codeine.

As the post-industrial economy develops, it is throwing more people back upon their own physical bodies as their last resort, working as cycle couriers or turning to sex work, in order to get by. The "gig economy," in which digital platforms create ultraflexible low-wage labor markets, farming out small chunks of work by the hour, treats work as something that lacks any broader social meaning, beyond its market price. Amazon warehouses are managed with scant recognition of the difference between worker and machine, with toilet breaks being timed, and new wearable technology on the way that will steer every small bodily movement in the most efficient path possible. The only social distinction that matters, from a libertarian perspective, is between the tiny minority of visionary entrepreneurs who are in control, and the millions of powerless bodies that are an object of control.

In the more extreme versions of Mises and Hayek's narrative, progress is guaranteed as the rich and powerful are unleashed to redraw the world as they see fit. These latter-day Napoleons have proved themselves stronger and more adaptable than the rest, and their vast wealth is testimony to that. By 2018, half of the world's wealth was in the hands of just forty-two people, representing a degree of wealth concentration not seen since the early twentieth century.[26] Jeff Bezos, founder of Amazon and the world's richest man, now makes several times more every minute than the average American makes in a year.

Today, *private* families and *private* companies (including hedge funds and private equity funds) control assets and money on a scale that, for most of the twentieth century, was only available to corporations listed on the stock market, which placed certain fiduciary duties and transparency upon the managers. Later in his life, Hayek was entirely open about his sympathy for intergenerational inequalities, hinting at a eugenicist justification for inheritance:

> there are some socially valuable qualities which will be rarely acquired in a single generation but which will generally be formed only by the continuous efforts of two or three. . . . Granted this, it

would be unreasonable to deny that a society is likely to get a better elite if ascent is not limited to one generation, if individuals are not deliberately made to start from the same level.[27]

In our new age of extreme personal wealth, billionaire owners of private companies such as the Koch brothers or Robert Mercer, the hedge-fund billionaire who has backed various populist and alt-right campaigns including Breitbart media, have huge political autonomy, without needing to be public about how they're using it. Facebook and Google are now listed on the stock market, yet their founders retain majority shareholding rights. The family becomes the most important political and economic institution for these new oligarchs, and will ensure that extremes of inequality outlive them. If they cannot achieve actual immortality (of the sort that Peter Thiel is hoping for) then achieving a dynasty becomes the best way of leaving a financial and genetic legacy.

To live in a Darwinian world is discomforting for everyone, including the winners. Even truths and great triumphs are temporary—as Napoleon discovered. The "founders" and oligarchs who now dominate our economies feel this as deeply as anyone. Why else would they strive so hard to keep their wealth away from the taxman, to stockpile it for their children, and their children's children? Why the hostility to the natural aging process? The psychologists who discovered that people become more politically authoritarian when reminded of death also found a tendency to become more acquisitive and materialistic at the same time.[28] They deduce that gratuitous devotion to accumulation is a means of denying one's own mortality. The hatred that many people feel for inheritance tax, regardless of whether they own enough to pay it, comes from the same place.

The financial economy offers one vivid manifestation of the Austrian economic program in action, with its constantly fluctuating prices, which respond to every rumor and tidbit of information, rewarding whichever investor moves fastest, until eventually that investor is actually a computer algorithm. Those at the front line of high-stakes financial trading rarely view it with the detached, objective eye of the economic expert, and are more likely to speak of it as a form of physical combat, a test of nerve. The trader's physical body becomes a resource to be optimized and maintained, using neural supplements and other types of

performance-enhancing drugs to sharpen focus. The financial economy
becomes a battle between physical brains, aided by financial models and
machines. Emotional resources, of courage, ambition, self-esteem, and
sheer greed, become invaluable for those pitting themselves against each
other in this environment. This is against a backdrop of perpetual anxiety,
that the global market is a machine that is always on.

But arguably, the ultimate destination of the Austrian ideology is a
system which starts to eliminate the market altogether, at least in the ordinary sense of companies competing to sell to the same set of customers.
New private empires are built to compete against rival private empires,
with attributes that appear more like those of states than typical businesses. The billionaire Elon Musk, for example, seized the initiative from
NASA and the European Space Agency and made traveling to Mars one of
his entrepreneurial ambitions. Amazon's relationship to retail markets is
becoming closer to that of a regulator than a competitor. Companies such
as Palantir and SCL, which founded the now defunct Cambridge Analytica with Mercer's financial support, straddle commercial, political, and
military domains of intelligence operations. The capacity for violence,
which for Hobbes was the preserve of the "sovereign," is shifting gradually
into private hands, with war, prison systems, immigration enforcement,
and border control increasingly delivered by commercial contractors.
Disruptors emerge, seeking to overturn all existing private empires, so
as to become the ultimate private emperors. The fact that companies are
now acquiring all the forms of surveillance and control that libertarians
originally feared in government does not seem to undermine this vision.
The main center of these Napoleonic disruptors is Silicon Valley, where
the goal is to establish a global nervous system with even greater sensitivity to our feelings than the free market.

7

WAR OF WORDS

From "facts" to "data"

During a question-and-answer session hosted on Facebook in June 2015, Mark Zuckerberg outlined a startling vision of where his company was heading. "One day, I believe we'll be able to send full rich thoughts to each other directly using technology," he said. "You'll just be able to think of something and your friends will immediately be able to experience it too if you'd like. This would be the ultimate communication technology." This prediction of telepathic communication was not just science fiction, but soon seemed to be informing Facebook's hiring strategy. Job listings were put out seeking engineers to develop "novel non-invasive neuroimaging technologies" and "realistic and immersive haptics experiences." Neuroimaging makes visible the activity of the central nervous system by brain scanning, while haptics is the science of touch-based human–computer interaction, of which the computer mouse is one familiar product. Sure enough, Facebook soon appointed Mark Chevillet, an applied neuroscientist from Johns Hopkins University, and Regina Dugan, a former head of the US defense research agency DARPA, who was hired to lead on "technologies that fluidly blend physical and digital worlds."

Technologies are emerging for limited forms of mind-reading. DARPA has invested $60 million in brain–computer interface technology, while a Boston-based start-up, Neurable, is seeking to develop technologies that can track "intentions" of users in virtual reality environments.[1] Elon Musk has founded a company, Neuralink, to develop "neural lace" technologies which will see chips implanted directly into the brain, so as to integrate thinking with computers. Among Dugan's projects at Facebook was the development of technologies through which users could send brief "text messages" using only their thoughts, and could "hear" similar messages through their skin, wearing a vibrating sleeve.[2] Discussing these new technological frontiers in April 2017, Dugan put a neat multicultural spin on the vision that Zuckerberg had laid out a couple of years earlier: "it may be possible for me to think in Mandarin and you to feel it instantly in Spanish."

Leaving aside the advanced technicalities of Zuckerberg's vision, his predictions revealed his own ethical and philosophical worldview. For Zuckerberg, telepathy would be the *ultimate* communication technology toward which all relationships are heading, and which Facebook intends to make available. This denigrates ordinary human languages, whether of a spoken or written form, as inefficient and incomplete, a sign of stunted technological development. The ultimate form of communication would involve no symbolic representation at all, but be an experience of total social intimacy, perhaps even of love.

Elsewhere, Zuckerberg laid out his vision of Facebook's abiding goal, namely "bringing us closer together and building a global community," not simply through facilitating greater connectivity or information sharing, but creating the types of "meaningful groups" that are people's primary basis for attachments and identities.[3] Progress, according to Zuckerberg, is a movement toward greater and greater social and psychological proximity. The end goal is the eradication of all boundaries separating one mind from another, creating a kind of blissful unity in which one doesn't even need to speak or swipe on a screen. It is also a pure intimacy between Facebook users and Facebook itself.

Telepathy can be imagined as a form of empathy, akin to physical intimacy. But it might also serve as a means of intercepting someone's thoughts against their will, and of encrypting communication for strategic purposes. Viewed more aggressively, the thoughts occurring in someone else's mind are a type of secret, that demand specialist techniques to detect or transmit. Nonverbal communication has long been crucial in warfare, for coordinating allies and sabotaging enemies, and the Cold War witnessed many outlandish experiments in telepathy. In 1964, Soviet researchers implanted electrodes in the brain of a female rabbit, and her babies were taken to a submarine several thousand miles away and then killed. According to the researchers, the mother's brain experienced a stab of pain at the precise moment the rabbits were killed.[4]

A memo from 1972 indicates that the US Defense Intelligence Agency was alarmed that the Soviets might actually have mastered psychic techniques of hypnosis and telepathy.[5] One fear was that they might be able to deliberately put American soldiers to sleep, through long-distance hypnosis. During the Korean War, the notion of "brainwashing" provoked panic among US defense officials, that American soldiers were being captured and scientifically converted to communism without their knowledge. In an attempt to meet psychic fire with fire, DARPA approached the Israeli spoon-bending psychic, Uri Geller, to explore whether he could apply his techniques to damaging Soviet weapons.

Thanks to the technical advances being made in Silicon Valley, the fantasy of brain-to-brain communication is becoming a reality, without requiring paranormal leaps. Unlike the Cold War fantasies, the vision of telepathy being pursued by the likes of Zuckerberg or Musk takes the symbolic codes of human culture and politics (the ones we consciously read, interpret, and understand) and replaces them with those of biology and computer software. The brain-to-brain communication of the future will depend on a form of language, just not one that most people are able to understand when they see it. The means of communication will have become privatized.

As with so many of Facebook's innovations, this provokes profound privacy anxieties. Most immediately, how could the user of such technologies avoid having *all* their thoughts read and shared? We all think and feel plenty of things we don't wish to communicate. Facebook says that the technologies will capture only those thoughts "that you have already decided to share by sending them to the speech center of your brain," but what would stop them from harvesting additional information from the brain? Facebook declined to say whether such technologies could be used for advertising, which is Facebook's central commercial purpose, after all.[6] Zuckerberg's vision of the "ultimate communication technology" may unite us in cohesive groups, but more likely it will serve as just a more advanced marketing infrastructure.

The broader philosophical fear is of a society in which people become readable pieces of data, without any recognized interiority. Communication becomes an entirely physical phenomenon, of getting data from one point to another as efficiently as possible, without ambiguity of meaning or understanding. Speech, for example, comes to be treated as the activity that links a brain to vocal cords, which produce vibrations that impact upon an eardrum and then transmit information to another brain. Thought and communication get reduced to their neural dimensions, the sensory networks that process and transmit them. It follows that these networks are amenable to technological augmentation and improvement, just as a walking stick aids someone with weak legs or spectacles improve eyesight.

The work of Charles Darwin and experimental psychologists in the 1870s began this process of rendering the mind observable by physical and behavioral indicators. But the twenty-first century is witnessing the final evaporation of Descartes' vision of the mind as a private, metaphysical entity. This has transformative implications for the nature of knowledge, which are spilling over into our politics and culture in complex and disorientating ways. In place of a mind that captures experiences, with certain distinguished individuals being recognized as experts, there is just a brain, a physical organ that receives impressions, and transmits expressions. Knowledge involves spotting patterns amid billions of such impressions—but that is something that computers can do better than humans.

Once our thoughts and words are reconceived as physical activities, their "objective" perspective becomes less credible. After all, if thinking is a physical activity, how can it be isolated from feelings and intentions? Why should thoughts be isolated from the rest of the body, to which they are connected by the nervous system? The expert claim to be able to separate "feelings" from "knowledge" becomes impossible to sustain, and their dispassionate neutral stance is then just one emotional state among many. Language and thought lose their fundamentally representational role (to reflect reality like a mirror) and become mere behaviors among many, to be tracked in search of something significant. The crucial question is who has the equipment to do the tracking, and whether they are doing so in pursuit of empathy or greater control. The most likely answer is that they are seeking both.

The physical mind

Computers are originally instruments of war, as are the networks that connect them to each other. From the early 1940s through to the early 1960s, the needs of the US military drove the development of digital computers, with academic centers (primarily MIT and Stanford) and commercial companies (primarily IBM) sweeping up many of the dividends. The first electronic computers were built during the Second World War at vast cost, to help produce more accurate antiaircraft guns. The threat of catastrophic aerial attack during the Cold War then led to the construction of Semi-Automatic Ground Environment (SAGE) in the late 1950s, a control room consisting of screens and visualization tools, aimed at detecting incoming enemy bombers. US defense agencies first sought to connect up university computers in the mid-1960s, creating an embryonic version of the Internet, on the assumption that a computational network would be more resilient to nuclear attack than a central hub.

It was only the emergency of the Second World War, then the Cold War threat of mutually assured destruction, that created sufficient political intensity for digital computers to be built at all. The Second World War brought the scientific and military establishments into a tight alliance which, in the United States at least, has remained intact ever since. The formation of the National Defense Research Committee in 1940 created the template for a new style of research investment, which was high-budget, high-risk, often classified, and aimed at matters of the greatest national urgency. This would later become known as "Big Science." It was also interdisciplinary, bringing together "pure" and "applied" scientists in a way that was essential for the development of computing. Under these high-pressure conditions, questions of "theory" and those of "engineering" were addressed simultaneously. The way in which digital culture straddles the material realm of technology and the abstract realm of codes and symbols is a legacy of how high-tech warfare brought mechanics, mathematicians, and philosophers into the same discussions.

Some of the logic behind this technological innovation would have been recognizable to Carl von Clausewitz, over a century earlier. Computers serve long-standing logistical needs, of coordinating one's own wartime resources and anticipating the enemy's. Just as Clausewitz believed a great general needed to be able to "scent out the truth," much of the computational capacity developed after 1940 was aimed at sensing what was going on, helping decision makers orient themselves in a fast-moving and hostile world. The problem of aerial bombing during the Blitz, followed quickly by the threat of ballistic missiles and nuclear bombs (later to be combined into nuclear ballistic missiles), meant that ordinary human perception and cognition was no longer adequate to keep track of enemy activity.

But digital computation extends well beyond the imaginings of Clause-witz in the mechanization of thinking itself. In the years immediately before the Second World War, various mathematicians, philosophers, and psychologists mused on whether human thought and communication could be modeled as mathematical formulae. The British mathematician (and subsequently celebrated code breaker) Alan Turing's 1937 paper, "On Computable Numbers," imagined a "Turing Machine" which could be programmed to perform basic instructions in response to different symbols that it was fed in a random order. While the Turing Machine was never built, this vision signaled the leap from the abstract mathematics of com-putation to its technological construction. Humans would be required to program such machines, but the machines could then perform various acts of calculation on their own.

This idea of a programmable machine is now so familiar to us, that we often fail to notice the peculiar assumptions on which it rests. First, it assumes that computation is an activity, like any other. As Ross Ashby, a British psy-chiatrist and associate of Turing, wrote in 1948, "the brain is not a thinking machine, it is an *acting* machine."[7] Mental processes are tasks, which can be split into a series of separate chunks: this is what it means to process some-thing *digitally*. These tasks can be pieced together in the form of code, which a machine can then execute one by one. Mark Zuckerberg's belief in telepathy ultimately rests on the idea that "thoughts" are nothing but a series of physical motions, whose patterns can potentially be read like the smile on a face or an encrypted message to be cracked. What things *mean* is really just a question of pattern recognition, that is, what order they appear in. In that sense, *all* interpretation and understanding is akin to code breaking.

Second, the programmer instructs the computer to abide by certain rules, which are then converted into commands to be executed. Activities are ruled by hierarchies, not unlike the military. Such instructions pro-duce a world that is—hopefully—more obedient to the wishes of the com-mander. The basic linguistic form of computational language is "NOW DO THIS." Both programmer and military commander fear that instruc-tions will fail to be transmitted clearly enough, and chaos will ensue. Clausewitz warned of the problem of "friction" which impedes military plans, as they come into contact with a messy and changing reality. Good instructions are those which are as clear and simple as possible, with mini-mal rhetorical or aesthetic flourishes.

None of this actually requires language, as it is conventionally understood. The success of communication depends on how effectively it travels from A to B. Napoleon's semaphore lines cut across Europe (the "chappe telegraph") using a chain of mechanical movements. Humans send instructions to cars using steering wheels and accelerator pedals. A smartphone conveys information to its owner by buzzing in their pocket. Effective human–computer interaction operates across various "interfaces," of which screens and text are only one. The goal of haptics, of the sort being explored by Facebook, is to render the division between the human and the digital less and less noticeable.

Understanding communication along such quasi-military lines has profound implications for the nature of knowledge and expertise. The most important capacity of the human mind or expert, from this perspective, is not to produce a valid image of reality, but to effectively issue or execute a command. Equally, the main political question that arises is not "can I trust this person to tell the truth?" but "will this person lead me to my destination?" If the iconic example of seventeenth-century knowledge was the map, produced according to strict principles of geometry, the twenty-first-century equivalent would be Google Maps, a technology that only requires us to know our destination, and then converts that into a series of commands to turn left or right. We provide Google Maps with a desired goal, and it provides us with instructions. The function of Google Maps is not to provide a portrait of reality, but to execute a plan.

Weaponizing the mind

As the Cold War progressed, the military expectations for computers continued to grow. Where SAGE had required human beings to monitor aircraft data, systems developed in the 1960s reduced the human involvement in nuclear defense systems. Computers could now potentially spot incoming missiles and launch a response on their own. These computers were large enough to fill a room, guzzling vast quantities of electricity and research dollars. But military researchers argued that only if defense intelligence could be raised to a superhuman level, could the West be safe from potential Soviet attack.

Intelligence gathering and effective communication had long been integral to effective warfare. But as aerial bombardment gave way to the threat of intercontinental nuclear ballistic missiles, the technologies of war outstripped the capacities of the human mind to anticipate and control them. These threats elevated the academic fields of computer science, game theory, and behavioral and cognitive science within US defense policy. Where so much hangs on one individual decision (as it does where nuclear weapons are concerned), the question of what is a "rational" course of action needs answering with the best mechanical and mathematical equipment available.

The RAND Corporation think tank achieved notoriety for its various simulations of nuclear war, developed in an effort to identify the optimal strategy if the day ever arrived. "Virtual reality" was born as a way of testing out different military strategies, because there was no opportunity for real-world trial and error. If Napoleon turned war into a conflict between national populations, the Cold War turned it into a conflict between national intelligence infrastructures, both in the sense of espionage and of "artificial" intelligence. That paradigm still obtains today. Vladimir Putin has expressed the view, regularly advanced by others such as Elon Musk, that the country that leads the world in artificial intelligence will dominate the twenty-first century.[8]

The initial question put forward by Turing was whether a machine could "think," which he argued it could. But this quickly flips into speculation as to what kind of "machine" is the mind. During the 1940s and 1950s, as computers were becoming imbued with almost metaphysical and humane characteristics, cognitive scientists reimagined humans as circuits of information. Mind and machine become directly comparable, and the question arises of which is superior for different purposes. Where a task involves speed of calculation or mathematical modeling (as it does when tracking and predicting aerial attacks), the machine inevitably outperforms its human creator. As computers have come to "learn" a wider variety of human languages, thanks especially to designing computers around the same format as the human brain, more and more cultural forms of communication can be digitized. At a certain point in this development, a human's sole function is to have feelings, intentions and desires, and technology will do the rest.

One of the most alluring qualities of computers, from the perspective of various Silicon Valley entrepreneurs and ideologues such as Ray Kurzweil, is that they don't necessarily die in the way that human bodies do. This suggests that with sufficient augmentation, a human could live for far longer, or even forever. If thoughts can be shared directly with other brains, thanks to technology, then at some point an entire human mind could perhaps be uploaded to a computer where it could potentially live forever. This bizarre fantasy, known as the "singularity," is symptomatic of the underlying military character of computing, whose initial *raison d'être* was to preserve "our" existence at any cost, and to destroy "theirs." Adapting Hobbes, this is a dream of life as nasty, brutish, and *long*. Here we see another manifestation of social Darwinism, in which truth is identified with sheer survival in the face of threats, rather than with reason or consensus.

In the immediate aftermath of the Cold War, it wasn't entirely clear what the Internet was *for* as a civilian technology, other than for those specialists in academic computer science departments. The launch of the World Wide Web in 1990 ushered in a brief period of idealism, that could scarcely have been more different from the Cold War paranoia that drove early networked computing. Dreams of "e-democracy" pictured a more inclusive public sphere. The main obstacle to achieving this was the "digital divide" between the connected and the unconnected, and therefore Internet access needed to be treated as a basic democratic entitlement. This imagined network computing in Enlightenment terms, as an advanced form of printing press or parliament, or perhaps some combination of the two. In any case, it proposed—optimistically—that its function was representational and democratic.

The Internet is now well established as a civilian technology, through which we shop, socialize, date, and access any kind of "content." The spread of smartphones in the twenty-first century means that concerns about the "digital divide" are no longer as pressing. Thanks to a growing range of physical digital interfaces, we are also connected to our urban environments, material artifacts, and bodies, in ways that we are largely oblivious to. But what is becoming increasingly clear, now that the early optimism surrounding "cyberspace" and "virtual community" has dissipated, is that the Internet retains something of its military character. Whether in the service of big business such as Facebook or of government agencies, it remains most effective as a tool of surveillance, pattern recognition, and control.

The way we are ensnared in digital networks, by apps and platforms, is with the promise of more efficient coordination: it's not that the world will become better *known* to us, but that it will become more *obedient* to us. Uber, for example, relieves us of the need to *know* taxi numbers, addresses, or maps, replacing them all with a technology of command. Zuckerberg's vision of telepathy is also one of commands, allowing the "user" to send thought A to person B, with minimal interruption or effort. Of course, in the process, the companies that facilitate this coordination are seeking to render themselves so indispensable to the social world that the ultimate capacity for control lies with them.

Digital networks certainly have the capacity to produce new forms of knowledge, thanks to the data we now routinely leave in our wake, but little of that knowledge is being made public. The secrecy in Silicon Valley invites as many conspiracy theories as Cold War defense agencies attracted in the 1950s or 1960s. By design, this is not a technology that supports scientific ideals of factual consensus or objectivity, but one that supports military ideals of effective coordination leading to victory. Its key traits are speed and sensitivity to change, providing the kind of knowledge needed in times of war, rather than the kind conducive to peace.

Between mind and world

Most Internet and smartphone users are aware that these technologies are instruments of surveillance, even if few of us spend very long reflecting on this. Services that are free to the user, such as social media platforms or search engines, make their money from the collection and analysis of data, which can then be used to sell targeted advertising space. As the privacy expert Bruce Schneier has said, "surveillance is the business model of the Internet."[9] This raises various political concerns about how companies will use this new power. In particular, Google, Apple, Facebook, Amazon, and Uber are acquiring unprecedented insights into our thoughts, feelings, movements, relationships, and tastes, of a sort that was never available to traditional social scientists, statisticians, or market researchers. When married to analytical algorithms, the predictive power of big data is now legion, and the potential uses and abuses of it are troubling. Life-changing decisions about policing, hiring, consumer credit, counter-terrorism, and much else can all be informed and shaped by data analytics, but this power is often invisible and lies mostly within an opaque commercial sector.[10]

Big data shares one thing in common with traditional statistics, in that both are numerical, but the political differences are stark. Traditional scientific societies, such as the Royal Society, and national statistics agencies involve a small group of experts producing knowledge, that is then made available to the public. This can provoke resentment, where members of the public feel unrepresented by the facts being produced. But with big data, things are effectively the other way around: the mass public are generating knowledge all the time with their search queries, movements, and Facebook statuses, which is then made available to a small group of experts. Since it is a commercial resource, there is no incentive to share this intelligence.

To really understand the transformative power of Silicon Valley, it's necessary to consider the ambitions of these companies in ways that extend beyond politics and economics. While Zuckerberg's comments about telepathy might sound far-fetched, they were also remarkably honest about the ultimate objective of Internet companies such as Facebook. Their real goal is to provide the infrastructure through which humans encounter the world. This is a philosophical intervention as much as a technological one, bringing computers to bear on the basic relation of "mind" and "world" that had caused Descartes so much doubt in the 1630s. According to this vision, when the mind wants to know something, it will go to Google; when it wants to communicate with someone, it will turn to Facebook. When we want to be somewhere else, we click on Uber; and when we simply want something, Amazon will make it arrive. And so on.

For evidence of the success of this project to date, witness the proportion of people in a train carriage immersed in their phones, and the number walking down a street while looking at a screen. Our "addiction" to our devices provokes a lingering cultural concern of what we may be failing to notice while staring at screens. If we treat these machines purely in terms of the knowledge or content they communicate to us, as if they were simply high-tech newspapers, we misunderstand their power. The allure of the smartphone derives from its military inheritance: the screen represents a world that is obedient to our commands. The scrolling and "swiping" hold our attention, until the intended function of the app or platform starts to dissolve into its constant, fidgety use. The addictive quality of smartphones derives from how they engage us physically (in this case via our hands) as much as mentally, via our eyes and minds. We study our screens more because they are under our control, than for whatever information they might impart.

In the longer term, screens will be too cumbersome to facilitate this ambition of mediating mind and world. Voice-recognition technologies, such as Amazon Echo and Apple Siri, make it possible to capture thoughts and wishes aurally, and turn these into data. Amazon has patented a technology that detects who is speaking at any moment, and gradually develops a profile of their personality and tastes. Showing a curious mixture of sensory metaphors, this is known as "voice-sniffing" technology. Wearable technologies, such as Apple Watch and Fitbit, capture the data emitted by our bodies as they respond to different environments or products. Amazon Dash is a small device that attaches to a wall, with a button to press whenever the user notices a household product has run out, which is then transmitted to Amazon as an order. What all these technologies do is to minimize the chance of an individual expressing their thoughts via some medium *other* than that owned by the platform in question. Needless to say, anything that could get directly to "thoughts" as they arise in the brain would be the most immediate of all.

The infrastructure being built by Silicon Valley is unlike the dystopian twentieth-century fantasies of the surveillance state, with oppressive secret police. Similarly, it is unlike statistical techniques of census, polling, or surveys, which require specialists to go out into society and ask questions, potentially inconveniencing respondents in the process. The difference is this: we welcome digital surveillance into our lives, because it promises to bring our personal lives under control. It allows us to issue orders: "we need more kitchen cleaner!," "send me a driver!," "tell me the weather forecast!" It is a bleak reflection on human psychology that we accept the growing global dominance of Uber and the rest, mainly because they offer us the chance to exercise small acts of dominance ourselves, over taxi drivers, information, and material goods.

Everything we do is leaving an impression. That impression is data. But data of this sort isn't quite the same thing as knowledge or facts. It is closer to the footprints that are left on a beach: evidence of some past physical activity. In the case of Silicon Valley's tech giants, the beach in question is open to the public, but privately owned and run, granting its owners exclusive rights to analyze the prints in the sand. In the utopia of Zuckerberg et al., every thought or emotion that passes through our minds will leave an impression, opening up the recesses of human psychology to inspection on a vast scale. Critics of Silicon Valley occasionally argue that data should really belong to the user, given that we produced it (as if ordering an Uber were like writing a poem). But if the beach analogy is correct, would it really make sense to say that my footprints are *mine*, especially if the sand itself was not? This is the crux of the problem. Unlike statisticians or social scientists, Silicon Valley is not seeking to create an accurate portrait of society, but to provide the infrastructure on which we all depend, which will then capture our movements and sentiments with the utmost sensitivity.

Advances in machine-learning techniques have improved sensitivity beyond that of human consciousness. "Sentiment analysis" involves training algorithms to detect different types of emotion in a given sentence, and can be used to monitor the emotions being expressed on Twitter, Facebook, email, or (due to voice-recognition technology) phones. "Facial analytics" does something similar to detect how someone might be feeling from the movements in their face, and can now apparently be used to detect a person's sexuality.[11] The entire field of "affective computing," which is transforming market research, uses machine learning to enable computers to identify emotions by means of body language and behavior. A wide variety of different data points can be analyzed together, such that our shopping habits can be correlated to our commuting patterns, and these to our political opinions. One study found that an average smartphone user touches their device 2,617 times a day, each of which is a potential data point of some kind, seeing as the screen is touch-sensitive.[12] Given so much attention to the physical body as an object of digital tracking, it is difficult to describe the Internet as a "virtual" or "unreal" space any longer.

The further surveillance reaches into our lives and across cultures, the more emotionally intelligent machines can become. The Boston-based affective computing company Affectiva boasted in 2017 that it had analyzed 4.7 million faces from seventy-five countries.[13] Another company spun out of the University of Washington named Megaface has a database of 5 million images of 672,000 people. Ira Kemelmacher-Shlizerman, a computer science professor advising Megaface, argued that "we need to test facial recognition on a planetary scale to enable practical applications—testing on a larger scale lets you discover the flaws and successes of recognition algorithms."[14] Endless expansion of surveillance is justified on the basis that it aids machine learning.

Analogue statistical techniques, such as surveys, require us to present our views and preferences in deliberate, objective, and coherent terms, often with a moment of reflection. By contrast, digital platforms only require us all to carry on emoting and demanding whatever and however we wish, and the algorithms will detect patterns in the mess that arises. No finite number of classifications or identifiers (such as "employed," "unemployed," "self-employed") needs to be selected in advance. Feelings do not need to be rendered conscious or verbal in order to be captured. Everything can be discerned from whatever words, images, and trails happen to be left lying around.

Data analysts now possess a huge advantage over traditional technocrats and bureaucrats. The hostility directed toward experts stems from a deep-lying sense that, in their attention to mathematical laws and models, they are not really interested in individual *people*, their desires, fears, and lives. Facebook doesn't suffer the same alienation, because its "front-end" and its "back-end" are so utterly different. Their users express themselves in their own words and feelings, presenting unique biographies. Behind the scenes, this is gobbled up and mathematically processed. As the math has become more and more sophisticated, the user no longer even experiences it as mathematical.

From science to data science

A curiosity of big-data analytics is that its specialists are relatively uninterested in whether the data is generated by people, particles in the atmosphere, cars, financial prices, or bacteria. Data scientists are more often trained in mathematics or physics than in social science. They generate knowledge about our behavior, but they don't profess any expertise about *people*, or *shopping*, or *finance*, or *cities*. They're not really paying attention to *us*. Their skill is to study those aspects of reality that have already been quantified, rather than to study reality itself.

This is generating a new type of expert from the one who was born in the seventeenth century. They don't study nature or society, in the way that the archetypal expert does, but seek patterns in data that computers have already captured. As opposed to a scientist, a data scientist might better be compared to a librarian, someone who is skilled in navigating a vast collection of already-recorded information. The difference is that the data archive is growing at great speed, thanks to the mass of nonhuman sensors that gather it, and can only be sifted algorithmically.

Take the example of psychology. Data science reveals a great deal that is of interest to psychologists, given the ability of algorithms to detect emotions, behaviors, and anxieties across populations. By design, Facebook generates psychologically revealing data, which is how they enable their advertising clients to target individuals with immense precision. After the 2016 US election, it was reported that it was possible to select from 175,000 versions of a political advert, and direct it at precisely the right person on the basis of 300 of their "likes."[15] And yet the data scientist needn't have any theoretical view on how political attitudes are formed or what political attitudes even are. Nor do they have any pre-held view of which ones are worth studying in the first place. They are simply able to detect how different behaviors, images, or words happen to correlate within a certain population.

The distinctive property of big data (its size) is also its defining challenge. The job of the data analyst is to help extract something meaningful from a data set, and ignore the rest. The analyst's value lies in pruning vast quantities of useless data, leaving only that which deserves our attention.[16] But if they lack any intrinsic interest in the topic at hand (other than the mathematics), they also have no view of their own regarding what "something meaningful" means—they are therefore in the service of a client. Alternatively, their biases and assumptions creep in, without being consciously reflected on or criticized.[17]

The clients for data science are multiplying all the time. "Quants" can make big money working for Wall Street banks and hedge funds, building algorithms to analyze price movements. "Smart city" projects depend on data scientists to extract patterns of activity from the frenetic movements of urban populations, resources, and transport. Firms such as Peter Thiel's Palantir help security services identify potential security threats, by isolating dangerous patterns of behavior. And then there are the murky cases of consultancies, such as Cambridge Analytica, who worked for political clients to help tailor messaging to particular voters. In every case, the data scientist can provide advice on what to do, to serve a particular interest or agenda, but they are rarely in the job of producing matters of consensual public *fact*.

Commercial analytics companies are inevitably concerned with commercial secrecy and client confidentiality. But where big data is concerned, it's not clear what a "fact" would actually mean: what data reveals depends on what you're looking for, which depends on who you are. Knowledge of this nature serves strategic goals, rather than producing a common reality. What truth is contained within vast and messy data sets depends partly on what you are hoping to see. Where so much of our behavior and history is captured automatically, it becomes possible for a cynic to curate a partial and misleading portrait of a person or event. This combines dangerously with racist and nationalist politics, which seeks to exaggerate cultural and moral divisions, marshalling carefully selected imagery to do so. Evidence doesn't even need to be faked, if the extraction of relevant data is done with sufficient political bias.

Stripped of strategic goals, the findings of data science have a strange banality, even an obviousness, about them. Google can tell us that people search "flu remedy" before they get sick. Uber knows that demand for taxis in downtown Manhattan is highest at a certain time on a Friday night. Facebook knows that forty-year-old men in a particular suburb of Bristol like craft beer and Radiohead. As facts, none of these is earth-shattering. But for anyone seeking to predict and control these activities (and to do so *quickly*, in real time), this information has tremendous value.

A central challenge for traditional statisticians is to ensure that their data sets and models are *representative* of the broader population they are aiming to portray. If a sample of the population is to be surveyed (for instance by a polling company), some efforts need to be made to ensure it is a sample that roughly mirrors the broader demographic of society. Techniques of representative sampling took off during the 1920s, and provided the crucial ingredient for the emergence of opinion polling soon after. Achieving representativeness is an implicitly democratic aspiration, as it aims to ensure that the facts about society treat everybody equally, taking everyone into account, although this can fail for various reasons. By contrast, digital data analytics typically studies the data that happens to have been captured—the question of who or what it "represents" is secondary. The civic dimension is therefore harder to sustain.

What it offers instead is immense sensitivity to fluctuating mood and activity, such as consumer sentiment, energy usage, indeed any movement or thought that might leave an impression. Rather than studying any "representative sample," it tracks as many people as possible, which for the tech giants—Amazon, Google, Facebook et al.—is a very large number indeed. Not only do these platforms track behavior of their users well beyond perceived use (for instance tracing an Uber user, even after the ride has ended, or a Facebook user when they are visiting Web pages other than Facebook), several of them also generate data profiles of individuals who don't have accounts with them, purely on the basis of traces those people have left elsewhere. Such blanket surveillance generates incredibly rich profiles of those it targets, but it's not typically employed for purposes of generating a representative portrait of society as a whole. Data analytics does not yield conclusive facts such as "youth unemployment" or "literacy," but detects clusters of feeling and trends that might then become targets of advertising or campaigning.

Such emotional sensitivity offers potentially acute forms of control for those seeking to influence the public. In 2017, Facebook issued a private report for advertising clients, boasting that they were able to identify teenagers who felt "insecure," "worthless" and in "need of a confidence boost," on the assumption that these would be more receptive to certain types of advertising.[18] Had that report not been leaked to the *Australian* newspaper in May 2017, this marketing technique would have remained secret from the public—just another "unknown known" shaping our everyday environment.

Digital technology means that virtually any cultural trait can now be quantified. The mechanical power to accumulate and analyze this kind of knowledge was developed in the face of specific hostile threats from the air, the like of which the human mind and conventional expertise were powerless to mitigate. Today our everyday lives are structured by techniques of intelligence that were initially developed to plan and resist nuclear attacks. The result is that, while certain aspects of our lives become more and more obedient to our personal whims, the possibility for peaceful consensus seems to be evaporating. Meanwhile, the capacity to mobilize people in some quasi-military fashion has reached unprecedented technical heights. One of the consequences of this is that political argument, especially when conducted primarily online, has come to feel more like conflict.

The pursuit of war by other means

Networked computing has always featured in-jokes. Through most of its history, these were jokes made between programmers, who found fun in the fact that they were able to communicate in ways that the rest of society could not understand. Pieces of code could be written in ways that included puns for the entertainment of other programmers. A classic computer geek T-shirt reads "There's no place like 127.0.0.1," a joke referring to the fact that 127.0.0.1 is the most common localhost IP address—or what is otherwise known as "home."

Humor does a couple of things here, which can have serious political consequences. First it serves to reinforce a common but exclusive identity. As the technicians who send instructions to computers, they connect senior decision makers to the means of executing those decisions. While programmers have little control over the whole system, they retain the power of sabotage. The in-jokes of geek culture often refer to gentle tactics of obstruction and slowing things down.

But geek humor also does something else. It plays with the fact that two different kinds of language are being employed. There is the language of human culture, involving metaphor, symbolic representation, and poetic description, as ways of grasping the complexity of human experience. And there is the language of machines, in which every chunk of information is a command to be executed, referring only to the internally computable world of data and algorithms. Computer coders are able to switch between the two, and create jokes out of the ambiguities and misunderstandings that arise. Things expressed in one domain can appear funny when transported to the other.

The same is true of other communities that interact heavily via computer networks, such as gamers. Gaming can facilitate a type of gleeful nihilism, in which nothing matters except in terms of how it contributes to the outcome. Violence becomes purely instrumental, shorn of any ethical conundrums, much as it was in Clausewitz's ideal of war. The cliché of the gamer is of the young man shut in his bedroom, who knows nothing of the physical reality of war. (In an age of drone strikes and automated weaponry, where foreign interventions can be executed from control rooms in Nevada, maybe that *is* the reality.) Yet the gap between the "virtual reality" of the game and the "material reality" of the civilian world outside produces a type of irony, in which features of one can be transported into the other, and vice versa, for comic effect.

For similar reasons, humor has also been central to the development of Internet trolling, and it is here that we start to see some of the connections to our broader political culture and the problems the Internet poses for it. Humor and memes allow trolls to create a sense of community, putting up a cultural fortress around themselves through clever forms of encryption. As with coders or gamers, trolls operate in an online space where everything is about point-scoring and controlling the outcome. When this comes into contact with ordinary Internet users using computers for day-to-day social activities, such as organizing events, sharing photos of their children, or grieving for loved ones, it can wreak havoc. Trolling is really a civilian form of guerrilla warfare, whereby those without any formally recognized power or status use the one power they have, namely of sabotage. This may result in some mirth, but it doesn't actually achieve anything, other than to highlight the vulnerability of social rituals and institutions to being trolled. Trolls weaponize ordinary cultural symbols and codes, for no other reason than to discover how far they can be weaponized.

Various aspects of troll culture have leaked into mainstream political discourse, which is becoming increasingly organized around concepts of meme and sabotaging of opponents. Arguments on Twitter often take on a game-like quality of seeking to hold other users up to ridicule or seeking to "own" them by highlighting the internal contradictions in what they've written. Those who express moral sincerity online are accused of "virtue signalling," as if all dialogue were a competitive game, in which every move aims to gain strategic advantage. Causing offense is often perceived as a form of victory, something which is taken to illegal extremes in the hateful and threatening messages that are now routinely sent to public figures, especially women and civil rights campaigners. These communities often seek as much harm as possible (treating words as weapons), then immediately retreat back to the alternative position, that this is all just a "joke" or "freedom of speech" (treating words as harmless symbols).

The central weapon in the armory of the troll is to mess with conventional norms of anonymity and identification for destructive effect. Those norms are (or were) absolutely central to how expert communities were first formed, and work as follows. An argument or scientific claim is put forward for evaluation by peers, but without much attention to the author's name, and sometimes without any author identified at all (in scientific publishing this occurs through blind peer review). The text is assessed on its own merits, and if it is deemed valid then the author becomes identified, and it contributes to their public reputation. The delicate interplay of anonymity and public identification is the legacy of the seventeenth-century etiquette in which experts took great pains never to impute bad character or intentions on the part of their peers. Similarly in journalism, the author's name accompanies a text, but the validity of the story does not traditionally hang on the moral character of the journalist.

Trolls maximize anonymity for themselves while maximizing identification of their target, even if it is not someone who is seeking public recognition at all. Platforms such as Twitter make it easy for individuals to participate in public discussions without revealing their identity. The extreme case of this unbalancing act in troll culture is known as "doxing," where the private and offline identity of someone is deliberately revealed for malicious purposes. "Call-out culture," in which individuals are publicly identified and shamed online for their identities or opinions, has become a problem, especially within student communities. Meanwhile, more and more information is revealed about public figures, to the point where it becomes virtually impossible to judge them on the basis of their public words alone. Social media archives and email leaks allow the world to view and criticize their behavior, whether or not it is obviously relevant to their public status and credibility.

The email hacking scandal known as "Climategate" saw thousands of emails being leaked from the University of East Anglia Climate Research Unit in 2009–11, aimed at undermining both the authority of climate science but also the neutrality and objectivity of climate scientists themselves. This form of trolling follows the logic of encryption and interception, and harnesses them as weapons of cultural war. The enemy is rendered as transparent as possible, while the perpetrator remains opaque. Forums that might traditionally have been viewed as civil spaces of reasoned dialogue become reconfigured as spaces of ad hominem attack.

Inequalities of anonymity are exacerbated by concentrations of private wealth which can be employed toward secretive political ends. Basic principles of accountability and transparency have become a disadvantage in these battles of exposure and obfuscation. This is why the specter of Russia and of private wealth haunt us, as we seek explanations for political upheavals and chaos: they offer the perfect base from which to wage informational war, being less constrained by public regulation. Reports of alliances between the Kremlin, billionaire owners of private companies (as opposed to shareholders of corporations), WikiLeaks, and firms, such as Cambridge Analytica, sometimes feel like conspiracy theories because— by definition and design—such entities are not subject to any expert or regulatory oversight. If the ideal of presenting facts in public in search of peaceful consensus has become a source of strategic vulnerability, then Western democracies are in serious trouble.

Sabotaging power

As for so many other insurgents, the objective of the troll is not to gain power but to inflict pain. Rather than as means of representation or reason, words become instruments of violence, which seek out human weakness then exploit it. Libertarians might argue that emotional harm is not "violence," but this is contradicted by the behavior of trolls, who pursue emotional harm with a militaristic and sadistic relish. The infamous alt-right troll Milo Yiannopoulos, who attracted attention for his extreme sexism, frequently sneered to those he offended that "I don't care about your feelings." And yet the entire careers of figures like Yiannopoulos depend on the assumption that people's feelings *do* matter, for otherwise his insults would have received no attention. The goal of a figure such as Yiannopoulos is to achieve real harm.

As states have found when fighting guerrilla wars or a "war on terror," it is extremely difficult to fight against the powerless, because they have no obvious centers of organization. This was precisely the original justification for the creation of the Internet: that if America were to come under nuclear attack, its computational capacity would be distributed across various nodes, and be more resilient as a result. But one legacy of this military technology for politics has been that it is extremely useful to anyone who feels ignored and powerless, as a way of gaining attention and wreaking havoc. Clause-witz observed that a disorganized but passionate army was a fearsome force. Where emotions run high, tight hierarchical organization isn't so necessary.

The Internet has turned out to be very effective at undermining estab-lished institutions of democracy, but less so when it comes to constructing new ones. It can pull down the old systems of representation, but it remains to be seen what new structures (if any) will replace them. This includes the attacks on the "mainstream media," which in its supposed commitment to "impartiality" and "objectivity" can be easily mocked and exposed for the hypocrisy or privilege of its individual journalists. Established political party machines and electoral processes can be "hacked," both in a literal sense (as Hillary Clinton's 2016 presidential campaign discovered) and in a less literal sense, as once-implausible figures such as Jeremy Corbyn and Don-ald Trump can impose themselves on institutions that previously shunned them. The logic in each case is the same, namely that the mechanisms of representation—be they parties, broadcasters, expertise—are deemed cor-rupted by their own power, and need disassembling. In these situations the technology of the Internet meshes perfectly with the anti-elitist instincts of populism, and especially with the resentful sentiments of nationalism.

From the perspective of the troll, it is more honest to conceive of politics as warfare than to do so in terms of the quest for consensus or peace. "Neutral" perspectives, whether adopted by journalists, experts, or leaders, are judged a sham. Once language itself is turned into a tool of violence (which is some-thing that arises as much from the logic of digital computers as from popu-lism or identity politics), it becomes impossible to sustain an independent or objective stance in a political argument. Every statement becomes a strategic move, one way or the other, something that trolls will eagerly demonstrate by going through the past statements of public figures for inconsistencies.

The flipside of this dialogue-as-warfare is dialogue-as-empathy. While one set of spaces emerges in which differences are expressed as a form of violence (metaphorical or otherwise), another is created to maximize empathy. Mark Zuckerberg's stated desire to unite people, not simply into a global information network, but into more "meaningful groups" assumes that people want minimal conflict in their lives, eventually leading to a total, silent intimacy between brains. "Our success isn't just based on whether we can capture videos and share them with friends," he writes in his 2017 open letter, "it's about whether we're building a community that helps keep us safe." But ultimately how different is that from nationalist projects of uniting people around their shared resentments and phobias? In an environment characterized by openness and global connectivity, the allure of sanctuaries becomes all the greater, not just for the weak and the victimized, but also (or especially so) for those who fear losing their power, wealth, and racial advantages. At the same time as the argument for "free speech" has collapsed into the nihilistic libertarianism of troll culture, the argument for "community" has morphed into a hyperdefensive valorization of intimacy.

Mining the crowd

The businesses that own the means of data production are acquiring an unprecedented level of power. In some sense this is traditional monopoly power, inasmuch as it allows them to control the prices of goods and services (such as advertising), in the way that economists warn monopolies will do. Like many wealthy corporations, these monopolies use their money to try and influence politics and civil society in ways that aren't always obvious. The Google Transparency Project, which aims to hold Google to account, identified 330 academic papers published between 2005 and 2017 which touched on public policy issues that are relevant to Google, and discovered that while 54% of the academics involved were funded by Google, most of them did not disclose that fact.[19] This type of power has led some to compare these new platforms to the oil conglomerates of the past. But this doesn't reflect the type of quasi-military power that is at stake in the digitization of everyday life.

Data secrecy can be countered by open data projects, in which data accumulated by public institutions (such as state departments and municipalities) is made available as a public good. It can also be alleviated by alliances between academic researchers and commercial platforms. Twitter, for example, makes a considerable amount of its data "stream" available for public analysis, while Google allows users to search trends in search data. Companies such as Facebook have hired academics to analyze their data, and many of these experts are still permitted to publish in academic journals. But these developments remain hindered by the ambiguities of public–private partnerships. For example, the IT infrastructure used to build e-government projects or "smart cities" comes from the commercial sector, and the companies that provide it often retain control over the data that results. The US government outsources IT services in areas of the greatest importance to national security, with Amazon Web Services hosting classified systems for the CIA for example.

Among the things we don't know is quite how effective platforms are in influencing our behavior, emotions, and preferences. This uncertainty is exacerbated by the marketing bravado of companies such as Cambridge Analytica, who had repeatedly exaggerated their political influence before they were disbanded. Most commercial websites engage in small forms of social experimentation all the time, seeking to know which of two different design layouts results in more click-throughs or purchases (what's called "A/B testing"). This is relatively innocent, but when combined with artificial intelligence that can interpret user-made textual and photographic content, then added to analysis of other behavior elsewhere, people become understandably fearful about the potential for social control. A sense of paranoia now surrounds some of the tech giants, especially Facebook, which was discovered to have sold $100,000 of advertising space to a pro-Kremlin Russian "troll farm" in the run-up to the 2016 US presidential election, which was then seen by 126 million Americans. This suggests Facebook may have been actively complicit in (and profiting from) the production of "fake news."

One interpretation holds that Facebook *needs* their users to become more and more emotionally expressive and volatile, in order for Zuckerberg's technological ambitions to succeed. First, only by having access to reams and reams of facial expressions, emojis, and emotional text, can artificial intelligence learn to interpret human beings. Our rage, glee, sorrow, and horror provide tutorials for machines learning how to behave like a human. Second, by expressing our most authentic feelings, we provide acute data about ourselves through which further advertising can be sold. The "attention economy," over which Facebook possesses immense monopolistic power, is fertile territory for transgressive and violent political expression to take root, turning rage and shock into engagement. Regardless of Zuckerberg's stated political views, there are undeniable overlaps between his company's financial interests and extremist political interests.

The scenario that results is a variant on the SAGE control room of the late 1950s, only now it is behavioral and emotional trends that are flitting across the screens of the commanders, rather than aircraft. Political turmoil and emotional upheavals can be viewed like weather events, tracked in real time, and studied in search of patterns. Silicon Valley has undoubtedly produced its own elites and its own experts, but they do not fit the template of mainstream political and professional elites, nor do they possess the same form of expertise as the statisticians, scientists, and economists who first emerged in the seventeenth century. The central difference is that, where those traditional elites and experts seek to monopolize the means of representation (as journalists, political representatives, scientists, statisticians, and so on), their digital successors seek to monopolize the means of *control*. Like military commanders but of everyday civilian life, they are stockpiling *intelligence*, but showing relatively little interest in conventional facts.

While we don't know exactly how effective these techniques of manipulation are, what is clear is that they transform political campaigning. Mass democracy in the age of broadcast media involved grand public messages (albeit targeted especially at swing voters in swing states). This has been gradually replaced by messaging aimed at niche demographics with immense precision, while being invisible to everybody else. The fear is that, with much more fine-grained emotional insight and demographic segmentation, it will become possible to tailor the emotional trigger for the individual, in ways that either change their vote or provide the catalyst for them to vote at all. Facebook especially is a medium that serves and normalizes "dog whistle" politics, in which content can be tailored to mobilize specific recipients, and bypass mass media.

A danger lurking in modern societies is that technologies can be unexpectedly repurposed as instruments of violence. Civic institutions that were taken for granted for generations can suddenly appear vulnerable to attack, if just one piece of the jigsaw is subverted. Rising technological complexity increases the opportunities available to the weak to make violent and disruptive interventions, whether these be termed "hacks," "terrorism" or "cyberwar." Digitization of everyday life seems to be offering rising opportunities for violence, but little additional capacity for power, other than for the tech giants that own and control the new infrastructure. This doesn't translate into physical combat so much as heightened nervousness.

The Internet has turned out to be an excellent weapon of sabotage. It provides us with the tools to verbally and emotionally attack each other, and it helps political disruptors to bring down the status quo. It renders many conventional industries unviable, or else completely dependent on infrastructures provided by the likes of Amazon and Facebook. Having no say in the overall direction or control of these infrastructures, the users only seek to exploit them as best they can, rather than shape or defend them. This is in contrast to the eighteenth-century Enlightenment, where the protagonists of the intellectual and political public sphere were always partly concerned with defending its own institutions, such as a free press and scholarly debate.

In place of society, the Internet offers us a selection of war games to play, for enjoyment, friendship, convenience, or to let off emotional steam. Worryingly, this menu of games now appears to include democracy itself, and some of the "players" may have been sold more powerful weapons than the rest of us. The boundary between politics and violence becomes blurred, as the purpose of argument is to wreak emotional harm and destabilize agreements. There is often an initial thrill of watching "elites" tumble when they underestimate both the resentment of the powerless and the violence of the new computational instruments in play. But the division between "war" and "peace," that was the prop at the heart of Hobbes's political philosophy, becomes weakened in the process.

8

BETWEEN WAR AND PEACE

Resisting the new violence

We regularly hear that elites and experts have lost the public's trust. But this blanket claim obscures some intriguing divergences in how trust is invested. The institutions whose credibility is in greatest trouble around the world are those that are professionally tasked with representing society in one way or the other: most crucially, the media and elected representatives.[1] Concentrations of governmental and technocratic power generate suspicion, especially where their remit extends across large and diverse populations, as in the European Union and the United States. Distrust of this nature is especially pronounced among economically struggling populations, sometimes to the point of rejecting representative democracy altogether.

Now consider some of the areas which are bucking these trends. People continue to express considerable trust in the military, doctors, and nurses, well beyond their confidence in other experts or officials. Supporters of populist parties also tend to back alternatives to representative democracy to a greater extent than the rest of the public. For example, 88% of those who support Podemos in Spain favor greater use of *direct* democracy, that is, plebiscites. Meanwhile, around 42% of people who support Silvio Berlusconi and the UK Independence Party are in favor of some form of autocracy, in which a strong leader makes decisions unimpeded by parliament or the judiciary.[2]

While these opinions stem from disparate parts of the political spectrum, there is nevertheless a pattern. In contrast to those elites who seem to deal only in words, those who are tasked with *rescuing* and *protecting* us still command widespread respect, especially where their role involves focusing on human bodies, either in battle or in hospital. Confidence in these heroic action figures may even be rising as confidence in representatives falls. One study conducted across Europe found that the experience of unemployment leads people to become less trusting in parliament, but *more* trusting in the police.[3] The elites who are in trouble are the ones whose lineage begins in the seventeenth century: journalists, experts, officials. They are the ones whose task it was originally to create portraits, maps, statistical models of the world, that the rest of us were expected to accept, on the basis that they were unpolluted by personal feelings or bias. Social media has accelerated this declining credibility, but it is not the sole cause.

This split reflects something about the role of speed in our politics. The work of government and of establishing facts can be slow and frustrating. It can often appear unresponsive or unsympathetic to the seriousness of people's needs and feelings *right now*. Populism speaks to a yearning for change that comes immediately, with an almost military speed, breaking free of the constraints of reason and evidence-gathering. The failings of technocratic politics are serious and real, but the danger is that they are exploited by political movements that value speed of action above all else, eliminating the need for evidence gathering or democratic consent, which are unavoidably slow. What Silicon Valley technology giants share with fascism is an insistence on fixing problems immediately, and not bothering to debate them first. That is a mentality with rising popular appeal right now.

Economic prosperity and reduced inequality would do much to keep these developments in check. But neither would arrest them altogether or reverse them. We are at a turning point. The project which was launched in the seventeenth century, of trusting elite individuals to know, report, and judge things on our behalf, may not be viable in the long term, at least in its existing form. Amid the political reactions against technocrats, there is a more profound philosophical change under way that is altering the role of knowledge and feeling in society. Central to the ambitions of Descartes, Hobbes, and the scientific pioneers was the idea that "nature" could be viewed as a separate entity, with an air of objective detachment. Privileged individuals would use their command over words and numbers to produce a version of reality that everyone could agree on, generating peace in the process. The knowledge provided by geometry, anatomy, astronomy, and statistics arose from the sense that nature was a God-given machine that would run forever according to eternal laws, that humans could observe but not change. For a number of disconcerting reasons, that is no longer the case.

Nature gets political

The dawn of nuclear weapons during the 1940s radically altered our understanding of the scope of possible violence, as well as the political status of nature and scientists. One obvious feature of the bomb was its existential threat to civilian life, finally obliterating the noble distinction between "combatant" and "noncombatant" that had been slowly fraying ever since the French Revolution. But another was the source of this threat: physical matter itself. Physicists had unleashed a type of violence that had lurked within the natural world all along, but never before been triggered. Inverting the progressive ideal of science, this was scientific knowledge in the service of annihilation. If anyone still harbored a belief that Western science was innately humanitarian, they could do so no longer.

This weapon also possessed the capacity to alter basic rhythms of the natural world in frightening and unpredictable ways. Scientists struggled to model the "fallout" of the weapons they had helped create. The development of the hydrogen bomb in the 1950s catalyzed significant early advances in computing power, as the US Defense Department sought to calculate the bomb's likely consequences. Scientists realized that nuclear weapons tests in the immediate postwar period were contributing to raised levels of carbon in the earth's atmosphere, and began to track this from 1950 onwards.[4] Among the findings was that the oceans were absorbing far less carbon than previously thought, meaning that the burning of fossil fuels might also be disrupting the global climate. Beyond growing public anxiety, questions about nuclear fallout led to the first attempts to monitor the global atmosphere in three dimensions.

If the Scientific Revolution of the seventeenth century saw nature submitting to civilian control, various military revolutions of the twentieth century saw science being put to the contrary use, of discovering ways of untaming nature, and triggering natural violence. Indeed, wreaking ecological disruption was integral to Cold War battle plans. Up until the early 1960s, US defense officials pushed for research into weather control, in the hope that negative weather events could be deliberately unleashed on the enemy. The US was accused of committing "ecocide" during the Vietnam War, with forests being destroyed by the chemical known as Agent Orange and rivers being deliberately polluted and diverted so as to render the natural environment uninhabitable.[5]

Nature's violence now intrudes into civilian life on a range of unintended fronts, regardless of military conflict. Once-in-a-thousand-year storms are becoming familiar news items. The earth's climate is already 0.85°C warmer than in 1880; only a rapid reduction in atmospheric greenhouse gases would avoid a rise to potentially catastrophic levels over the twenty-first century. Even the upper limits of warming aimed for by the Paris climate accord (c. 1.5–2°C above pre-industrial levels) could have an impact on sea levels and agriculture that would produce mass migrations, famines, and resource wars. Cities such as New York, with its 520-mile coastline, are severely imperiled by rising seas. Increased global temperature levels have already had a measurable impact on public health, from the impact of extreme heat on the elderly and the greater prevalence of dengue fever.[6]

If this weren't frightening enough, resistance of diseases to drugs is rising steadily. The use of antibiotics in farming, combined with improper disposal of agricultural waste, is creating swamps filled with antibiotics in which new strains of "superbug" can develop. By 2017, the number of people dying due to drug-resistant infections was around 700,000 a year globally, but current trends suggest this will rise to 10 million a year by 2050. Antibiotics are now integral to the safety of many standard medical procedures, from caesareans to removal of an appendix and chemotherapy treatment. The discovery that has done more than any other over the past 400 years to save and prolong human life is becoming less and less effective.

Elsewhere, hints are emerging that our ecosystem is tipping into something never seen before by scientists. A study of flying insects in Germany discovered that they had declined by 75% in twenty-seven years.[7] As pollinators and prey for other wildlife, these insects play a crucial role in the balance of life, and insects make up about two-thirds of all life on earth. This discovery led one scientist to express concern about "ecological Armageddon," but there's no clear explanation of why it's happening. Pesticides are one likely culprit, signaling the extent to which scientific "advances" and attempts to control nature are at the heart of the new crises we face today.

The hubris of Western science is partially to blame. The belief that natural processes can be transparent to the rational human mind is the same one that advocates unending plunder and manipulation of natural resources. The seventeenth-century vision of nature and politics as separate parallel worlds, only mediated via experts, is no longer tenable, now that nature begins to intrude unexpectedly and violently into spheres of civilization where it was never invited. It transpires that the Industrial Revolution triggered something just as violent and dangerous to human life as any weapon. Climate change is a case of what the environmentalist Rob Nixon refers to as "slow violence," but it is only slow relative to human biography.[8] Relative to geological history, it has been like a gunshot. In the process, nature has become unavoidably political without becoming civil. Hobbes's vision of the state of nature as a "warre of all against all" is breaking out all over again, only now with various nonhuman combatants involved.

In 2000, the geologists Paul Crutzen and Eugene Stoermer suggested that the earth had entered a new epoch which they christened the "Anthropocene," as its climate appeared to have changed irreversibly as a result of human (anthropic) activities. The build-up of carbon dioxide in the atmosphere, plastics in the oceans, and production of new radioactive materials contributed to an epochal shift. Aside from the geological significance of such a break, this has deep philosophical and political importance: nature is not something pure and separate from culture, but already bears the stamp of human activity. Others have pointed to 1945 as the key year in the rise of the Anthropocene, as Hiroshima made manifest humanity's capacity to rapidly destroy their own world.

The point is that it no longer seems possible to constrain the natural world within tidy expert categories, to be inspected through neatly planned experiments, and subjected to mathematical modeling. Nature no longer waits patiently to be represented by facts and figures, but demands attention according to its own frenetic timetable and chaotic geography. The scientific question of what is objectively true can no longer be divorced from urgent political questions of how to survive in peace. Problems such as global warming and antibiotic resistance usher in a phase of what two science-policy thinkers have termed "post-normal science," in which "facts are uncertain, values in dispute, stakes high and decisions urgent."[9]

To say that "facts are uncertain" is not to endorse cynicism toward climate science or any other type of science. It is to acknowledge that things are unfolding with a speed and complexity that cannot be easily settled with traditional expert authority. Problems straddle natural and social sciences. There are no simple measuring devices or experimental situations of the sort that launched the Scientific Revolution 350 years ago. And we are now living with the consequences of previous scientific advances. In matters of "post-normal" science, few things stand still long enough to generate hard truths, and the audiences that need convincing are a mixture of experts and nonexperts. This is attractive territory for conspiracy theorists and lobbyists, who sow suspicion on scientific consensus, and attempt to debunk the entire scientific enterprise.

The facts alone won't save us

The election of an American president who believes "the concept of global warming was created by and for the Chinese in order to make US manufacturing non-competitive" was horrifying for anyone who trusted the evidence on climate change. Trump's announcement that the United States would withdraw from the Paris climate accord, combined with his extravagant support for carbon-intensive industries, represented a reactionary force at a pivotal moment in the history of the earth's climate. It did, however, serve as a reminder of how the most urgent scientific and political challenges are now entwined. How to respond? This question provokes a deep and uneasy dilemma.

One path is to reassert our commitment to scientific objectivity and institutions in even bolder terms, as figures such as Harvard psychologist Stephen Pinker and British biologist Richard Dawkins have demanded. In the face of nationalist reaction, this strategy offers faith in facts as the only means of resistance. It assumes the unrivaled capacity of rational argument among qualified experts will save us from demagogues and nationalists. The ideals of professionalism and expertise, namely of putting objective knowledge to work in the public interest, thus need defending at all costs. For the more aggressive defenders of Western progress, rationality becomes a type of weapon through which to attack critics and doubters, on high-profile debating platforms and the "marketplace of ideas."

This renewed commitment to scientific expertise ostensibly targets the lies of conspiracy theorists and disreputable media outlets, using the hard evidence of academic science—methodical, apolitical, objective—to do so. Factchecking, evidence-based policymaking, statistics, diagnostics, expert audit, transparency initiatives, and critical peer review are the instruments through which the liars and manipulators will be found out and dismissed. This renewed commitment also requires a de-escalation of tactics associated with "identity politics," such as "no-platforming" and campus "safe-spaces," which exclude distressing ideas and speakers. The argument against these practices is that intellectual argument is harmless, and any restraint on it therefore constitutes censorship.

Bravado rationalism assumes that, with sufficient freedom of speech, consensus will be re-established, so long as people accept certain rules of discourse, as the gentlemen of the Royal Society were required to do in 1660. Fact will overwhelm fiction, and truth will displace lies. We know that water boils at 100°C, and objectivity should similarly surround knowledge of climate, physiology, or, for that matter, economic policy. In response to those who want to politicize the "facts," political institutions should celebrate the aloof, apolitical, unyielding nature of the rational expert. Democracy comes second.

The machismo that often accompanies these arguments exists partly to conceal the difficult truth, that elite appeals to objectivity are growing more vulnerable all the time. Such appeals ignore the copious forces that for over a century have been progressively undermining the seventeenth-century philosophy of knowledge, which treats the mind as a neutral "mirror." In recent years, neuroscience—led by the work of the Portuguese-American scientist Antonio Damasio—has demonstrated the impossibility of isolating the rational from the emotional functions of the brain. Damasio's most influential book carries the title *Descartes' Error*. While this body of research has been cause for great excitement in the worlds of marketing and communications since the 1990s, the full cultural and political implications are only now being realized. The division between how we feel about things and how we think rationally about them has been steadily eroding, and this is accelerated by the spread of increasingly intelligent devices and sensors in our physical environments.

If the authority of experts cannot be guaranteed simply from their credentials, perhaps it can be reasserted in the heat of public debate. To this end, polemical defenders of scientific method, such as the British journalist and businessman Matt Ridley, promote "free speech" as the most cherished principle of Western civilization. But the very notion of "free speech" has become a trap. Neo-fascist or alt-right movements now use it to attack alleged "political correctness," using the principle of free expression to push hateful and threatening messages toward minority groups. The movement known as "new atheism," led by Dawkins, has some troubling commonalities with nationalist and Islamophobic movements, namely in their deep hostility toward identity politics. Whereas intellectual freedom was once advanced in Europe as the right to publish texts that were critical of the establishment, it has now become tied up with spurious arguments surrounding the "right to offend." A recent valorization of "debate" as a spectacle, in which public "bouts" are staged between intellectual "heavyweights," rests on the historically doubtful supposition that progress and enlightenment are fundamentally driven by conflict. Rather than resurrect reason, which is slow and aimed at developing consensus, this new industry of ideas makes do with mere disagreement.

Elsewhere, "free speech" has become a cloak for corporate lobbyists, who hide behind the principle to disseminate ideas that further their own economic interests. Goading experts into positions of alleged hypocrisy, in which they condemn certain views and positions out of hand and refuse to debate them (which then allows them to be painted as intolerant), is the ultimate victory of the troll and the libertarian think tank. If the original principle of a free intellectual public sphere is to be rescued, it cannot be reducible to an ethos of gratuitous disruption and offence.

Even on a basic philosophical and physiological level, the idea that we can establish some absolute line between the realm of speech and that of action (and therefore potentially of physical harm) belongs to the past. As the silent "language" of bodies, brains and nature becomes increasingly readable, and the interaction of "social" and "physical" human experiences becomes clearer to see (as the example of PTSD testifies), the ideal of "free speech" as something that always transcends our physical selves and the natural world is now a relic. We have to find a way to live with that reality, and to trust institutions such as student societies to navigate it.

The seventeenth-century model of the scientist was of the gentleman who'd learned a certain manner of formal speech, and was able to speak about what he'd witnessed while simultaneously excluding himself from the narrative. It rested on a delicate balance of anonymity and identification. However, this unavoidably elitist model preserves for a select group the task of representing nature and society. A small and privileged minority are granted the right to express the truth. The rage it inspires from some disenfranchised political quarters speaks of something real. In the digital age, we now have a full spectrum of media outlets and quasi-experts, between those still straining toward the seventeenth-century ideal of apolitical facts and those seeking to subvert it. We can side with the former, but it is no longer possible to ignore the latter. For a large part of the population, it is becoming impossible to distinguish between "authentic" expertise (understood in terms of credentials, methods, and transparency) and the alternative offered by lobbyists and think tanks serving vested interests.

This confusion points toward a different perspective altogether: should the defenders of science and rationality mount a more nakedly political defense of their procedures and values, as occurred with the 2017 March for Science, for example? Or is that to cave in to the agenda of their antagonists, and demonstrate that experts really are no better, calmer, or more "objective" than anyone else? The reality is that experts have no choice, given how their monopoly over the means of representation has been disintegrating over time. They cannot simply expect that monopoly to reassemble itself—not without political engagement, anyway. But this is where the defenders of expertise are often at their weakest. Precisely because they have spent much of the past 350 years refusing to incorporate politics in their project, they are unable to understand why people become politically alienated from it. By contrast, populists grasp the cultural underpinnings of expert power only too well.

The desire for war

Trust in the scientific establishment still polls well but it holds little emotional appeal, in contrast to nationalism, heroism, and nostalgia. Despite ample education, elites seem to have precious little understanding of why.

Having spent too long believing that facts can speak for themselves, their capacity to defend their own political vision is stunted. Events such as the April 2017 March for Science may be a sign of a new type of democratic mobilization for expertise, but are not adequate by themselves. Elites are hamstrung by a simplistic understanding of how nationalism connects, and of the type of truth that it offers. Technocrats assume that populists are bad policymakers only with better anthems, more exciting rallies, and fewer qualms about naked lying. Judgments regarding the supporters of populists are often even harsher, and imply a complete lack of independent thought, or just incurable bigotry.

A contrasting view starts by considering some of the key historical and philosophical characteristics of nationalism, which are inexorably tied up with the cultural and psychological dynamics of modern warfare. Recognizing these characteristics does not commit us to sympathizing with nationalists or racists, let alone endorsing them. But it demystifies political movements currently seen as "irrational." The first thing to reflect on is that nationalism originates as a left-wing, revolutionary phenomenon (following the French Revolution), offering the promise of solidarity and equality amidst economic systems that otherwise corrode those things. The emotions in play are not merely the trickery of marketing experts, but relate to real yearnings for community and popular power that are otherwise not available. Those yearnings do not respond to "evidence" because they are not looking for anything objective in the first place. Part of the seduction of war, at least in the imagination, is that it offers a type of togetherness and shared sentiment that can't be reduced to facts.

Secondly, the lurking promise of nationalism—and of the type of world-changing war invented by Napoleon—is that ordinary individual lives acquire meaning. A great leader promising total war offers escape from the ennui of civilian life, in which death is simply the end of a meaningless existence. Instead, each life will be valued, remembered, and commemorated. In the absence of religion, war provides the rituals and institutions to publicly acknowledge and soothe pain. To understand resurgent nationalism, we need to ask where pain has come from and why established political and media institutions have not given it more voice or better served its memory. Part of the answer lies in the connections that exist between ill health, rising mortality rates, and authoritarian sympathies.

One may recognize facts as valid and experts as trustworthy, but if one suffers a collapse in one's community and sense of existential significance, then authoritarianism and nationalism become more ethically and politically attractive. When an entire political and economic system appears rotten, a flagrant liar can give voice to an underlying truth. If there is one thing more important than prosperity to people's well-being, then it is self-esteem. Those suffering a collapse of self-esteem, for whatever reason, are often the most receptive to nationalist rhetoric. For those living with fear and with pain, the idea of a quasi-military mobilization acquires almost therapeutic properties, placing those feelings into a grander public framework. "Progress" does not recognize let alone valorize pain, indeed it is embarrassed by it. Heroism, potentially involving physical or emotional violence, does the opposite and thus acquires tremendous appeal.

In the second half of the seventeenth century, in the wake of civil and religious wars, states of "war" and "peace" were held apart by a range of new institutions. But there is a limit to how successfully this division can be sustained, as the tools and psychology of war have gradually reappeared in economic, political, and civil institutions. War of one kind or another feels almost inevitable today. In some respects, such as "cyberwar" and the "full spectrum" strategic approach adopted by Russia, it is already under way. If peace is no longer so peaceful, and war is no longer so warlike, could it be that war provides a more meaningful and more effective metaphor for addressing today's most pressing concerns? Might it be time to take a leaf out of the playbook of the populists and nationalists, and accept that we are all in a situation of quasi-war, albeit with very different forms of violence from those that Thomas Hobbes was desperate to eliminate from political life in 1651? Beyond reasserting facts and expertise, maybe the "culture wars" need to be joined from both sides. This isn't necessarily as frightening as it might sound.

One immediate benefit of such thinking would be to relieve the pressure to establish a general public consensus around the facts. The primary concern in situations of war is to gather intelligence quickly, and to ensure that it is "actionable." Knowledge captured this way has no need of a public audience, indeed it often remains at the status of an "unknown known"—or a secret. Its primary virtue is its sensitivity and immediacy. Meanwhile, public knowledge is geared to mobilize people as much as to provide factual reports. The hunger for a faster, more engaging politics is not about to abate. One question is whether it could be diverted toward something non-violent.

While today we may feel ill-served when it comes to slow, thoughtful, reasoned debate of issues, of the sort which emerged in the clubs and coffee houses of commercial Europe in the seventeenth century, we are only too well served by possibilities for rapid detection and analysis. Public debate might descend into irresolvable conflicts, but the intelligence powers of business, computing, and the military expand all the time. The good news is that, at least in terms of technical equipment, we could scarcely be more capable of dealing with the uncertainties and dangers of the Anthropocene. Even if consensus on nature and society seems further off than ever, *coordination* of responses is still eminently possible. We are endowed with a global information nervous system, allowing us to detect change and react at great speed. An example of this is how financial markets are harnessed as environmental policy tools, with new markets and derivatives in carbon being constructed, in the hope that the sentiments and guessing games of the financial economy will spontaneously steer us toward a sustainable path. But this is not enough.

Diverting war

Around 2008, various writers and campaigners began to suggest that only the equivalent of a state-led wartime mobilization, similar to that seen during the Second World War, could prevent a level of global warming with serious negative consequences for civilization. As the environmentalist Bill McKibben wrote in 2016, "it's not that global warming is *like* a world war. It *is* a world war. . . . The question is, will we fight back?"[10] The alternative to "fighting back" is to accept temperatures 2°C or more above pre-industrial levels, something that—in addition to the submergence of many coastal cities beneath water—would render current global levels of agricultural production impossible. Fighting back is therefore essential.

The Climate Mobilization is an environmental advocacy group that seeks to draw together lessons from the Second World War to consider how a rapid decarbonization of the economy might work in practice. They point to

the way car manufacturers rapidly retooled to become arms manufacturers
to demonstrate that widespread "mobilization"—including divestments and
reinvestments—is possible. Such action does require vast levels of state intervention, of up to 45% of total GDP (US defense spending peaked in 1944
at 44% of GDP). The Climate Mobilization claims that, unlike the Second
World War, there would be no violence or "dehumanizing propaganda" in
this war. But given the way in which fossil-fuel interests have poured billions
of dollars into denialist research institutes and anti-regulation lobbying vehicles, an information counteroffensive would seem necessary as well.

The Pentagon is already one of the branches of government that takes
climate change most seriously. In a 2016 directive, "Climate Change
Adaptation and Resilience," the Defense Department made the case for
considering climate change as one of the main threats confronting global
security. The document was immediately contested by pro-fossil-fuel
voices, including the Heritage Foundation. NATO has also identified climate change as a "threat multiplier." While Hillary Clinton was running
for president, her campaign flirted with the idea of declaring "war" on
climate change, and at one point promised there would be a "climate war
room" in the White House. Clinton shifted gears when addressing the
scale of the threat, promising—in vain, of course—to deploy half a billion
new solar panels over the course of her first term.

It may sound odd to be speaking of military mobilization and the US
global security agenda as sources of hope. Then again, compared to some
of the projections of the consequences of climate change over the next
century, this may now be what hope looks like. What political economists Geoff Mann and Joel Wainright term "climate Leviathan" is not an
entirely happy vision, but nor is it the worst of the possible scenarios that
await us.[11] The issues at stake are existential, well beyond standard technocratic policy fare about optimizing economic output or achieving margin-
ally better health outcomes. The arrival of nature as a violent force in our
politics demands a *practical* response. The success of populists, on both the
left and the right, should tell us that the hunger for changing course and
achieving collective security is of a far greater importance to people than
the hunger for factchecking.

Perhaps the most urgent question posed by "climate mobilization" is
whether technologies designed to destroy life should be repurposed for the

sustenance and protection of life, both human and nonhuman. As in situations of "total war," the task is to coordinate experts and amateurs working toward shared goals. "Citizen science" and "citizen journalism" might sound like a mild, if not dubious, form of mobilization, but they are one essential ingredient in how research and politics can be recombined. DIY air-monitoring practices, carried out by activists, have been instrumental in raising public concern about certain fracking sites and car emissions in city centers.[12] The discovery that flying insects in Germany had fallen by 75% was made thanks initially to a club of amateur entomologists, establishing traps around the countryside. The origins of climate science itself lie in a series of complicated alliances between local weather forecasters, space agencies, and Cold War atmospheric monitoring.[13]

As participants in a popular mobilization, experts need to express their political commitments and feelings more openly. This is uncomfortable territory, as it confirms the populist suspicion that experts have an agenda—but then all the more reason to articulate it properly. In truth, science has always been accompanied by a moral vision. The original attempt to model nature's mechanics was rooted in a Protestant theology which saw "useful knowledge" of the natural world as a way of getting closer to God. What *is* the equivalent now? We need to be told. A project called "Is This How You Feel?" has collected written letters from climate scientists describing their feelings about their work. One writes that "It is probably the first time that I have been asked to describe what I feel, rather than what I think" about climate change. The letters frequently include words such as "overwhelmed," "tired," "fear," but also several references to "hope" and "excitement."

The Anthropocene epoch offers a different political role for science, which could connect with the emotions that are otherwise channeled into more tribal forms of politics. Throughout its history, modern science has been vulnerable to the charge that it is aloof, amoral, and oblivious to ordinary people. Science, from this perspective, turns nature into something mechanical, abstract, and distant. But the entangling of politics and science, and the unruliness of climate in particular, today put an end to that. A rescue mission is under way, and experts are at the heart of it. New forms of "emergency service" may be required, aimed at protecting people and nature from disruption, and preventing their spiraling. As ecological problems escalate, rescue operations will occupy a more prominent role in society. Scientists are dealing with mortal systems whose decline and disappearance is an emotional issue, which should be recognized as such.

The division between large cities and rural areas is central to the cultural and political conflicts that are reshaping democracies around the world. While economic factors are important here (major metropolises have become engines of growth, while small towns and rural territories struggle), there is an arguably more important split in how recognition is distributed. All too often, communities that are distant from metropolitan centers have been treated as having nothing of interest to say. Their knowledge and culture have not been valued by major media outlets, universities, or expert institutions, but rather they've been passive recipients of handouts and information. Ecological emergency and the dawn of the Anthropocene potentially changes this: those who live and work with nature, rather than accumulating facts and theories about nature from afar, have know-how that could become increasingly valuable as nature becomes more politically problematic. In parallel to "citizen science," harnessing the nonexpert knowledge scattered across rural populations will be both necessary and politically beneficial.

What the wartime mind-set offers above all, together with aggressive technologies and strategies, is speed of response. The hunger that populists seek to satisfy, but which technocrats cannot, is for action that takes place *immediately*, rather than later, after all the evidence is in. As the former Pentagon employee Rosa Brooks has observed, one reason why the US military spreads its tentacles ever further into American policymaking is that "Americans increasingly treat the military as an all-purpose tool for fixing anything that happens to be broken."[14] The challenge of fixing a violent and rapidly self-destructive relationship to the natural environment has greater historic importance than any other. Whatever confronts this task, if not the actual military, will have to be something with many of the same characteristics as the military.

Making promises

Thanks to the sudden progress of "neural networking" techniques of AI (or deep learning), we now face the potential prospect of computers matching the powers of the human mind. This is perhaps the most daunting prospect for expertise today, threatening to replace a wide range of "white collar" and "knowledge-intensive" jobs. The professional work of journalists, lawyers, accountants, and architects is already vulnerable to automation, as machine learning grows in sophistication, thanks partly to the vast quantities of data we produce. Risks to national security and financial stability are increasingly gauged by data analytics.

Some of the resentment that is heaped on the professional classes and highly educated elites stems from the perception that their well-remunerated services are protected from the ravages of technological change by cartel-like arrangements, but such privileges are not permanent. A passing glance at the news about the impending robot revolution suggests to many we may not need experts or professionals at all. It is difficult to claim public authority on the basis of one's knowledge, when machines possess vastly more information and are incomparably quicker at processing it. Before too long, we fear computers will perfectly mimic human thought and behavior, while also being capable of vastly superior alternatives to it. The fear of robots is always a dual one, that they are both the same as us and unimaginably different. What do we have left that is *ours* as a species?

There is one problem confronting humanity that may never go away, and which computers do nothing to alleviate: how to make *promises*. This problem produced Hobbes's deepest anxieties regarding humans in a "state of nature." He feared that, while everyone may be better off if they honored their promises to each other, there would be no way to verify that they all would. Words alone are not enough. Violence would swiftly ensue, he lamented, unless some kind of powerful third party—the modern state— could provide a set of rules backed by force, that would allow promises (such as contracts) to become reliable. Writing in the 1880s, the philosopher Friedrich Nietzsche concurred, albeit with a dash of cynicism:

> To breed an animal that is entitled to make promises—surely that is the essence of the paradoxical task nature has set itself where human beings are concerned? Isn't that the real problem of human beings?[15]

Regardless of Hobbes's pessimism or Nietzsche's sarcasm, the act of making a promise has a unique, almost magical property to it. A promise made to a child or loved one, or a promise made before a public audience, has a peculiarly binding power. It's not that it cannot be broken, but the breaking of it registers as a distinctive type of breach, that can leave deep emotional and cultural wounds.

The expert communities that emerged during Hobbes's lifetime were really just another solution to the problem he diagnosed. Crucial to the public status of bookkeepers, natural scientists, statisticians, journalists, and anatomists was that they made *promises* regarding what had been witnessed, using standardized techniques of record keeping and reporting. We become seduced by heroic tales of individual genius, but the key ingredient of the Scientific Revolution was the institutional innovation which allowed evidence and arguments to be judged on their merits according to fixed rules, rather than on the moral character of the person presenting them. The result was knowledge, but the prerequisite was a system of trust. The achievement of institutions such as the Royal Society was to entrench a culture of promise-making and promise-keeping within its highly select bunch of members, and then to communicate and publish this reliably.

Can a computer make a promise? This is an intriguing philosophical question. If Google DeepMind were to take data on 100 million "promises" that had been made (perhaps legal contracts, informal agreements via email, videos of people "shaking on a deal," friends promising to be somewhere at a certain time) and feed it to an AI, what would it make of it all? Would it understand? In a manner of speaking, it would. No doubt handshaking, contract-signing, and the bodily signals of sincerity are not hard to "learn." But then what? Unlike in a competitive game, where the purpose is to outdo an opponent, a promise involves a momentary leap of faith that is not rooted in strategic acumen or calculation. To put that another way, a promise which was wholly reducible to strategic acumen or calculation *wouldn't really be a promise.* And for that reason, it's difficult to imagine that a computer could ever really learn how to make a promise.

The global financial crisis of 2007–9, which left prolonged economic stagnation in its wake, occurred because of a steady corrosion of promise-making within the financial sector. The explosive, albeit very profitable, mistake was to redefine debt as an asset, that is, merely as a source of future income rather than a type of interpersonal bond that endures over time. The "securitization" of loans, in which the right to receive income from a debtor can be repackaged and sold, meant that bankers lost interest in whether money was being lent to people who were likely to repay it. Failure to repay was simply an opportunity to develop new insurance products to cover such a risk, which could also become valuable assets to be bought and sold. Institutions established to facilitate commitment and trust were effectively "gamed" by bankers for profit, and trashed in the process. Friedrich von Hayek's ambition to replace expert judgment with market indicators succeeded, but left society with little to cling to once the market imploded.

Social media platforms, especially Facebook, do something equally cynical. Relationships of trust and friendship, on which people depend and draw comfort, become a basis for surveillance and hence advertising. The bonds that connect us to each other are "securitized" and sold to marketers or political propagandists. Facebook is an astonishing, purpose-built *engagement machine*. But it only achieves the results it does because of the pre-existing commitments and care that we have for each other, in addition to the more egocentric urges to show off. By inserting itself into our daily social—and increasingly our political—lives, Facebook has achieved a unique type of global power, but what damage has it done to social and political trust in the process?

An alternative perspective on financial securitization and Facebook is that they are further cases of "weaponization" of everyday institutions and promises. They exploit and weaken norms of trust, without building adequate replacements. Debt, housing, friendship, and democracy have been around for thousands of years; the contribution of the financial sector or Silicon Valley over the past thirty years has been to find ways of manipulating and destabilizing them, so that society no longer feels so secure. Nothing permanent is constructed by the invention of mortgage-backed securities or Facebook, but a great deal is damaged. In Hannah Arendt's distinction, this is the logic of violence, not of power.

If we think of experts only as carriers of knowledge, we miss something arguably more important about their public role: they serve to overcome conflicts. Religious wars of the seventeenth century were overcome, albeit with terrible suffering along the way. Cultural and informational wars of the twenty-first century might also be overcome, but this requires us to abandon a vision of heroic scientific truth-seekers, and to think carefully and constructively about the types of institutions we can build in order to support promise making today.

Institutional innovation

Whether we like it or not, the starting point for this venture will be the same as it was for Hobbes: the modern state, issuing laws backed by sovereign power. It is difficult to conceive how promises can be made at scale, in a complex modern society, without the use of contracts, rights, and statutes underpinned by sovereign law. Only law really has the ability to push back against the rapidly rising tide of digital algorithmic power. It remains possible to make legal demands on the owners and controllers of machines, regardless of how sophisticated those machines are.

It is hard to see how giant technology platforms will be checked other than by legal intervention. Populism, understood as a non-class-based mobilization against concentrations of "elite" power, originated in Kansas in the 1880s because of resentment against monopolistic railroad and oil companies. The birth of modern antitrust law followed soon afterward, allowing large economic powers to be broken up by legal intervention. Busting cartels and monopolies continued to be a way that political leaders of various parties demonstrated their populist credentials, right up until the 1970s.[16] But since the 1970s, competition law in Europe and the United States has become increasingly technocratic in nature, focusing on intricacies of economic efficiency that are entirely invisible and incomprehensible to the public. Expertise (in particular, complex fields of economics and game theory that shape antitrust nowadays) has made regulation more opaque to the public. At the same time, monopolies have prospered, with Silicon Valley giants being among the principal beneficiaries.

A new wave of populist legal interventions for the twenty-first century could rein in the power of the new monopolists, and not only through breaking them up. One of the political dangers of Facebook, for example, is that there is no available means for a member of the public to see the full range of political campaign ads that are being disseminated, but only those which are tailored for them. The public sphere is presented in a personalized form, for each individual user, and there is no way to see it in its impersonal form. Treating platforms as "information fiduciaries"[17] or enforcing a principle of "platform neutrality"[18] (similar to net neutrality) are possible routes to reining in platform power using legal means.

One precondition of such interventions would be for regulators to move beyond their narrowly defined economic criteria of what counts as a problem in the first place. The Silicon Valley dream, of building the machines which mediate mind and world, is dashed, once companies are restricted to serving specific markets and clearly articulated human needs.

Much of the lure of populists, both of a left- and a right-wing variety, is their willingness to make promises. In many cases, these promises might be rash, as when Donald Trump campaigned around de-industrialized regions of the Midwest promising to bring back traditional manufacturing jobs. But for those who have studied the supporters of such politicians, the appeal of this type of rhetoric makes sense. The sociologist Arlie Russell Hochschild's exploration of the lives of Tea Party enthusiasts in Louisiana revealed to her a "deep story" underlying their political views.[19] On a fundamental emotional level, these people felt that some basic moral agreement had been broken, whereby their patience and hard work was no longer adequate for them to be deemed respectable citizens. Crucially, at least for their political reaction to this, they blamed government rather than business for the fact that a promise had not been honored.

In this climate, policymakers must rediscover the political capacity to make simple, realistic, and life-changing promises. Either that, or nationalists will show them how it's done. Highly complex policies, developed by experts with sophisticated modeling and delivery mechanisms, cannot satisfy the current demand. Today policies predicated on universality—of treating everyone equally—have growing political appeal. The British Labour Party's unexpected surge in the 2017 general election campaign was fueled by extremely simple promises, that had no conditions or strings attached, such as free school meals *for all*, free university tuition *for all*, and so on. Much of the appeal of "universal basic income" is the simplicity of paying everybody a fixed amount of money, with no strings attached. Sufficiently simple and universal promises are able to withstand political attacks and media distortions, even in an age of rising online propaganda.

Politics has always been awash with liars and broken promises. Of course there are some outrageous liars in the political realm today, and some of them have become very powerful and influential. But one of the conditions that allowed this to happen was that politics (and policymaking in particular) became too technically complex to sustain a common sense of reality. The best hope for breaking the cycle of cynicism and distrust might be just one or two policies that are so simple, so deliverable that they reconnect the words of elected representatives with the experience of citizens. Had governments introduced a policy of "helicopter money" instead of quantitative easing in 2009, this would have seen the sum in every individual savings account increase by a set figure, using the same technical means as the one employed for quantitative easing. Who knows if this would have worked (who knows if quantitative easing *worked*?) but it would have had a populist quality with valuable symbolism.

Societies have renewed their capacity to make wide-ranging promises in the past, both legal and otherwise. But they usually do so in response to prolonged warfare. The birth of modern government and scientific expertise occurred in the aftermath of civil and religious wars in the seventeenth century. The devastation of the Second World War was followed by unprecedented efforts to guarantee peace at an international level (most significantly by the formation of the United Nations) and social peace at a domestic level, through the expansion of the welfare state and socialized health care. There is no reason to assume that the capacity to produce new institutions of social contracts and peace has evaporated. Threats to peace today are less tangible and harder to trace, operating digitally, emotionally, and atmospherically, at a global level. The current direction of travel is from metaphorical and quasi-wars to literal war. The question is whether this can be averted by entrenching a new set of international and social guarantees now, thereby pre-empting violence rather than reacting to it.

Nonviolence

How are objective facts possible? The immediate answer lies in the skills, methods, and funding of professional research and reporting. These are things that have been progressively undermined, by a combination of technology, market forces, and political opposition. It is tempting to think that these things can simply be reversed. What if we could backtrack a little, perhaps to the heady days of the 1990s? But then again, why stop

there—why not go back to the 1950s, when American science was flush
with Cold War military investment? This is a seductive idea, that reason
can be pieced back together again, by eliminating the alien forces that have
invaded politics, so as to return to a state of normalcy. This is tempting,
but is ultimately another form of nostalgia. Not only that, but it extracts
the wrong kinds of lessons from the past. The challenge facing us today is
how to establish and discover a shared world in the future, inhabited by
beings who are feeling and thinking, not how to reassert the elite power of
the past. What is known as "objectivity" is just one way of settling disputes
and, ideally, avoiding recourse to violence. Expertise plays an indispensable role in this reconstruction work—but it cannot pretend to possess a
monopoly over how society and nature are described. Less still can we rely
on experts for the answers to divisive democratic questions.

The categorical division between "reason" and "feeling" no longer functions because Descartes' idea of the disembodied rational mind is dead.
But we can still draw distinctions between different speeds of reaction, and
strive to defend slowness. Impulsive reactions can be paranoid and aggressive, whereas more careful ones can be more understanding and attentive to
context. The phenomena known as "fake news" and "post-truth" are really
just symptoms of arguments accelerating to the point where only superficial
judgments are possible. Factcheckers can fight these forces in the short
term, but the grander task of building and safeguarding slower spheres
of discussion is a political one. Language needs to be de-weaponized,
and turned back into a tool of promise making, if democracy is to feel—
and be—less warlike in the future. But this will only be viable if the
urgency of our social, economic, and environmental situation is taken seriously, and if the feelings that situation elicits are recognized.

Simply recreating a previous political model, with all the slowly
emerging conflicts that were latent within it, will fail. The 1990s are no
more of a model for the future than the 1950s or the 1920s. An alternative
is to conduct the following thought experiment: imagine if we had just
emerged from some kind of war *today*, what *new* rules and policies would
we seek to establish for peace? Avoiding violence will require a leap of
imagination toward a future settlement, rather than clinging to a previous
one. Existing centers of elite power must now open their worldview to
understanding some of the processes that they've dismissed as "irrational" or

"post-truth," and to throw their considerable influence behind a different social and economic settlement.

An idea that might help such a thought experiment is that of nonviolence. This is not the same thing as "freedom of speech," "rationality," "human rights," or any of the other totemic values of Western civilization. "Nonviolence" typically refers to forms of activism and protest, in the tradition of Mahatma Gandhi and Martin Luther King Jr. It means actively and physically intervening in society, to both publicize and protect human and nonhuman bodies that are under threat. One could include various rescue services within this, in which experts and brave individuals act rapidly to prevent harm. By recognizing that people must be mobilized, it shows where political hope must lie for the future. The mistake of progressive policy tools, such as statistics and economics, is to assume that human action is reducible to hedonistic impulses, seeking more and more contentment. But the relief of pain and fear is a more potent force in human psychology, and undoubtedly a more politically effective one. People can be mobilized around transgression, which needn't have anything to do with aggression.

The modern ideal of civility, expressed forcefully in the work of Hobbes, is that everyone has a right to safety and to life. This ideal was always exclusionary (of colonized and enslaved populations, not to mention nonhuman lives) but today this ideal of civility risks being abandoned, rather than expanded. We live in a time when the life expectancy of many poor populations (notably many of the same ones that have swung behind right-wing populists) are in decline, while Silicon Valley billionaires speculate wildly and financially on innovations that might extend human life indefinitely. This is not ordinary economic inequality, it is an existential inequality, which is at the heart of the conflicted political times we inhabit.

Where life is not being adequately supported in a medical and scientific sense, then there is a widening opportunity for others to come in and offer to support it in a deeper ethical and metaphysical sense, while promising more exclusionary forms of protection. Ideals of nationhood and community have important corporeal dimensions, and cannot be understood entirely at the level of facts. Contemporary nationalism is tightly bound up with problems such as physical pain, aging, chronic illness, and a sense of deep pointlessness, that otherwise finds outlets in addictive and self-destructive behavior, through which feelings of meaning and personal control can be briefly achieved. The urge for violence is often a distortion of the urge for safety. While the experiences of morbidity and mortality continue to diverge as they do at present, politics will continue to be disrupted by forces that appear "irrational," including nationalism. Only some overarching new approach to the provision of healthcare will change that.

Elsewhere, politics is also becoming increasingly organized around vital needs and demands, which come down to matters of life and death. A movement such as Black Lives Matter gives a glimpse of the sort of political movements that will likely dominate the twenty-first century, aimed at highlighting inequalities in the defense of life itself. The central claim of Black Lives Matter is brutally simple: the American Leviathan does not deliver on its function of protecting all lives equally. It is almost certain that the number and scope of such political demands is going to multiply in the coming years, especially as climate-related mass migration increases. Threats to life do not need to be as direct as those publicized by Black Lives Matter in order to be politicized. The Missing Migrants Project has sought to count the number of migrants who have died or gone missing while migrating, initially in response to the mounting humanitarian crisis of boats sinking in the Mediterranean. Applied retrospectively, the project estimates that 60,000 people disappeared between 1997 and 2017 as a result of migrating.

One can imagine more extensive global security measures to reduce some of these risks, but such measures will probably benefit wealthier countries seeking to keep migrants away. By contrast, the recognition of common and equal humanity is a far more exacting ethical and political demand, which requires us to view suffering as something that we share, rather than as the exclusive preserve of our own group. Nevertheless, it is a demand that will be pressed with ever greater urgency over coming decades, especially as the inhabitable territories of the planet shrink. The question is whether disparate movements based on demanding a basic equal right to safety and life can become joined, and to what end exactly. The demand could fuel a different version of populism in the West, built on the truthful recognition that many marginalized populations are being physically and mortally harmed by the present model of progress. Faced with the evidence of how austerity and economic disruption are damaging

public health, the American health-policy expert Ted Shrecker has suggested that a different populism could be organized around the simple
cry of "Stop, you're killing us!"[20] The first step toward preventing harm is
simply to recognize it.

Against such a backdrop, it becomes hard to still credit the Enlightenment vision of humanity seizing powers of modern science and technology
to move forward as a single, united species. The fallout of modern science
and technology includes the gravest dangers facing us today. There will be
ultraprivileged elites who seek (and largely manage) to hoard the resources
and benefits of scientific progress, in the form of greater protection from
natural disasters, insulation from political upheavals and longer, healthier
lives. The new generation of Napoleonic high-tech entrepreneurs may
attain their dreams of living to 150 or 200 or longer. These "founders" may
build empires that outlive them. Some may manage to colonize Mars, as
Elon Musk insists they must. If this is the future of progress, then it cannot be something that includes most people, and much of its impetus is
to escape the fate that awaits the rest of us. Libertarian dreams ultimately
mean divorcing scientific from social progress.

What does hope look like, once divested of some constantly moving
frontier of technological control over nature, and ever more personal vitality for a minority? To the rationalist mind, progress only means more of
things: more life, more prosperity, more pleasure. Such an ideal requires us
to take a cold, emotionless look at history—how objectively better things
are now than in the past. But fear, pain and resentment never got eliminated altogether, nor can they be silenced in the long run. At a moment
when these forces seem to have invaded our politics anew, we have an
opportunity to listen and understand these features of human beings, as an
alternative to either more data on the one hand or more lies on the other.

Acknowledgments

This book emerged from a conversation with my agent, Karolina Sutton, whose enthusiasm and support has been invaluable at every step since. I'd like to thank her, and her colleagues at Curtis Brown, for all their work on making this book happen. I was fortunate to have a superb editor, Bea Hemming at Jonathan Cape, whose overall vision of the book and judgment remained steady throughout, and who showed admirable faith in how it was all going to turn out. My second editor, Tom Mayer at Norton, was critical in helping me identify the core threads of my argument, and has convinced me never to use the word "decimate" again (unless I mean it). I want to thank both of them for their hard work and tireless commitment to the book.

David Milner's copy-edit was based on unusually careful reading and greatly improved the text. André Spicer read a draft manuscript when it was at a difficult stage, and I am deeply grateful to him for his thoughtful insights and friendly advice.

The book was written over 2017 and early 2018, mostly in Husk, Muxima, and Poplar Union cafes in East London and in the British Library. I'd like to thank all the staff of those establishments for being friendly and welcoming, and providing the spaces where the slow work of writing can happen.

My colleagues and students at Goldsmiths have been a source of intellectual stimulation and camaraderie for many years. Thank you, Goldsmiths, for remaining uniquely interesting.

Finally, I want to thank my family. While small children aren't exactly a productivity hack, I am grateful to Martha and Laurie for keeping me endlessly entertained and exhausted. I hope that Martha enjoys finding her name at the front of this book when she goes into bookshops. And most of all to Lydia, thank you for being there with love, patience, ideas, and support throughout the ups and downs of the writing. I couldn't have done it without you.

Notes

Introduction

1 This is what Daniel Kahneman refers to as "system 1" thinking—see D. Kahneman (2011), *Thinking, Fast and Slow*, Allen Lane.
2 H. Arendt (1993), *Between Past and Future*, Penguin Books, p. 263.
3 2017 Edelman Trust Barometer.
4 Ibid.

Chapter 1: Democracy of Feeling

1 "The Corbyn Effect: Huge vote share boost where Labour leader held General Election rallies," *Huffington Post*, 9 June 2017.
2 "Globally, broad support for representative and direct democracy," Pew Research Center, 16 October 2017.
3 G. Le Bon (2006 [1895]), *The Crowd: A Study of the Popular Mind*, Cosimo Classics, p. 15.
4 Ibid.. p. 25.
5 Ibid., p. 10.
6 Ibid., p. 18.
7 Ibid., p. 74.
8 Ibid., p. 30.
9 E. Bernays (2005 [1928]), *Propaganda*, IG Publishing, pp. 127–8.
10 "Freedom on the Net 2017," Freedom House.
11 D. Lazer et al. (2018), "The Science of Fake News," *Science*, Vol. 359, Issue 6380.
12 Le Bon (2006), p. 21.
13 Le Bon (2006), p. 17.
14 A 2017 Pew survey showed that average support for autocracy ("a system in which a strong leader can make decisions without interference from parliament or the courts") is 26% around the world. It is 24% in Hungary, 15% in Poland, and 26% in the UK. "Globally, broad support for representative and direct democracy," Pew Research Center, 16 October 2017.
15 A. Livingston (2017), "The World According to Bannon," *Jacobin*, 2 July 2017.
16 W. Brady et al. (2016), "Emotion shapes the diffusion of moralized content in social networks," *Proceedings of the National Academy of Sciences*.

17 "Alt-white: How the Breitbart machine laundered racist hate," BuzzFeed, 5 October 2017.

18 H. Arendt (1970), *On Violence*, Houghton Mifflin Harcourt, p. 65.

19 O. Hahl et al. (2018), "The Authentic Appeal of the Lying Demagogue: Proclaiming the Deeper Truth about Political Illegitimacy," *American Sociological Review*, Vol. 83, Issue 1.

20 2018 Edelman Trust Barometer.

21 R. Barnes et al. (2018), "The effect of ad hominem attacks on the evaluation of claims promoted by scientists," *PLOS ONE*, 13(1).

Chapter 2: Knowledge for Peace

1 S. Puhringer & K. Hirte (2015), "Financial Crisis as Heart Attack," *Journal of Language and Politics*, January 2015.

2 "Loss of income caused by banks as bad as 'World War,' says BoE's Andrew Haldane," *Telegraph*, 3 December 2012.

3 See Bank of England (2012), "The Distributional Effects of Asset Purchases;" and N. Gane (2015), "Central Banking, Technocratic Governance and the Financial Crisis," *Sosiologia*, 4/2015.

4 See R. Merton (1970), *Science, Technology and Society in Seventeenth Century England*, Harper & Row.

5 T. Hobbes (1996 [1651]), *Leviathan*, Cambridge University Press, p. 28.

6 T. Hobbes (1998 [1642]), *On the Citizen*, Cambridge University Press, p. 186.

7 Quoted in R. Rorty (1980), *Philosophy and the Mirror of Nature*, Princeton University Press, p. 62.

8 Hobbes (1996), p. 29.

9 Ibid., p. 47.

10 Ibid., p. 87.

11 Ibid., pp. 88–9.

12 Ibid., p. 120.

13 See E. Becker (2014), *The Denial of Death*, Souvenir Press.

14 For the definitive history of this category, see M. Poovey (1998), *A History of the Modern Fact: Problems of Knowledge in the Sciences of Wealth and Society*, University of Chicago Press.

15 See A. Hirschman (1973), *The Passions and the Interests: Political Arguments for Capitalism before Its Triumph*, Princeton University Press.

16 See W. Letwin (2003: 89), *The Origins of Scientific Economics*, Routledge.

17 W. Eamon (1985), "From the secrets of nature to public knowledge: The origins of the concept of openness in science," *Minerva*, 23:3, pp. 321–47.

18 See Poovey (1998), p. 116.

19 The resulting philosophical and personal battle is the topic of S. Shapin & S. Shaffer (2011), *Leviathan and the Air-Pump: Hobbes, Boyle, and the Experimental Life*, Princeton University Press.

20 Quoted in Letwin (2003), p. 129.

21 Quoted in Merton (1970), p. 103.

22 S. Shapin (1994), *A Social History of Truth: Civility and Science in Seventeenth-Century England*, University of Chicago Press.

23 H. Arendt (1993), "Truth and Politics" in *Between Past and Future*, Penguin, p. 250.
24 J. Brewer (2002), *The Sinews of Power: War, Money and the English State 1688–1783*, Routledge.
25 E. Strauss (1954), *Sir William Petty: Portrait of a Genius*, Routledge, p. 193.
26 W. Petty (1992 [1690]) *Political Arithmetick*, Open Access version at McMaster University Archive for the History of Economic Thought, available at https://socialsciences.mcmaster.ca/~econ/ugcm/3113/index.html (accessed 24 April 2018).
27 T. Raines et al. (2017), *The Future of Europe: Comparing Public and Elite Attitudes*, Chatham House.
28 See K. Cramer (2016), *The Politics of Resentment: Rural Consciousness in Wisconsin and the Rise of Scott Walker*, University of Chicago Press; A. Hochschild (2016), *Strangers in Their Own Land: Anger and Mourning on the American Right*, The New Press.

Chapter 3: Progress in Question

1 "When the facts don't matter, how can democracy survive?," *Washington Post*, 17 October 2016.
2 J. Faulkner Rogers (2015), "Are conspiracy theorists for (political) losers?," YouGov.
3 "Just 1 in 4 people trust Government to present statistics honestly," *Independent*, 27 February 2017.
4 R. Porter (1999), *The Greatest Benefit to Mankind: A Medical History of Humanity*, W. W. Norton.
5 Hobbes (1996), p. 231.
6 Quoted in J. Scott (1989), *Seeing Like a State*, Yale University Press, p. 11.
7 J. Bruno et al. (2014), "Statactivism: Forms of action between disclosure and affirmation," *The Open Journal of Sociological Studies*, Vol. 7, No. 2.
8 F. Alvaredo et al. (2017), "Global Inequality Dynamics: New Findings from WID.world," *American Economic Review*, American Economic Association, Vol. 107(5).
9 R. Florida (2017), "Welcome to the Great Divergence" Citylab, 14 February 2017.
10 M. Muro & S. Liu (2016), "Another Clinton–Trump divide: High output America vs low output America," Brookings, 29 November 2016.
11 T. Hazeldine (2017), "Revolt of the Rustbelt," *New Left Review*, 105, May–June 2017.
12 O. Vardakoulias & F. Balata (2016), "Turning back to the sea," New Economics Foundation, 17 November 2016.
13 B. Milanovic (2016), *Global Inequality: A New Approach to Globalization*, Harvard University Press.
14 "Up to 70% of people in developed countries 'have seen incomes stagnate'," *Guardian*, 14 July 2016.
15 J. McLaren & S. Hakobyan (2010), "Looking for Local Labor Market Effects of NAFTA," NBER Working Paper No. 16535.
16 M. Davis (2017), "The Great God Trump and the White Working Class," *Jacobin*, 2 July 2017.
17 E.g., M. Ruhs & C. Vargas-Silva (2017), "The Labour Market Effects of Immigration," COMPAS.

18 "How wages fell in the UK while the economy grew," *Financial Times*, 2 March 2017.

19 "A Question of Polling," ASI Data Science, 5 May 2017.

20 See W. Davies et al. (2015), "Financial Melancholia," PERC.

21 E. Hobsbawm (2010), *Age of Revolution: 1789–1848*, Abacus, p. 91.

22 See K. Payne (2017), *Broken Ladder*, Viking.

23 T. Pettigrew (2017), "Social Psychological Perspectives on Trump Supporters," *Journal of Social and Political Psychology*, Vol. 5, No. 1.

24 Y. Algan et al. (2017), 'The European Trust Crisis and the Rise of Populism,' Brookings Papers on Economic Activity.

25 "BP settles Gulf of Mexico oil spill lawsuit," *Guardian*, 3 March 2012.

Chapter 4: The Body Politic

1 "Torture, reasonable dress code results,' YouGov, 26 January 2017.

2 S. Solomon et al. (2016), *The Worm at the Core: On the Role of Death in Life*, Penguin.

3 E.g. Mori Veracity Index 2016; Gallup's annual poll on "US views on honesty and ethical standards in professions."

4 Quoted in I. Illich (1995), *Limits to Medicine: Medical Nemesis: The Expropriation of Health*, M. Boyars, p. 190.

5 R. Descartes (1995 [1641]), *Meditations on First Philosophy: With Selections from the Objections and Replies*, Cambridge University Press.

6 "Trump succeeds where health is failing," *Economist*, 21 November 2016.

7 A. Case & A. Deaton (2015), "Rising morbidity and mortality in midlife among white non-Hispanic Americans in the 21st century," PNAS, 112 (49).

8 "Mortality in the United States, 2015," NCHS Data Brief, No. 267, December 2016; "Life expectancy in US down for second year in a row as opioid crisis deepens," *Guardian*, 21 December 2017.

9 "A new divide in American death," *Washington Post*, 10 April 2016.

10 C. Becker et al. (1998), "The Demographic Crisis in the Former Soviet Union," *World Development*, Vol. 26, No. 11.

11 "Rise in life expectancy has stalled since 2010, research shows," *Guardian*, 18 July 2017.

12 L. Hiam et al. (2017), "Why has mortality in England and Wales been increasing? An iterative demographic analysis," *Journal of the Royal Society of Medicine*, Vol. 110, Issue 4.

13 D. Dorling (2017), "Austerity and Mortality," in V. Cooper & D. Whyte (2017), *The Violence of Austerity*, Pluto.

14 Ibid., p. 49.

15 M. Marmot (2017), "The UK's current health problems should be treated with urgency," *BMJ Opinion*, 13 September 2017.

16 "'Alarming' rise in early deaths of young adults in the north of England—study," *Guardian*, 8 August 2017.

17 M. O'Hara (2017), "Mental health and suicide," in V. Cooper & D. Whyte (2017).

18 D. Stuckler & V. Basu (2013), *The Body Economic: Why Austerity Kills: Recessions, Budget Battles, and the Politics of Life and Death*, HarperCollins.

19 E. Gray (2017), "Health and social care spending cuts linked to 120,000 excess deaths in England," *BMJ Open*, 15 November 2017.

20 Stuckler & Basu (2013), p. 103.

21 "More and more women are now dying in childbirth, but only in America," *Vox*, 8 August 2016.

22 "French election results: Macron's victory in charts," *Financial Times*, 9 May 2017.

23 A. Fayaz et al. (2016), "Prevalence of chronic pain in the UK: A systematic review and meta-analysis of population studies," *BMJ Open*, Vol. 6, Issue 6.

24 E. Scarry (1985), *The Body in Pain: The Making and Unmaking of the World*, Oxford University Press, p. 29.

25 Ibid., p. 13.

26 See K. Wailoo (2014), *Pain: A Political History*, JHU Press.

27 M. Bair et al. (2003), "Depression and pain comorbidity: A literature review," *Archives of Internal Medicine*, Vol. 163, Issue 20.

28 D. Blanchflower & A. Oswald (2017), "Unhappiness and pain in modern America: A review essay and further evidence, on Carol Graham's *Happiness for All?*," NBER Working Paper No. 24087.

29 See J. Bourke (2014), *The Story of Pain: From Prayer to Painkillers*, Oxford University Press, p. 275.

30 See M. Benzer (2011), "Quality of Life and Risk Conceptions in UK Healthcare Regulation: Towards a critical analysis," CARR Discussion Paper 68.

31 S. Quinones (2015), *Dreamland: The True Tale of America's Opiate Epidemic*, Bloomsbury.

32 Ibid.

33 The seminal article in establishing this was R. Melzack & P. Wall (1965), "Pain Mechanisms: A new theory," *Nature*, Vol. 150, No. 3699.

34 See Bourke (2014).

35 Quoted in Bourke (2014), p. 10.

36 The other four are body temperature, pulse rate, respiration rate, and blood pressure.

37 See A. Horwitz & J. Wakefield (2007), *The Loss of Sadness: How Psychiatry Transformed Normal Sorrow into Depressive Disorder*, Oxford University Press.

38 See G. Bendelow & S. Williams (1995), "Transcending the dualisms: Towards a sociology of pain," *Sociology of Health and Illness*, 17:2.

39 S. Freud (2015), *Beyond the Pleasure Principle*, Dover Publications, p. 11.

40 Ibid., p. 30.

41 See B. Kolk (2014), *The Body Keeps the Score: Mind, Brain and Body in the Transformation of Trauma*, Penguin.

42 S. Tams et al. (2018), "Smartphone withdrawal creates stress: A moderated mediation model of nomophobia, social threat and phone withdrawal context," *Computers in Human Behaviour*, Vol. 81, April 2018.

43 See G. Lukianoff & J. Haidt (2015), "The coddling of the American mind," *Atlantic*, September 2015.

44 M. Teicher et al. (2010), "Hurtful words: Association of exposure to peer verbal abuse with elevated psychiatric symptom scores and corpus callosum abnormalities," *American Journal of Psychiatry*, Vol. 167, Issue 12.

45 See S. Chaney (2017), *Psyche on the Skin: A History of Self-harm*, Reaktion Books; C. Millard (2015), *A History of Self-Harm in Britain: A Genealogy of Cutting and Overdosing*, Springer.

46 J. Watts (2017), "Why do people self-harm? You asked Google—here's the answer," *Guardian*, 6 September 2017.

47 "The family that built an empire of pain," *New Yorker*, 30 October 2017.
48 "How the opioid epidemic has affected the US labor force, county-by-county," Brookings, 7 September 2017.
49 Quinones (2015).
50 See N. D. Schull (2012), *Addiction by Design: Machine Gambling in Las Vegas*, Princeton University Press.

Chapter 5: Knowledge for War

1 Around 1 million people died over the course of the Napoleonic Wars, compared to 600,000 in the American Civil War of 1861–5 or around 8 million in the Thirty Years War—Hobsbawm (2010), pp. 92–3.
2 Quoted in D. Stoker (2014), *Clausewitz: His Life and Work*, Oxford University Press, p. 11.
3 Quoted in H. Strachan (2008), *Clausewitz's On War: A Biography*, Grove Press, p. 19.
4 C. Von Clausewitz (2013 [1832]), *On War*, Simon & Schuster, p. 101.
5 P. Edwards (2010), *A Vast Machine: Computer Models, Climate Data, and the Politics of Global Warming*, MIT Press.
6 Clausewitz (2013), p. 163.
7 Ibid., p. 101.
8 See S. Weinberger (2017), *The Imagineers of War: The Untold Story of DARPA, the Pentagon Agency That Changed the World*, Knopf Doubleday.
9 A. Gonzales (2002), "Memorandum for the President: Decision re application of the Geneva Convention on prisoners of war to the conflict with Al Qaeda and the Taliban."
10 Galison (2010), "Secrecy in Three Acts," *Social Research: An International Quarterly*, 77:3.
11 Weinberger (2017), p. 17.
12 D. Edgerton (2011), *Britain's War Machine: Weapons, Resources, and Experts in the Second World War*, Oxford University Press.
13 Ibid., p. 100.
14 C. Darwin (1872), *The Expression of the Emotions in Man and Animals*, John Murray, p. 31.
15 W. James (1884), "What Is an Emotion?," *Mind*, Vol. 9, Issue 34, p. 190.
16 See E. Hobsbawm (2010), *Age of Empire: 1875–1914*, Hachette.
17 Clausewitz (2013), p. 341.
18 Quoted in Strachan (2008), pp. 25–6.
19 T. Hippler (2017), *Governing from the Skies: A Global History of Aerial Bombing*, Verso.
20 Clausewitz (2013), p. 146.
21 "Since all these events [Napoleonic wars] have shown what an enormous factor the heart and sentiments of a Nation may be in the product of its political and military strength, in fine, since governments have found out all these additional aids, it is not to be expected that they will let them lie idle in future Wars." Clausewitz (2013), p. 295.
22 Ibid., p. 337.
23 Ibid., p. 341.
24 Ibid., p. 325.

25 Hobsbawm (2010), p. 75.
26 Clausewitz (2013), p. 150.

Chapter 6: Guessing Games

1 P. Thiel (2009), "The Education of a Libertarian," *Cato Unbound*, 13 April 2009.

2 P. Thiel (2014), *Zero to One: Notes on Startups or How to Build the Future*, Virgin Books, p. 106.

3 Ibid., p. 5.

4 "Peter Thiel's Apocalypse," *San Francisco Magazine*, 29 September 2017.

5 C. McKenna (2006), *The World's Newest Profession: Management Consulting in the Twentieth Century*, Cambridge University Press.

6 "This shadowy company is flying planes over US cities," BuzzFeed, 4 August 2017.

7 O. Neurath (2005), *Economic Writings: Selections 1904–1945*, Springer.

8 L. Von Mises (1990), *Economic Calculation in the Socialist Commonwealth*, Ludwig Von Mises Institute.

9 J. Schumpeter (1934), *The Theory of Economic Development: An Inquiry Into Profits, Capital, Credit, Interest, and the Business Cycle*, Transaction Publisher, p. 85.

10 Ibid., p. 93.

11 L. Mises (1922), *Socialism: An Economic and Sociological Analysis*, Mises Institute, p. 42.

12 See P. Mirowski (2002), *Machine Dreams: How Economics Became a Cyborg Science*, Cambridge University Press; P. Mirowski & E. Nik-Khah (2017), *The Knowledge We Have Lost in Information: The History of Information in Modern Economics*, Oxford University Press.

13 Quoted in A. Ebenstein (2014), *Friedrich Hayek: A Biography*, St Martin's Press.

14 F. Hayek (1945), "The Use of Knowledge in Society," *American Economic Review*, Vol. 35, No. 4.

15 Ibid., p. 522.

16 F. Hayek (1943), "The facts of the social sciences," *Ethics*, Vol. 54, No. 1.

17 F. Hayek (2002), "Competition as a Discovery Procedure," *Quarterly Journal of Austrian Economics*, Vol. 5, No. 3.

18 J. Meyer (2016), *Dark Money*, Doubleday, p. 9.

19 Ibid., p. 71.

20 N. Oreskes & E. Conway (2011), *Merchants of Doubt: How a Handful of Scientists Obscured the Truth on Issues from Tobacco Smoke to Global Warming*, A&C Black.

21 "Exxon knew about climate change almost 40 years ago," *Scientific American*, 26 October 2015.

22 F. Hayek (2012), *Law, Legislation and Liberty*, Routledge, p. 179.

23 R. Henderson et al. (1998), "Universities As A Source Of Commercial Technology: A Detailed Analysis Of University Patenting, 1965–1988," *Review of Economics and Statistics*, Vol. 80, Issue 1.

24 F. Hayek (2006), *The Constitution of Liberty*, Routledge, p. 378.

25 "208,500 additional deaths could occur by 2026 under the Senate health plan," *Vox*, 3 July 2017.

26 "World's witnessing a new gilded age as billionaires' wealth swells to $6tn," *Guardian*, 26 October 2017.

27 Hayek (2006).

28 S. Solomon et al. (2016).

Chapter 7: War of Words

1 "DARPA devotes $60 million for a Brain-Computer interface," *InfoScience Today*, 14 February 2017; "Controlling VR with your mind," *MIT Technology Review*, 22 March 2017.

2 "Facebook has 60 people working on how to read your mind," *Guardian*, 19 April 2017.

3 M. Zuckerberg (2017), open letter, available at https://www.facebook.com/notes/mark-zuckerberg/building-global-community/10154544292806634/ (accessed 22 March 2018).

4 This story is recounted in S. Ostrander & L. Shroder (1970), *Psychic Discoveries Behind the Iron Curtain*, Prentice-Hall.

5 "DIA worried Soviets might try to 'intercept' them," *Muckrock*, 23 March 2017.

6 "Facebook won't say if they'll use your brain activity for advertisements," *Intercept*, 22 May 2017.

7 Quoted in T. Rid (2017), *Rise of the Machines: The Lost History of Cybernetics*, Scribe, p. 63.

8 "Putin says the nation that leads in AI 'will be the ruler of the world'," *Verge*, 4 September 2017.

9 "On Internet privacy, be very afraid," *Harvard Gazette*, 24 August 2017.

10 See C. O'Neill (2016), *Weapons of Math Destruction: How Big Data Increases Inequality and Threatens Democracy*, Penguin.

11 "Advances in AI are used to spot signs of sexuality," *Economist*, 9 September 2017.

12 "Putting a finger on our phone obsession," *dscout*, 16 June 2016.

13 "Tech is becoming emotionally intelligent and it's big business," *SingularityHub*, 2 November 2017.

14 "The Age of AI Surveillance is here," *Quartz*, 27 August 2017.

15 F. Maschewski & A. Nosthoff (2017), "Order from Noise: On Cambridge Analytica, Cybernetic Governance and the Technopolitical Imaginary," *Public Seminar*, 20 March 2017.

16 This essential problem, of how to cope with overabundant information, is explored by M. Andrejevic (2013), *InfoGlut: How Too Much Information Is Changing the Way We Think and Know*, Routledge.

17 O'Neill (2016).

18 "Facebook told advertisers it can identify teens feeling 'insecure' and 'worthless'," *Guardian*, 1 May 2017.

19 Google Transparency Project (2017), "Google Academics Inc."

Chapter 8: Between War and Peace

1 Pew (2017), "Globally, broad support for representative and direct democracy;" 2018 Edelman Trust Barometer.

2 Pew (2017).

3 Y. Algan et al. (2017).

4 Edwards (2010).

5 B. Weisberg (1970), *Ecocide in Indochina: The Ecology of War*, Canfield Press.

6 N. Watts et al. (2017), "The *Lancet* countdown on health and climate change: from 25 years of inaction to a global transformation for public health," *Lancet*, Vol. 391, No. 10120.

7 C. Hallmann et al. (2017), "More than 75 percent decline over 27 years in total flying insect biomass in protected areas," *PLOS ONE*, 12(10).

8 R. Nixon (2011), *Slow Violence*, Harvard University Press.

9 S. Funtowicz & J. Ravetz (1995), "Science for the Post-Normal Age," *Futures*, Vol. 25, Issue 7.

10 B. McKibben (2016), "We need to literally declare war on climate change," *New Republic*, 15 August 2016.

11 G. Mann & J. Wainright (2018), *Climate Leviathan: A Political Theory of Our Planetary Future*, Verso.

12 J. Gabrys (2017), "Citizen sensing, air pollution and fracking: From 'caring about your air' to speculative practices of evidencing harm," *Sociological Review*, Vol. 65, Issue 2.

13 Edwards (2010).

14 R. Brooke (2016), *How Everything Became War and the Military Became Everything: Tales from the Pentagon*, Simon & Schuster, p. 20.

15 F. Nietzsche (2013 [1889]), *Genealogy of Morals*, Penguin.

16 M. Stoller (2016), "How Democrats killed their populist soul," *Atlantic*, 24 October 2016.

17 J. Balkin (2016), "Information Fiduciaries and the First Amendment," *UC Davis Law Review*, Vol. 49, No. 4.

18 F. Pasquale (2016), "Platform Neutrality: Enhancing Freedom of Expression in Spheres of Private Power," *University of Maryland Legal Studies Research Paper* No. 2016–24.

19 A. Hochschild (2016), *Strangers in Their Own Land: Anger and Mourning on the American Right*, The New Press.

20 T. Shrecker (2017), "'Stop, You're Killing Us!' An Alternative Take on Populism and Public Health," *International Journal of Health Policy Management*, Vol. 6, Issue 11.

Index